T0328830

Agriculture, peasantry and poverty in Turkey in the neo-liberal age

Agriculture, peasantry and poverty in Turkey in the neo-liberal age

Murat Öztürk

Wageningen Academic
P u b l i s h e r s

ISBN: 978-90-8686-192-7
e-ISBN: 978-90-8686-748-6
DOI: 10.3920/978-90-8686-748-6

Cover photo:
Village in West Anatolia
by Zeynep Üstünipek

First published, 2012

© Wageningen Academic Publishers
The Netherlands, 2012

Table of contents

List of tables

List of textboxes

List of appendices

Foreword

Andy Hilton

By way of providing a context for this work, some thoughts and explanations are provided here regarding the background to the subject mater. First, a consideration of the term 'peasantry' is offered, as its significance cannot be assumed as unproblematic. Essentially, a dual analysis is suggested of narrow and wide meanings, the latter of which is invoked in contemporary discussion. There then follows a historical narrative focusing on the rural issue in Turkey. The place of the village and the peasantry in the state's desire to shape the country and promote its ideal of rural development contextualises the later unfolding of government policies as recounted in this book, coupled with the more immediate factor of the onset of migration from the countryside to the cities. Next, some of the issues around the introduction of neo-liberal policies to the agricultural sector in Turkey are mentioned. Important here are the inheritance of state involvement and the particular confluence of events and processes with which neo-liberalism was introduced into agriculture in Turkey. Finally, a note is added in respect to the impact of neo-liberal policies, with mention of effects in developing countries in the context of the issues addressed.

The 'peasantry'

The historical development of agriculture might be characterised by socio-economic stages of settlement (with village based arable farming), feudalism (with formalised ownership of land), and capitalisation (linked to industrialism). The peasantry is generally associated with the second of these, associated with terms like 'serf' as synonym and 'lord', 'noble' and suchlike in terms of property and social relations, attendant upon what may be referred to as the decommonising of the natural resource of land. For this reason the concept of peasantry is widely regarded as redundant now in the developed world, let alone in those non-developed (developing or undeveloped) territories where feudal type arrangements never have prevailed. The word 'peasant' is a relic from the past, that is, left over from of a previous (agricultural) era, and referring to the period of feudal arrangements on the path to modernity, a rather specific (socio-political) form characterising a largely Eurocentric model of (universal, unilinear) development (along with a pejorative undertone referencing the pre-modern lack of universal education, suffrage and human rights – the peasant, that is, as uncultured, unworthy and fundamentally backward).

Previously, the material homogeneity of the peasantry as a socio-economically defined category of people has enabled its conceptualisation as a class. In European socio-economic analysis, it was the underlying dynamics structuring this class in the context of capitalist development that gave rise to what became formulated as 'the agrarian question.' Presenting various types of problem as clarified by Kautsky, the peasantry was nevertheless susceptible to a Hegelian specification in terms of class consciousness. After all, peasant insurrections had dotted, if not exactly littered the pages of history in Europe at least since the technological development and accumulation of capital that saw the development of feudalism and statehood. Not by coincidence was the Medieval Industrial Revolution, as it is sometimes termed, accompanied by, among others, the Peasant Revolt in early fourteenth century Flanders, and the later Industrial Revolution by the 1831 English Peasants' Revolt, when Wat Tyler demanded that 'there should be... no serfdom' (Oman 1906: 201). Equally, the emerging proletariat of industrialized Europe interacted with other traditions of resistance to help fan the flames of discontent internationally, such as in the late nineteenth century Jun Mountain Peasant Rising in the Yangtze delta region of (still feudal) China (Le Mons Walker 2003).

This history of resistance is invoked in contemporary usage of the category 'peasant', in which the possibility of a continued class consciousness is premised upon (the ambiguity of) a loose delineation of peasants: those people of few means who subsist by working the land. This is an expanded concept, suggesting no more than small scale, typically family and/or community (village) based operations, which of itself neither infers feudal structure nor even necessarily precludes modern farming conditions. Clearly, the term 'peasant' has come to be the subject of some equivocation, with small scale farming at its definitional core, but shifting in meaning between the narrow – the original or archetypal (of farming folk in the feudal context) – and the broad – with a range that encompasses extremes of, on the one hand, subsistence farmers in basic, settled (non-nomadic) conditions irrespective of the wider socio-political structure (i.e. in non- or pre-feudal contexts), and on the other, those with a lack of access to sufficient means for significant capital acquisition (or interest in aiming for this) even though they might employ the latest technology for highly specialised production (i.e. in the context of advanced – post-feudal – economies). In other words, according to this wider definition, peasants might be found anywhere, in all lands at all stages of development and virtually any type of political arrangement.

Clearly, this definitional broadening of the peasantry results in a fragmented category far beyond the old complications of sub-classes like the Medieval freemen, villeins and cottars or the subsequent development of petty bourgeois types of agrarian labour relations. And the picture is yet further muddled nowadays by a host of recent developments in capital access and enterprise culture (with subsistence farmers in non-developed contexts, for example, co-developing the products of advanced biotechnology) and various new forms of intervention (such as the market guarantees for those local farmers involved in school feeding programmes), as well as the post-modern advances of agricultural ludditery, if it may be named thus (with small farmers in the West employing organic, permaculture, slow food, etc. approaches that may decry both technological aids and/or product specialisation). The amalgam as 'peasants' of those from the poorest (least developed) territories with those from the richest (most advanced) may appear problematic. Against this, however, is posited a shared condition of all small scale farmers as determined by material relations, by virtue of their position, that is, in labour as opposed to capital. Simply, while peasants of old were indentured to their local lord, now they are beholden to international market forces.

Thus it is that some writers on agricultural development, rural sociology and the like are motivated to employ the concept of the peasantry in the contemporary context, finding commonality as it does in the global situation of smallholders today in their struggle with the forces of the 'corporate food machine', and indicating the social space for a political agenda advocating for different forms of development, with 'alternative relationships to the land, farming and food' (McMichael 2005). Others, however, draw an opposite conclusion, interpreting this as a denial of political economy, ones that identifies the 'people of the land' as (if) the 'international proletariat', in a vacuous generalisation, that is, of 'farming populations everywhere', and when actually it is in the very nature of the operation of capital to disassemble and disunite (Bernstein 2008). Ultimately, one imagines, the issue may be settled by the relative dynamism of the material forces at play in the 'generative entrenchment' (Wimsatt 1983) constituted by the present revivification of 'peasantry'. The entrenchment of the old category of 'peasantry' here takes the generative form of a reclamation by national and international movements seeking to develop a new front against various modernising forces that tend towards increased scales of production, and one that can extend even to contemporary conditions of high as well as low development (and thus anything in between). A contemporary class consciousness, in fact. The success of the present revivification of 'peasantry' or 'new peasantry' (Van der Ploeg 2008) could yet come to depend more on its expression in action than academic debate, on the longevity and vitality of organisations like Via Campesina, MST and its anti-capitalist brethren in the alter globalist movement.

The current construction of the peasantry as a class is not really very different in the Turkish situation to that elsewhere, at least in other (higher level) developing countries. Its employment in this book should not be taken as a clarion call to arms, however, but rather as an observation of enduring realities, both analytical and material. Murat references the issue rather than takes sides. Indeed, he specifically observes a lack of class consciousness among the Turkish peasantry today, and without any emphasis or interpretation. In this sense his analysis is scientific rather than political. Nevertheless, there clearly is a political dimension to his work, and it seems to be precisely the issue of the peasantry that is key to this. Looking at the listing of agriculture, peasantry and poverty as given in the title, it is the second of the three that seems to hold the triple subject together. The peasantry is the common denominator linking agriculture to poverty.

Turkey's rural issue

Primarily comprising the peninsular of Anatolia, the fairly large, rather mountainous country of Turkey is blessed with a long coast. The conventional division of the nation is made on a longitudinal axis, with a poor, traditional, rugged East compared to the European oriented West, but a seaboard/interior division is just as valid. While the heartland tends to be dry and dotted with small, the generally more developed coastal area has offered opportunities for international movements of goods (trade) and people (culture) since time immemorial. Today, this is augmented by – or takes the modern form of – tourism. Turkey's western (Aegean) and southern (Mediterranean) resorts in particular have become international holiday resorts, while the northern coastline is also popular domestically. The tourism phenomenon is such that population figures for the top country's holiday destinations like Antalya or Bodrum are commonly given in two forms, the official (year round, out of season) residence and the mostly temporary summer number, when the local populations are doubled, trebled and more by the influx of holiday makers and their associated service sector workers. More interestingly perhaps though, description of the country's inland villages has begun to follow a similar format. Increasingly, after years of urban migration and rural depopulation, people are returning to their villages, to visit, organize their family property and re-establish community during the summer months before returning back to their everyday lives in the city. Their native settlements become known, sometimes ironically, as 'summer' or 'holiday' villages (*yazlık*, yayla, *tatil köyü*). This is just one of the phenomena observable in Turkish rural life today. Indeed, it is one of the ways in which agriculture can no longer be assumed to define the village through the peasantry in terms of poverty.

Historically, the village was the heart of the country, feted by nationalists during the early days of the republic. Whereas the Ottomans had been associated with Rumelia (the Balkan and west Anatolian heart of the empire centred on Istanbul), and with the cultured urban elites who could read and write the Ottoman Persian-Arabic fusion, the new nation state centred in Ankara, in the middle of Anatolia, espoused a people's 'democracy' of Turkic culture, which included the mythologisation of a central Asian heritage, the institution of the folk traditions of the people, adoption of the vernacular (Turkish) as the official language and esteem for village life. Much of this remains in place even today. Turkey is still renowned for the genuinely live and populist tradition of its regional folk dancing, for example, and most Turks believe they come from Ural-Altaic stock (although genetically this only about 20% true). The village as cornerstone of culture, however, was rapidly problematised.

In 1924, a few months after the victory of Ataturk's forces and the signing of the Treaty of Lausanne, which formerly ended the Ottoman Empire and brought the Republic of Turkey into existence, Law no. 442, the Village Law (*Köy Kanunu*) was passed. This established an administrative system for the formal political arrangement of rural life, and listed requirements related to things like water and drainage, including construction of a school and a mosque, and enforceable through financial penalties. Even after the Second World War, however, the law was not only still largely ignored, but found to be 'remarkable for it irrelevance' (Stirling 1950: 271). Indeed, the overwhelming majority of villagers remained illiterate, marriage ceremonies did not generally follow the civil code and there was no cadastral register, with the local records of land deeds typically incomplete and out of date. Villages were 'amorphous', with little formal organisation of any kind. Rural enterprise was family based and social organisation widely (ethno-religiously) sectarian or clan oriented. Thus, although 'tax farming' was largely a thing of the past, by all other standards the peasantry was very much in existence, and represented what was easily the largest population block in the country.

It was in order to tackle this Kemalist version of the agrarian problem that a national system of 'village institutes' was established under a legal framework constructed from the late 1930s to early 40s. Directed towards the production of teachers for village primary schools, the village institute system was specifically aimed at educating the rural population, but broader aims included also a modernisation of social relations, improvements in agriculture and reduction of poverty. Over time, however, the institutes became a focus of ideological conflict, and the system was closed down in the mid 50s when the institutes were seen to be supportive of leftist ideals. Assessment of the successes and failures of this system tend to depend on political perspective. Even educationally, evaluation may either focus on the thousands of teachers produced and village schools established across the country, and the hundreds of thousands of rural children who thus received a basic level of education – or else on the twenty thousand or so villages that remained without schools, only 60% attendance where there were schools and problematic position of the teachers in the villages (as outsiders with varying levels of pedagogic quality pushing a foreign doctrine), and a continued rural illiteracy rate, therefore, of around 80% (Weiker 1973: 266ff). The significant place of the village institute system in the republic's history of developmental planning, however, is not disputed.

Fashioning the territory, meanwhile, took various forms, including population movements and the reorganisation of settlement and administration structures. The establishment of modern Turkey was in many ways predicated on a national, religious based ethnic cleansing, with Christian Armenians and Greeks escaping or removed from and Muslim Turks entering the new national space in a series of events described by terms ranging from 'genocide' to 'population exchange' that involved hundred of thousands, perhaps millions of people. Large tracts of land changed ownership, and farming communities were lost and/or replaced, or squeezed into smaller areas. Populations were and moved around the country in processes of assimilation and incorporation. Muslims from the ex-Ottoman southern Balkans were placed in various specified parts of the land (where they often found themselves having to learn entirely new agricultural practices), while the 1934 Settlement Act divided the country into zones according to political sensitivity, with Zone 1 areas (along borders, near railways, etc.) targeted for those nearest the hegemonic ideal of (Sunni Muslim) ethnic Turks. Recalcitrant Kurds in the Southeast were shifted hundreds of kilometres to the west. Thus was a nation born.

The concentration of the citizenry into fewer, larger and planned population centres was also seen as progress, as part of the passage of history. Intriguingly, and rather instructively, one of the stipulations of the Village Act was for villages to have two routes that met at a crossroads. Presumably intended to mark the village centre, this evidences the very early desire of the political elite to determine the basic layout even of small communities. In similar vein were designs made in the 1930s for 'model villages' (typically organised around a village centre). Indeed, the issue of how to organize and rationalize rural communities into a better integrated system for more efficient administration, development and control was a central theme of state planning during most of the republican period. Envisaged ever since the 1930s, plans to modernise the spatial framework of the nation were never far from the agenda (Jongerden 2007: 122ff). In the early 60s, for example, exploratory research into a full-scale rural redevelopment was made with a costing of the resettlement of the entire rural population into settlements of 10,000 houses (and put at something like 120 billion dollars). In 1982, the State Planning Department (DPT) analysed the relationship between the state and the people in terms of the administrative distance, with a bureaucratic hierarchy descending from five main centres (cities) through levels of regional, sub-regional and small town centres to village group centres, which were the local hubs for villages (DPT 1982). Ideas were promoted during this period aimed at better integration at the lowest levels (or, expansion at the levels of small town and village group centres), through the development of 'centre villages' (*merkez köy*), 'village-towns' (*köy-kent*) and 'agricultural towns' (*tarım kent*).

Mostly housing less than six hundred people, the existing stock of villages did not tend to be augmented by new ones created 'naturally' through the second half of the twentieth century, or be reduced by village decline and death for that matter – records and estimates vary little in putting the number of villages at around 35,000. The number of hamlets, on the other hand, seemed to be increasing, from around thirty thousand in 1950 to over thirty-eight thousand in 1970 and more than fifty thousand by 1985. Reasons for this included the demographics of the rise in population and need for land along with social factors like the increased desire to live independently and family feuds.

More recent considerations related to the rationalisation of rural settlement tended to refer especially to the Kurdish issue. The history of ethno-nationalist separatism in the Kurdish dominated south-eastern part of the country has generally underscored the general narrative of nation building, but with its aspect of 'creative destruction' more evident. The assimilationist and/or oppressive approach to minorities that tends to characterise nationalism has been state policy in the Turkish Kurd case with a harsh order imposed from the centre ever since the first rebellions in the 1920s and 30s were put down and their leaders and families and communities forcibly evacuated and resettled. This became particularly clear in the decade between the mid 1990s and 2000s when the state responded to the success of the separatist guerrilla army of the Kurdish PKK by literally clearing the countryside. In order to counter the rural based insurgency, the army 'emptied' over thousand villages (evacuating the people and part destroying the buildings and crops), a figure expanded to more than seven thousand settlements with the inclusion of hamlets, effectively depopulating the land by a million people or more and leaving or laying to waste hundreds of thousands, millions even, of hectares of countryside used for arable farming, grazing and forestry. During this time, preparatory research was made and schemes drawn up for a nationwide rural redevelopment, for which European Community and World Bank funding was found – but then withheld upon the realisation that in the Southeast this support was implicitly financing a state policy of resettling people internally displaced by the military. Other 'return-to-village' and urban resettlement reconstruction plans were developed in order to deal with the issue, but never implemented beyond a few pilot projects. Again, these involved a tighter administrative organisation enabled through an increase in size and reduction in number of settlements (including the eradication of hamlets).

In the end, the Kemalist modernising rationale in the countryside was probably more widely and profoundly implemented culturally through privately owned mass media than state education, and socially by the sea change of urbanization based on a population boom rather than government approaches to spatial design. Market liberalisation policies during the 1980s enabled a flourishing of newspapers and television channels that quickly reached people countrywide, albeit generally constricted by a hegemonic ideology informed by the national education system and general culture, and enforced by censorship. This may be said to have had a relatively strong 'civilising' effect on villagers, whose access to television in particular can be dated from this period. In terms of demographics, population growth in the country had been slow until WWII, and public policy directed to increasing it. Thereafter, it was rapid, averaging 2.5% p.a. for the period 1945 to 1980, with the total population doubling during the quarter century 1950-75. Birth-rates were significantly higher in rural areas, which, combined with relatively low income rates – the fundamental linkage between agriculture and poverty – along with other factors such as improved transportation, resulted in large scale rural-to-urban migration, roughly in line with the global trend at this time. Thus, while the rural population grew by around 40% in the three decades 1950-80 (from around fifteen to twenty-five million people), the urban population quadrupled and that in the cities of ten thousand plus residents saw a five-fold increase (from four to twenty million) (Demir and Çabuk 2011). Steering cultural life and driving economic development, Istanbul was the main magnet for this exodus from the countryside, but all the major cities saw exponential growth during this period, even relative to the exponential overall rise in population. The population of Ankara, for example, rose by a half in the 70s alone, a decade in which well over half a million people annually were migrating to the large cities. Large areas of squatter development or shanty housing (*gecekondu*) sprang up. Mass poverty had become a defining characteristic of the new urban society.

For Turkey as a relatively poor country on the borders of Europe, the latter part of the twentieth century also saw the phenomenon of large scale emigration. People travelled to the then EEC and other European countries – especially to Germany on its guest worker programme – as these entered the post-war reconstruction and economic development period of the fifties and sixties with a booming demand for labour. The outflow of people to Europe – primarily of the rural poor – contributed to a further dampening of what became a very slow population increase in the Turkish countryside, especially as compared to the rocketing figures in the cities. In fact, the combined migration to the cities and the West not only saw the number of city dwellers nationwide finally outstripping that of villagers during the 80s, but also the beginning of an overall decline in the country's rural population. Nevertheless, even at the turn of the millennium, still something approaching a half of all working people in Turkey were active in the agricultural sector. And this at a time when no other developed country had proportions of the labour force in farming above 10 to 20%. For all the change wrought by waves of migration, nothing compared to the tsunami about to descend, which is the story told here.

Introducing neo-liberalism into Turkey

Because of the centralist system inherited from the period of the establishment and development of the republic, farming was quite strongly supported and controlled by the state. As in many newly independent (often ex-colonial) countries during the twentieth century, state involvement had established what was in some respects a command economy. Turkish governments had determined financial development in the 20s, organised economic survival during the Depression years and then, after WWII, structured a reasonably rapid growth. In respect of the agricultural sector, the financial system established with national state banks included a reformed Agriculture Bank (*Ziraat Bankası*), which facilitated the movement of credit in rural areas, including supports to agriculture from the treasury, while state and semi-state run systems had overseen the speedy recovery of agriculture after the turbulence of the collapse of empire with large production rises (cotton output, for example, saw a seven fold increase between 1930 and 1945).

Neo-liberal policies had been on the Turkish agenda since the 1980s, but farming had largely been spared (eventually as a function of the extension granted to developing nations by the Agreement on Agriculture part of the WTO Uruguay Round, which gave them until 2004 to meet reduction targets for customs duties, domestic supports and export subsidies). At the very end of the millennium, the government negotiated a stabilisation program with the IMF, which was itself flawed. A financial crisis followed, peaking in December 2001. The Turkish economy was protected by IMF loans, to the tune of some twenty billion dollars, the price for which was a new, concentrated round of neo-liberal policies, and which were now expanded to included the agricultural sector. As free market orientated reforms were suddenly catapulted into the forefront of economic policy, so too was Turkish farming flung more into the new world order.

The introduction of neo-liberalism in Turkey occurred in a context that was both general and specific. Of note in terms of the former, was the zeitgeist of a retrenchment of capital and capitalist values as the 70s scourge of inflation was defeated by monetarism (championed by Milton Freidman over Maynard Keynes), the socialist ethos thwarted (eventually symbolised by the collapse of the Soviet bloc), and a resurgent right augmented by Christian conservatives (leading to a fundamentalist ethic advocating 'small government' and 'traditional values'). Politically, neo-liberalism was no less neutral than the social liberalism it replaced. If it appears that we now entering the beginning of the end of the era of neo-liberalism – which I think we are – this is for a variety of reasons no less complex and varied and interlinked as those that ushered it in. The coupling in this book of agriculture to poverty through the peasantry is thus entirely within the scope of neo-liberalism as the prevailing economic model for globalisation, itself the primary socio-cultural force of our times.

The specific context for the introduction of neo-liberalism in Turkish agriculture concerns the particular combination of factors that came together. Crucially, the WTO Uruguay Round process came to a head. Completions and conclusions had been reached and processes and reviews initiated in the area of market access negotiations for the maritime sector and government procurement of services (in 1996), for telecommunications and financial services (1997), and textiles and clothing and the harmonisation of rules of origin (1998), along with developments in negotiations around the issue of patenting and intellectual property (with developing countries set to meet the TRIPS stipulations in 2000). Also, it was just a few months before the onset of the 2001 crisis that the agricultural agreement commitments came into effect for developed countries.

Important in respect of this last factor was the issue of the European Union. In 2000, this organisation of highly developed countries was finally implementing the GATT (WTO) bargain (with up to 50% reductions made that year in its Common Agricultural Policy export subsidies), in addition to preparing its Agenda 2000 programme for further CAP reform (with the beginning of a shift in supports away from traditional production and towards environmental protection and rural development), and pushing for 'multifunctionality' at the Millennium (later Doha) Round (with proposals for subsidies on the basis of non-trade concerns and tied to programmes limiting production). At the same time as this strategic shift was taking place, Turkey was entering the stage prior to accession negotiations, having finally received the green light from Europe. Included among the preparations for enlargement announced by the Helsinki Council in mid December 1999 – with these following an outlining of closer integration plans, which was itself prefaced by a call for the need to tackle unemployment – was recognition of Turkey as a candidate state destined to join the Union.

The dream of European acceptance had long figured in the Turkish psyche – initially since its previous imperial incarnation had become dubbed Europe's sick man and disregarded by the Powers, and certainly since the establishment of the republic, when it was European models and conventions that were adopted for the wide range of national systems and public institutions introduced. There was, therefore, no little irony in the fact that it was such a short time before what was probably the gravest financial crisis in the history of the republic that the European club was finally signalling the possibility of acceptance. Following the singing of Customs Union Agreement in 1995 between Turkey and the EU (which excluded agriculture and automotive sectors), the Copenhagen Criteria, toward which the Turkish state had already been moving, now assumed unparalleled importance in the country's political and economic life. Europe, for its part, commenced regular reports on Turkey's progress. The generally worded requirement for 'a functioning market economy', the 'capacity to cope with competitive pressure and market forces within the Union' and 'adherence to the aims of... economic... union' was assessed in respect of agriculture by the mid 1999 EU Turkey report with notes on Turkish 'import restrictions' on bovine and beef, its generally 'high support and protection' of the sector, and the 'lack of progress' regarding the 'abolition of state involvement in marketing and processing of agricultural produce', followed by a statement of the strategy of bringing Turkey's farm policy 'into line' with the CAP and announcement of the commencement of this (EU 1999: 32-33). It was no accident, therefore, that the World Bank stated a few years late that 'Turkey must continue to make improvements in its agricultural sector so as to comply with European Union requirements'.[1]

Developments regarding the WTO, WB, IMF and EU coalesced when the final piece of the jigsaw fell into place, the political situation at home: the 'Islamic' AK Party swept to power in the 2002 general election with approaching half of the popular vote and a commanding majority in parliament. The AKP government was rooted not only in the moral conservatism of the Anatolian heartland, but also in the economics of liberalization. It was also committed to EU membership, both as proof

---

[1] Available at: http://www.worldbank.org.tr/external/default/main?pagePK=64193027&piPK=64187937&theSitePK=361712&menuPK=64187510&searchMenuPK=64187282&theSitePK=361712&entityID=000160016_20051122163001&searchMenuPK=64187282&theSitePK=361712.

of its modernising credentials and insurance against further military intervention (the only previous Islamic government had been forced out of office after just a few weeks in 1997 by the army in what became known as the 'post-modern coup'. Economic neo-liberalism was thus confirmed as the only game in town. The republic had experienced a changing of the guard, in which a novel political situation had seen the forces of the new economic order propelled forward by a new social order.

Neoliberalism and development

The intervention of the IMF in Turkey's economic management can be regarded as a further stage in the capitalization of the national system – or, the command by capital of this – which had hitherto been significantly state bounded, with high levels of central government intervene and public ownership/management. As recognised by the two-tier phasing in of the WTO Agriculture Agreement, farming has a special place in the structure of developing countries. It constitutes a major part of economic activity in the nation and is the source of subsistence for a major part of the population. Development, in the dominant model to have emerged in recent human history, involves a reduction of this. Where state financial inputs into the agricultural sector are significant (as a proportion of GDP, for example), then the drive for development as conventionally determined combines with the imperative of neo-liberalism to produce a confluence of change that sweeps the nation. Not only is the countryside, primary site of agricultural enterprise, the likely site for business consolidation, but a rapid depopulation of rural areas is to be expected, with major implications for urban society also. At least, as Murat explains in this book, this seems to have been the case in Turkey over the last decade.

Clearly, neo-liberalism does not mean the same thing in a relatively poor country like Turkey as it does in the richer West. Rolling back the state in a developing economy does not necessarily extend to a major reduction in state welfare programs. On the contrary, these tend to start from a position of under-development. The tax situation is also framed very differently. Whereas in the West the movement away from state intervention has resulted in a raising of the populist cause of low taxation to the status of something like a moral prescription and sharply circumscribing political possibilities, in Turkey it is the levels of tax collection that have been problematic (leading to the setting of high levels of underpaid tax and resulting in the need for windfall type consumer taxes, such as irregular mobile phone tariffs). Moreover, Turkey did not start from a position of inefficient heavy industry based on highly unionised, relatively expensive labour, which has characterized the restructuring that has been taking place in some Western (and CIS) countries. This is not to say that the introduction of neo-liberalism in developing countries does not include social programmes being transferred away from state provision, capital gains taxes going unreduced and workers' rights being eroded. On the contrary, all of these have occurred in Turkey, much of which Murat refers to. Nevertheless, it is developing countries that are most vulnerable to the interests of international capital, even as they enter a new age of comparative prosperity. And starting from the position of a prominence of the agricultural sector, it is the rural economies that are most affected by the transformation effected by capital, and it is the fabric of village life that is most torn and ripped apart and partially patched back together in new ways by the ending of supports and opening of markets; it is urban migration and the metamorphosis or death of the village that most defines the socio-economic restructuring that occurs as a result, and it is the consequent transformation of poverty and the peasantry that characterises the human dimension of this. These are the changes documented here for Turkey.

References

Bernstein, H. (2008). Who are the 'people of the land'? Some provocative thoughts on globalization and development, with reference to sub-Saharan Africa. Presented at conference on *Environments Undone: The Political Ecology of Globalization and Development*, University of North Carolina, Chapel Hill, NC, USA, Feb 29 – March 1, 2008.

DPT (1982/2000). *İhtisas Raporu*. Ankara: Devlet Planlama Teskilati, cited in Jongerden, J. (2007).

Demir, K. and S. Çabuk (2011). Türkiye'de Metropoliten Kentlerin Nüfus Gelişmi (The population growth of metropolitan cities in Turkey). *Sosyal Bilimler Enstitütsü Dergisi* 28: 193-215.

EU (1999). 1999 Regular Report from the Commission on Turkey's Progress towards Accession. Available at: http://ec.europa.eu/enlargement/archives/pdf/key_documents/1999/turkey_en.pdf.

Jongerden, J. (2007). The settlement issue in Turkey and the Kurds: an analysis of spatial policies, modernity and war. Leiden: Brill.

Le Mons Walker, K. (2003). Peasant insurrection in China reconsidered: a preliminary examination of the Jun Mountain peasant rising, Nantong county, 1863. *Journal of Peasant Studies* 20(4): 640-668.

McMichael, P. (2005). Global development and the corporate food machine. In: Buttel, F.H., and McMichael, P. (eds.) *New directions in the sociology of global development, Vol. 11, Research in Rural Sociology and Development*. San Diego: Elsevier JAI, pp. 269-303.

Oman, C. (1906). *The great revolt.* Oxford: Clarendon Press.

Stirling, P. (1965). *Turkish village.* London: Weidenfeld and Nicolson.

Van der Ploeg, J.D. (2008). *The New Peasantries: Struggles for Autonomy and sustainability in era of empire and globalisation.* London: Earthscan.

Wimsatt, W.C. (1983), Von Baer's law of development, generative entrenchment, and scientific change. Unpublished manuscript, Department of Philosophy, Chicago: University of Chicago, cited in McLaughlin, P. (1998). Rethinking the agrarian question: the limits of essentialism and the promise of evolutionism. *Human Ecology Review* 5(2): 25-39.

Weiker, W.F. (1973). *Political tutelage and democracy in Turkey: the free party and its aftermath.* Leiden: Brill.

Preface

The agrarian question had been much discussed in Turkey in the 1960s and 70s. Essentially, the focus of this debate was on whether Turkish agriculture structure was semi-feudal or capitalist in character. Those of us interested in agriculture, from academic or political viewpoints, caught the end of these discussions during the 1980s. Meanwhile, along with the most of the rest of the world, Turkey was taking another route, that of neo-liberal globalization. In this new context of international capitalism, the agrarian question took on new dimensions. It is this to which the present work is principally addressed.

The study started in earnest in 2008 with a review of the old agrarian debate and historically development of Turkish agriculture. Using data from the State Statistics Institute, a first article was produced and published in the Turkish edition of the Monthly Review (Öztürk 2010). The core of this comprises an enhanced version of that study. Upon completion of the initial study, it soon became clear that detailed new research was required in order understand the changes that the Turkish countryside had experienced and was still undergoing. A research project was designed and funds secured through Kadir Has University in Istanbul, where a research project was established on 'Agricultural transformation in Turkey since 1980'. The completed qualitative stage of this, as well as new information gathered from fieldwork, is included here together with the initial findings of the project.

The change in agriculture and rural Turkey in under neo-liberal policies indicated another area of focus, that of poverty. With millions of people leaving village life for the city, the problem of poverty had clearly taken on new features. To understand further the socio-economic impact of the effects of neo-liberalism on agriculture – in short, the transformation of the peasantry – the issue of poverty, focusing especially on urban poverty, also needed to be reconsidered. Thus, as a corollary of the work on agriculture and the rural situation, a study of poverty was made. This was presented namely 'Neo-liberal policies and poverty: effects of policy on poverty and poverty reduction in Turkey', at the first International Conference of Social Economy and Sustainability, held at Maringa University, Parana, Brazil, 21-26 September 2010, a developed version of which was then published (Öztürk 2011). The final chapters of this book are drawn from that study.

Joost Jongerden, Ahmet Çakmak and Murat Çokgezen read and criticized the draft for this work and suggested some new approaches. Metin Çulhaoğlu helped with the translation of a part of study into English. Andy Hilton proofread the final draft and suggested many ideas for the data, rebuilding the text and compiling the book and adding a foreword. Mike Jacobs and his colleagues from Wageningen Academic Publishers offered further helpful suggestions and prepared the book for publishing, I want to thank them all for their contributions.

Chapter 1. Introduction

This book represents a case study of agriculture, peasantry and poverty in the neo-liberal age. As a 'developing' country, the case of Turkey stands as an example of the paradigmatic socio-economic transition of the present era, the modernising upheaval of a society wrenched from its deeply rooted, inherited agrarian base in a short space of time through processes of industrialisation and urbanisation facilitated by state support of international capital transfers and a globalised 'free trade' regime. There has been a seismic shift in agriculture and its place in the country, constituting also a transformation of the peasantry and radical restructuring of poverty. The present study thus focuses on changes in and linkages between its chosen topics of agriculture, peasantry and poverty in the Turkish context, rather than detailed analysis of them individually (in which respect they are different research areas and already have a rich literature). Firstly, a historiographic analysis of agriculture in Turkey is presented. The focus here is very much on developments specific to the current period of neo-liberalism. Then, relations between agricultural and rural development are considered, along with their impact on poverty. Inevitably, the issue of poverty cannot be handled in the context of the agricultural and rural development alone, and demands that other (urban) phenomena associated with and constitutive of the problem also be addressed.

The underlying dynamic of change in the three subjects as examined here is that defined by the framework of neo-liberalism. Neo-liberal policies have many common characteristics, exhibited and followed the world over. On the other hand, changes in agriculture, peasantry and poverty attendant upon neo-liberal policies do also exhibit different particularities in different countries, including those specified as generalities by developmental level. Some changes, that is, are ubiquitous (the long-term trend away from agriculture as a primary means of subsistence, for instance, accelerated by neo-liberalism through policies like the withdrawal of direct state support for farmers); some are particular to developing countries (such as large-scale internal migration and extremely rapid urban growth, strongly linked to the neo-liberal thrust for economic 'development'); and some specific to the case of Turkey (including details related to quite how the state has been rolled back, and the specific ways in which rural life and poverty have altered in its various regions). Clearly, a complex field of analysis is indicated. It is with this in mind, therefore, that the present study follows the methodology of political economics, The nexus of agriculture, peasantry and poverty is analysed in the context of a nation (Turkey) and specific historical period (post 1980), taking farming and the equation of farmer with peasant as its starting point, along with the socio-spatial representation of this in the rural, manifested especially through the village as a place where farming communities composed of small scale operations (essentially family-based, subsistence enterprises) live and work the land. This equation conceptually grounds a focus of interest in poverty, to which agriculture and peasantry have strong internal ties.

Processes and dynamics of physical production may be considered from the perspective of social relations. In any such examination of relations, both (or all) sides obviously have their own specificities. This is valid also for agriculture and peasantry analysis, which needs to handle these both separately, as two different items, and together, as a unitary dyad, notwithstanding the fact that it is only in the recent past that they have become decoupled in any important way (in the non-developed territories that comprise most of the world, that is). In this book, agriculture and peasantry are viewed as distinct (albeit interconnected) entities. The reasons for this analytical distinction are mostly related to the evolution of the peasantry out of agriculture: rural based populations no longer live solely or even primarily off the land, while, people living off the land no longer necessarily live in villages. Smallholder families in Turkey today, for example, often include members who are employed outside the agricultural sector off-farm jobs, while geographical and social mobility stretches the traditional ties of extended family and fractures the traditional communal solidarity of village life (the lived reality of the peasantry as a social class). There is another category of people who live in towns or even large cities but earn (full or part) incomes from farming activities, mostly on family (small plot, inherited) land but related especially to enterprise culture rather than subsistence. And again, rises in the numbers of people who live on pensions and income supports, perhaps also with major contributions from migrant family members (including from out of the country), further complicates the identification of categories like farmer and peasant, or agriculture and peasantry as (single) units of analysis. It is developments like these that challenge traditional modes of conceptualisation and require the analytical separation of agriculture from peasantry, and vice versa.

Rural populations today are no longer bound by farming for their subsistence as they once were. In Turkey, as elsewhere in the world, the diversification of economic activities and income sources of the traditional peasantry is increasingly evident, necessitated especially by changes in the globalizing economic environment. Coupled with adjustments to farming practices, as peasant farmers entering and operating in the local market are also increasingly forced by the commercial pressures of agribusiness to become resilient entrepreneurs functioning as lean and flexible enterprises, this differentiation of villagers' economic activities and income sources is bringing about changes in their relationship to land, the means of production and thus to their own specification as a social class. In a country like Turkey, where the agriculture sector had been dominant until the very recent past (and still continues to be hugely important in the country as a whole), this transformation constitutes a major change in social structure. It is a transformation that includes a diversification not only in rural peoples' subsistence practices but also in property relations and the usage of yielded incomes. This implies a need for these phenomena to be analysed together (with, at the same time, of course, cognisance of the differences between them).

The ties between poverty and agriculture and peasantry are many and varied. For one thing, a large proportion of poor people live in rural areas (or, surplus value is primarily produced in urban contexts, or, population centres are also the sites of concentrations of wealth). This remains the case despite the fact that farming with one's own means of production enables nutritional and housing requirements to be more easily met for the rural poor than the urban, and even though the effects of poverty are ameliorated in rural areas through family solidarity and communal ties among neighbours. Secondly, one main source of (the character of) poverty in a country like Turkey is rural-to-urban migration (of the peasantry, that is, from agriculture and, often enough, into the ranks of the city poor). Thirdly, neo-liberal policies have negative impacts on all these areas (agriculture, peasantry and poverty), insofar as they have destructive effects on small scale farming which increases rural poverty while at the same time being linked to growth policies that cannot create employment for the urbanised ex-peasantry. This also implies a need to consider the historical background to the issues in question, prior, that is, to the neo-liberal period.

The present work is divided into two parts, the first looking at developments in agriculture in Turkey and the second focusing on changes to rural life and poverty. Each begins with a theoretical context for the review that follows. The first chapter of Part I presents a précis of conceptual frameworks and theoretical explanations that deal with the transition from pre-capitalist to capitalist social formation and analysis of subsequent (contemporary) agricultural and rural transitions. Discussion of the transformation of the peasantry – or 'petty commodity producer', or 'small scale agriculture producer', or just 'smallholders' – from pre-capitalist to capitalist production relations has been a subject much considered since the development of the capitalist system in Europe and its diffusion through the world at large. The present work thus opens with an overview focusing on some recent perspectives on this 'agrarian question', as it became formulated.

Differentiations of agriculture and peasantry have, of course, progressed parallel to the development of capitalism, and the agrarian question has been reframed accordingly. In order to understand the current transformation in agriculture and the peasantry, therefore, one needs to look at the contemporary characteristics of capitalism. Foremost among these is the integration at world scale, termed 'globalisation', which includes among its main economic characteristics the financialisation of economic life and rising instability in financial markets, the anonymity of international trade, and changes in the organisation of economic activities with the usage of new information technologies and the production, supply and sales strategies of multinational companies.

Some of the primary issues in the area(s) of agriculture and the peasantry in the process of globalisation can be listed thus:
- the liberalisation of the agricultural products trade;
- speculation dependent on the forward transaction of agricultural products and therefore floating agricultural product prices;
- diminishing agricultural supports, corporate monopolisation of the global agricultural input and food sectors, and the effects of the these corporations on nourishment supply, sales and farmer and consumer practices (related to 'food security' and 'food sovereignty');
- the development of property rights on herbal genetic materials, and its corollary, bio-piracy;
- declining biodiversity and environment problems generally;
- health concerns related to industrialised food production;
- the long-term sustainability of the present system (Bernstein 2010: 102-106).

Drawing on the work of writers such as Philip McMichael and Jan Douwe van der Ploeg as well as Henry Bernstein, Chapter 2 introduces the present work with observations on the economic and social aspects of the transformation in agriculture and peasantry that have been occurring as a result of – and as a part of – this global capitalist development.

The next chapter (Chapter 3) provides a background for the Turkish situation, with a brief review of the development of agriculture in the Republic from its foundation after WWI until the new era. One of the main structural characteristics of Turkish agriculture has been small scale land ownership. Inherited from the Ottoman Empire, this basic structure did not change so much during the main part of the period of the Turkish Republic. When the modern state of Turkey was founded, agriculture had a big share in the economy, and the urgent need in the country in the context of an impoverished and broken land, wracked with starvation, disease and poverty and depopulated by war, genocides and expulsions was for essential produce like food and cloth. This shaped agriculture policy in the nascent state, and was fundamental to its economic strategy. Public institutions founded to buy, process and sell agriculture products, enact price support mechanisms, and deliver education in the framework of these policies guided the development of Turkish agriculture and dominated the economy up to about 1950. Thereafter, industrial processes and the manufacturing sector began to become significant, mechanisation was introduced into agriculture, slowly at first but gaining speed later, and combining in the 1960s with the green revolution to lead to rises in the amount of cultivated land and levels of productivity.

This sets the scene for the following chapters of Part I, which consider developments in agriculture in Turkey after 1980, reviewing, in other words, the particular expression in this sector of neo-liberalism. The neo-liberal policies applied in Turkey since 1980 and especially after 1999 have had profound effects on its farming economy and village life. Deep, structural changes have occurred that partly represent a continuation of historical development, but also indicate novel characteristics. The analysis of agriculture during this period presented here in order to get at this mainly employs official statistical data in focusing on agricultural enterprises (enterprise scale), mechanisation and technology, productivity employment and the state financing of agriculture.

Fundamental to contemporary globalizing progress has been the establishment of international institutions and mechanisms and the (multi-)national implementation of policies in line with the approach of neo-liberalism. The essential proposals of neo-liberal policies targeting various macro-economic and institutional changes can be summarised thus:

- removal of state price intervention in product and factor markets;
- liberalisation of foreign trade: abandonment of quotas and reduction of duties;
- privatisation of public economic enterprises (SOEs);
- liberalisation of finance markets, promotion of direct foreign capital investments and external financial flows;
- extension of privatisation in social services provision (education, health, etc.);
- expansion of tax base with the help of tax rate reductions;
- market determination of interest rates;
- emphasis on competitive exchange rates;
- generalised deregulation of the economy;
- regularisation of property rights;
- ensured flexibility of labour markets.

These policies were designed mostly with regard to the interests of international capital and, when developing nations slow to implement them came unstuck in the new climate of globalised capital movements, were introduced through IMF prescription and structural adjustment programs. Approaches developed by the World Trade Organisation, it might be added, did not contradict this framework. In Turkey's case, liberalisation was initiated at the beginning of the 1980s, but progressed slowly during the 1990s when a series of weak coalition governments prevented radical adjustment. However, a massive financial and economic crisis at the end of the 90s enabled the IMF to dictate an extremely rapid pace of change. This dovetailed into Turkey's ongoing integration of EU norms and the coming to power of a new, moderately Islamist (or 'conservative') party (the AKP), whose political franchise was outside the old Republican elite. In other words, a combination of external and internal political developments and economic events coincided to facilitate the implementation of a relatively rapid neo-liberal restructuring in Turkey during the first decade of the millennium. From a macroeconomic perspective, it may be noted, this has resulted in a period of strong growth and reduced national debt as measured by GDP, along with a large balance of payments (current account) deficit and heightened vulnerability to swings in the international money markets and withdrawals of corporate investments.

Historically, agricultural development has followed different paths according to the stage of capital accumulation in combination with administrative (national government) policies and international (institutional) approaches. As a fundamental shift in the way agriculture is done in the sense of the capital/labour relationship, this process inevitably impacts on and is affected through concomitant changes in the socio-economic structures linked to agriculture and the way farming is done. Chapter 6 provides a resume of the main findings in this respect from Part I. Interestingly, perhaps, considering that Turkey is sometimes categorised as a 'newly industrialised country' (NIC), small scale farming is statistically shown to be still a determinate characteristic of the country's agriculture. The question begged, therefore, is (even acknowledging that small scale farmers cultivate less than land in the past) how is it that, despite reduced state supports, uncertain market conditions and new competitive actors, they continue to rebuff rationalisation and the economic imperative of capital towards scale economies – and survive? The concluding passages of Part I therefore point to some of the survival mechanisms small scale farmers, which also directs attention to the (non-)unity or equation of farmer as peasant. The kind of developments described in the first part of this book thus indicate some of the new explanations that are needed, which will have to include the new complexities in global economic conditions.

The further introduction of economies of scale and rationalisations of business in the agricultural sector leave a deep impression on the countryside, and the second part of this book comprises an investigation into that and its linkage to poverty generally. As mentioned, Part II is introduced by a theoretical perspective on socio-economic changes in Turkish agriculture and rural structure Chapter 7 comprises a review of the literature on this. In the context of agricultural income rises and the beginnings of rural-to-urban migration after 1950, rural sociology in Turkey focused especially on migration and rural transformation, generally approaching this from a developmentalist or modernist point of view. The peasantry and its environment were problematised, with consideration of issues around rural education, infrastructure, unemployment, health provision and, of course, migration. More recent work has begun to look at some of the contemporary complexities – questioning the village and peasantry as unit of analysis, for example, and looking at the widening income generation base in villages – which here serves as a launching pad for an investigation into the socio-economic structures and dynamics of rural life today.

Changes in the rural population and its primary settlement unit, the village, comprise the subject matter of Chapter 8. Turkey has a young and fast growing population, but obviously, like anywhere in the (developing) world today, this increase is centred on the cities. The numbers of people living in Turkey's villages and hamlets have not risen as they have in urban areas during the last decades – in fact, the upheaval in agriculture has seen them fall, sharply. While this recent history marks both a continuation of historical process (urbanisation), the scale of the urban migration and consequent rural depopulation represents a qualitatively new dimension. But population changes are not just gross numbers, they are demographics: that is, the people moving between rural and urban areas are not necessarily a perfect cross section of the populace. Chapter 8, therefore, investigates this. How is the rural population changing? What is happening to the village? And, by implication (as a continuation of the theme of the peasantry), what is happening to the small scale agriculture producer? Inquiry into these matters takes the form of an analysis of migration, economic activities, incomes and the reshaping of the rural population of peasant farmers as a social class.

Although rural population decrease has led to a reduction in agricultural activities, around a quarter of the labour force remains employed in agriculture. This labour force, however, is not necessarily domicile in rural contexts. Urban migrants continue to farm the land, either directly, returning to their villages during seeding and harvesting time, or indirectly, renting their land to neighbours and other farmers still living in the area (village or local town, or even both, on a seasonal basis). And while some villages have just died, losing their entire populations, a limited number of villages have witnessed a rise in the number of people living there. These are mostly retired people and the villages situated on the coast. Indeed, ageing village populations generally represent another trend, one that indicates a grim future. Another important area of change is in the structure of the rural population employment. Non-farm and off-farm employment are rising rapidly, and due particularly to the participation of women in such paid activities, traditional forms of unwaged employment are waning in importance. And another conspicuous fact that is the proportion of handicapped people is higher in rural areas. These and other factors go to indicate that villages have a special social function as asylums for the weak.

Considerations such as these afford insights into the future of the farm and village life. Predictable trends include the continued survival of smallholder farming – due in part to the extent of mountainous terrain in Turkey, which operates in various ways as a preventative to economies of scale – but an erosion of the peasantry as social class as their means of subsistence diversifies, thereby fracturing their integrity as a single grouping and mitigating against simple class analysis. Testimony to this is the lack of politicisation of the peasantry in Turkey after the manner of the Via Campesina movement. Small land owners will farm less and farmer numbers decline in line with capitalistic development, with a continued increase in the number and size of large scale farms. Some villages will become living and holiday areas rather than farming spaces, or dual living places, with families split between village and urban lives – in respect of which the Turkish bent to long summer sojourns in a second home, including in the family village (the 'homeland', or *memleket*), represents an important cultural phenomenon. Another phenomenon of the future may be the continued increase of urban farmers, while the (often reverse) migration of retired people (seasonally or permanently) from cities to rural environments suggests that 'pension villages' will not only survive but increase in numbers. Meanwhile, at the same time as the development of villages as asylums for the weak, as centres of unemployment and residence for those out of the labour force, there will also be further movements of urban wealth to rural areas, both through tourism, indigenous and also foreign (as in many emerging and developing economies, the tourism sector is a major income source for Turkey), and also through satellite development linked to urban conurbations and industrial, service and trading centres.

When the huge changes in agriculture and consequent loss of rural population are considered, the question of how the rural people and rural migrants survive is clearly a huge social issue. In fact, the 'progress' in agriculture is one of the main reasons for the rise of new kinds of poverty, in rural and urban areas (i.e. as outlined, but also further to these types of changes). Neo-liberal policies, that is, play a major role in determining the new character of poverty at the start of the new millennium. What remains to be considered in the present study, therefore, is this residual problem of poverty, residual in the sense that neo-liberalism, it is quite clear now, is no magic solvent for hardship, as well as in the sense that much of the traditional poverty of the peasantry remains but situated now in the city, moved through migration to an alternative social setting, that of the new urban underclass. This by product of the neo-liberal distillation of agriculture then nourishes the capitalist project itself with massive supplies of labour, which feed the cycle of poverty with depressed wages and unprotected working conditions. By way of an analysis of this situation, its underlying dynamics and the response, the final chapters here consider the neo-liberal approach to poverty (Chapter 9), and the structuring of poverty and recent history of pro-poor and poverty reduction policies in Turkey today (Chapter 10).

The neo-liberal approach to poverty is essentially constituted by emphasis on wealth production as the best route to a worldwide reduction in the numbers and hardships of the poor. Economies grow their way out of poverty (or, the global economy makes mass extreme poverty a thing of the past). This tends toward non-engagement with the actual problem as it manifests, while the dogma of non-state intervention leads to a stress on self-help and an understanding of the issues involved that suggests piecemeal charity rather than the developed social security systems built through social struggle and financed by taxation. This approach, in the eyes of many, has reached its limit. Neo-liberal does not, in fact, address underlying causes of poverty such as structural inequality as an integral part of the capitalist system of wealth production, and its one notable positive policy, the championing of micro credit systems, is little more than window-dressing, excellent for a relatively small number of people and groups with entrepreneurial ideas and vitality on the borderlines of poverty, but no more than scratching the surface of the problem as a whole. This holds for Turkey, too. The *lack* of success of neo-liberalism in dealing with worldwide poverty to date is reviewed in Chapter 8, taking the UN Millennium Goals as a starting point. Even according to this minimal index, it is argued, results are less impressive than may be assumed. A brief critique of the foundations of the neo-liberal approach to poverty is then developed, including in this the perspective of distribution, or social justice.

As outlined in Chapter 10, Turkey's current poverty reduction policies have been maintained with IMF/World Bank supports, and continue to follow a course parallel to the neo-liberalizing poverty reduction policies of these institutions. Pro-poor policies since 1980 have increasingly consisted of aids from charitable institutions, municipalities, non-governmental organisation and public institutions, rather than employment creation and income protection. These have thus failed to impact on a distinctive character of the new poverty in Turkey's cities. The old type of urban poverty constituted by the migration from village to city was possible to escape – indeed, this was expected – through employment and support from the informal support network of family and village coupled with that of the social security system. The massive influx of migrants from the countryside during the neo-liberal dismantling of the country's agrarian base and the lack of concern of this approach with positive policies for job creation or employment protection combined also with other but linked factors (such as in the area of housing) has meant that this is no longer so. People cannot escape urban poverty, and do not expect to, or even hope to. This transition – characterised here as a move from 'rotation poverty' to 'permanent poverty' – has also led to the development of various forms of exclusion. Chapter 10 concludes with a review and critique of the implementation of the Turkish government's social policies related to poverty and exclusion.

The end of this study (Chapter 11) is comprised by a general evaluation of the developments in agriculture and countryside and the historical place of the smallholder in Turkey in the present context of depopulation and depeasantisation. It is uncertain how the transformations of capitalism propelled by neo-liberalism will end, and the current dynamics of development suggest questions like how many of today's villages will still exist in a couple of decades, how will these survive villages and what kind of places will they be? Contrary to the negative implications behind these questions, however, the further development of peasant (smallholder) survival strategies, increases in the non-agricultural usage of villages, and various forms of population movements to rural areas have the potential to reduce poverty in the countryside. It is entirely conceivable that effective policies might be able to utilise and maximise these potentials and support the reduction of urban overcrowding while also supplying a better living environment for the elderly in particular.

Part I
Trends in Turkish agriculture since 1980

The first part of this book seeks to identify the major trends in Turkish agriculture during the period since 1980. It begins with a brief look at the classical agrarian question and new approaches to the question with reference to an environment in which neo-liberal policies dominate and the tendency to globalisation prevails in the world economy. Developments in Turkish agriculture after 1980 are addressed through these conceptual tools. Chapter 3 provides a historical overview on the development of agriculture in Turkey prior to the introduction of neo-liberal policies, while the fourth reviews developments since then. Then follows in Chapter 5 an analysis of the trends in Turkish agriculture over the last three decades, employing arguments made in the literature and empirical data. The sixth, concluding chapter assesses the developments in Turkish agriculture after 1980 in the context of classical views and others that address the issue in the light of the contemporary global circumstances. While classical approaches still have some explanative power in understanding recent developments, new approaches offer more in this respect. Nevertheless, there is a need for new field studies to test and/or consolidate the elaborations introduced by these new approaches.

Chapter 2. The agrarian question

This chapter begins with the overview of the agrarian question. The literature on this subject is extensive, and here it is only introduced by way of establishing a conceptual framework, with a presentation just of the first (classic) exposition and recent revisions of the agrarian question that are. Parallel to the major, ongoing transformation in agriculture we witness today, understanding and explanation of it are improving too. Until the recent past, the main questions had related to the ways in which agriculture and the rural environment changed with capital accumulation. Sociological concern nowadays focuses on how smallholder agriculture and rural life survive. Current explanations include the global dimension of contemporary capitalism in their analysis of agrarian change, and international circumstances thus receive extra attention here also. It is the aim of this chapter to give basic theoretical information summarising agrarian and rural processes, to look at the main arguments of the original and current explanations, rather than engage in detailed discussion.

Peasant-farmers and change

Analyses of peasantry and agricultural structures in the process of capitalist development have been an important and highly debated issue. Dubbed the 'agrarian question', this 'focuses on how in the context of a capitalistic world system or a social formation where capitalism is dominant, pre-capitalistic forms of production and enterprise types, particularly the existence of petty production, can survive and exist and how this persistence can be associated with capitalism' (Boratav 1981: 106).

The development that can be expected to take place in agriculture when the process of capital accumulation starts to operate in a given economy can be put simply as the emergence, on the one hand, of peasants turning into workers having to sell their labour force after having lost their land, and on the other, of capitalist farmers who expand their land by appropriating others' and strive to maximise their profit by investing in agricultural production. Another component of the same process is that production is no longer employed for the needs and subsistence of the farmer, but for markets. Within this overall scheme there is another issue that should be mentioned, namely small farming or peasant production. The peasant producing for the market on the basis of his/her family labour and with his/her own instruments of production has been addressed both as an enterprise engaged in production and as a unit of demographic analysis (Boratav 1985: 10).

Discussions on the agrarian question came to the fore at the end of the 19th and the beginning of the 20th centuries. In Lenin and Kautsky, followers of Marx, peasantry is not taken up as a distinct issue for analysis: the peasantry is merely addressed as a composition of mixed classes and groups (see Aydın 1986: 133). Capitalist development does not mean the complete expropriation and proletarianisation of rural families: they are able to sell their labour force without being expropriated (Kautsky, cited by Aydın 1986: 138). This development, according to Lenin, offers the possibility for infinite combinations of various types of capitalist formation and evolution. When the laws of capitalist accumulation start to operate in agriculture, the liquidation of the peasantry can take place in several forms. These include:
- forceful liquidation (the British model);
- landlords become capitalist farmers and serfs losing their land move into wage labour (the Prussian model);
- small farmers increase in numbers and come to constitute a petty bourgeoisie (the American model) (De Janvry *et al.*, cited by Ulukan 2009: 33).

Some of the leading classical views concerning the peasantry and its transformation are represented by Alexander Chayanov, Teodor Shanin, Samir Amin, Kostas Vergopoulos and Henry Bernstein. According to Chayanov (1966), the peasant works not for profit but family subsistence. S/he is thus incapable of engaging in capital accumulation. Peasants are transformed into commodity producers, linked to the market by commercial capital and placed under the control of capital. Shanin (1982, cited in Chris Hann and Ildiko Beller Hann 2001) argues similarly, that peasant communities are essentially static, and that change is exerted from without through such factors as nature, the market and the state.

According to Samir Amin (2009), farmers in peripheral countries are not small commodity producers. Both the state and capital intervene in the process of production and de facto control it. While seemingly owning their instruments of production, therefore, they can neither control production nor decide what to produce on the basis of relative prices. They have the status of 'proletarians working at home'. Vergopolos (1978, cited by Ulukan 2009) maintains that family farm is the most successful form of production, transferring the maximum possible surplus to urban capitalism. In this form of simple commodity production in articulation with urban-origin capitalism, resources flow from rural to urban areas. Again, as in Amin's view, rural farmers are regarded as akin to wage labourers even though they appear to be the owners of instruments of production. It is market mechanisms that transfer surplus out from this mode of production.

According to Bernstein (2008), in the model of peasant economy there can be no reference to a mode of production. Since the household is taken as the producing unit, social relations are examined at household level. The *social relations of production* which is the crucial part of the concept of *mode of production* is absent in this theory. Relations of production comprise the form of appropriating surplus, distribution and use of social output as a whole. This totality does not really correspond to the position of peasant farmers. Bernstein does hold that the process of capitalistic commodity production creates the conditions for the development of a peasant economy becoming a part of its organisation and activities, and that some forms of small scale production disappear with the development of a capitalist division of labour. However, the dynamics of development (i.e. capitalist competition, accumulation, concentration) continuously create new areas in this division of labour for small scale commodity production. Efforts on the part of peasants to reproduce their instruments of production and labour are moulded in the context of access to land, credit and markets, of relations with powerful groups or individuals, of natural conditions and of government policies. The peasant continues to produce both use value for him/herself and commodities for markets. This use value causes the devaluation of household labour time and thus the value of goods produced for market. In the face of declining terms of trade (the ratio of the prices of agricultural products to those of industrial products), the household either reduces consumption or intensifies commodity production or both. The exploitation of the peasantry is explained through the devaluation of working time, and, based on this, peasants are identified as 'wage labour equivalents' (Ulukan 2009: 33-48).

Summarizing the above, what and who the peasant/small producer is and how change occurs can be expressed thus:
- *Small producer/peasant*: unable to accumulate (Chayanov); a proletarian working at home having no control over production, which is controlled by the State and capital (Amin); akin to wage labourer, with surplus pumped out through market mechanisms (Vergopulos);

produces use value for himself while also producing for the market; equivalent to wage labourer (Bernstein).

- *Change* can take place in various ways and combinations; transformation given effect by commercial capital (Chayanov); comes from without, through nature, the market, the state, etc. (Shanin); efforts on the part of peasants to reproduce their instruments of production and labour are moulded in the context of various forms of material access (to land, credit, markets) and social relations (with powerful groups, individuals) along with natural conditions and government policies (Bernstein).

Globalisation, imperialism and agriculture

Reconsidering the agrarian question in our present day, classical arguments clearly have an obviously weaker explanative power now given that agrarian socio-economics are now shaped by the global context. Contemporary views dealing with agriculture and the peasantry refer to such concepts as 'the diminishing peasantry', 'the demise of the peasantry' or 'the new peasantry' to signify a new framework and differentiate it from the classical. Developments that lie behind these ideas are associated with the impact on agriculture of neo-liberal policies and the tendencies of globalisation that became prevalent from the late 70s, but their origins are earlier than this (c.f. the models listed above).

According to the historian Eric Hobsbawm (1995), the demise of the peasantry was one of the most dramatic events of the 20th century. Yet, the peasantry remains, even in parts of Europe and certainly in the Middle East (and most of the rest of the world). In Turkey, it has been shrinking (a phenomenon that is also widely observed), but still constitutes an absolute majority of the rural population.[2] As a generalisation, therefore, it can be stated that worldwide trends hold also for Turkey.

According to Samir Amin (2009: 89-91) there are, in fact, three billion peasant-farmers worldwide. These three billion people engaged in subsistence farming, it is theorised, could be replaced by thirty million farmers engaged in the production system (i.e. without effecting food security). In other words, the *actual* death of the peasantry would involve

---

[2] In Turkey, as elsewhere, the rural population generally has been (is) in decline, not only as a proportion of the national population (the demographic phenomenon of mass urbanisation), but also in absolute terms (as a result of the industrialisation of agriculture and various migrations) (see Chapter 7).

the reduction of the population working in agriculture to just 1% of its current number. Whether such a complete transformation is at all likely in the foreseeable future (let alone desirable) is, of course, highly speculative (and contentious), but it would certainly involve the continuation of some historical global trends on a massive scale. The preconditions for such a transformation would include:
- the transfer of fertile lands to capitalist farmers;
- capital endowment (for materials and equipment);
- access to consumer markets.

With the emergence of such trends of fundamental change, any analysis of the issue requires an equivalent revision of fundamental concepts. As McMichael states, 'Explanations on the agrarian question in its original form cannot be applied to the change taking place today. While states were organised on the principles of political economy for a period starting from the late 19th and early 20th century, in the 21st century capital became the organizing principle (McMichael 2008: 205).

Defined in a broader context, the 'agrarian question' today tends to focus on the following: the detrimental effects of internationally directed food policies on small farms; the appropriation of local farmers' information by seed monopolies through copyright law; and the ruthless attack on peasant smallholders in the context of new balances determined by financial relations and globalised industrial-retail commodity chains ('agribusiness'). Agriculture is turning into 'world agriculture' as the globalisation of agricultural companies ousts peasant farming which is replaced by company-commodity chains. As a result of economic liberalisation, newly emerging patterns of food(stuff) production and trading ruthlessly eject small farmers from their niches, causing the displacement of labour and thus further flexibility in employment conditions (McMichael 2006: 407-409). The globalisation of the world's markets and state withdraw from economic activities other than macro-economic management (from public ownership, import protection, subsidised supports, etc.), has provided ideal conditions for transnational corporate imperialism. For these brave new empires, agriculture is a major colony.

The institutional food regime rests especially upon the deregulation of financial relations shaped by privatisations in indebted countries along with a heightened (worldwide) mobility of labour. It becomes effective on the basis of a political context in which world prices diverge from labour costs. Prices of agricultural goods are artificially suppressed in a regime of over-production and redundancies (supported by the glaring anomaly of US and EU subsidies). The liberalisation in world prices (generalised reduction of subsidies and duties, and corporate hegemony of markets) combine with a relative decline in the commodity value of agricultural products to further increase the vulnerability of farmers to expropriation (McMichael 2006: 409).

> There are three key issues here. First, peasant trajectories are conditioned by world, rather than national, history. Second, as an instrument of legitimacy, the development narrative's enabling of an intensified peasant dispossession under a virulent neo-liberal regime has become the focal point of a contemporary peasant mobilisation. Third, conventional (liberal and Marxist) attempts to schematize modern history in developmentalist terms run aground on the shoals of stage theory – democratic outcomes, nationally imagined, are as partial as representations of peasants as historical relics (McMichael 2008: 206).

In redefining the agrarian question as one of social reproduction rather than capitalist transition, Bernstein abandons the classical agrarian question of capital on the grounds that globalisation involves centralizing capital and fragmenting labour under conditions of 'massive development of the productive forces in (advanced) capitalist agriculture.' That is, the material (but not social) question of food supply is resolved, even as global labour is impoverished by tenuous employment conditions. The 'agrarian question of labour' is now 'manifested in struggles for land against 'actually existing' forms of capitalist landed property' (Bernstein 2008). A question here is why labour would struggle for land rather than employment, or, if the strugglers are indeed peasants of one kind or another, why represent the struggle through a lens that invokes (only) the capital/labour relation Robert Johnson's scenario echoes Bernstein in suggesting that capital turns its back on its margins – for him, present developments testify to an incomplete development project, which suspends the peasantry in a negative logic of bare subsistence (McMichael 2006: 410).

Another approach seeking to explain the contemporary process has been developed by Jan Douwe van der Ploeg. According to Van der Ploeg (2008a), world agriculture is characterised by three major trajectories, which fundamentally contradict one another. These trajectories are associated with specific components of agriculture, which, with and their reciprocal relations, which can be conceptualised thus:

1. *Peasant farming*: based on preserving natural capital and rural life; multi-functional, dependent on family labour and owning major instruments of production; production both for market and reproduction of family and the agricultural unit concerned.
2. *Enterprising agriculture*: distinguished by its use of credit, industrial inputs and technology; larger scale necessary; also, market-oriented specialised production, market dependency in terms of inputs and adaptation to modern agricultural policies developed by the state, etc.
3. *Corporate agriculture*: large-scale, international capitalist agriculture; mobile corporate farming with large networks, using wage labour and gaining further strength upon support accorded to export-oriented agriculture model.

All of these trajectories are currently to be found, coexisting and evolving, but there is also a movement through them (as stages of development), which might be termed 'the industrialisation of agriculture'.[3] The industrialisation of agriculture is characterised generally by processes of enlargement (realizing economies of scale), intensification (maximizing profit), specialisation (tending to monoculture) and artificialisation (fertilisation, biotechnology, etc.) (Van der Ploeg 2008a). Along with industrialisation, argues Van der Ploeg, comes diminishing agricultural activity and repeasantisation (see below). Individually, these trajectories have different, sometimes contradictory impacts, but industrialisation as a process through them does tend to have a common effect on several areas, including employment (increasing wage-labour but decreasing total agrarian labour input), the level of production (raised), the environment (damaged, polluted), nature(controlled, limited), biological diversity (reduced, lost) and the amount (increased) and quality (reduced) of food. In relation to the characteristics of these development trends, Van der Ploeg comments briefly on how industrialisation effects what he effects what he represents as the definitive break of the connection between food production and consumption. But space for food production is likely to become a problem with still rising consumption (population).With their

---

[3] This is not necessarily to imply incremental development – indeed, agricultural development in many parts of the world has been characterized by a move straight from trajectory 1 to 3, as multi-national companies have moved into and expropriated traditional (peasant based) farming environments.

spatial and temporal delinking, the problem of the relation between food production and consumption dissipated.[4]

Other current developments in agriculture associated with the move to corporate farming include: deactivation (a process that implies a reduction and eventual elimination of agricultural activities); falling output (contrary to the primary historical trend of industrialisation, in which the move from peasant farming to enterprise agriculture has generally been associated with a rise in production, the reverse seems to be the case in the move from enterprise to corporate agriculture); the transformation of agricultural resources into finance capital and their investment in other sectors and activities; the loss of agricultural land (due to an expansion of urban centres encroaching on farming lands; and land speculation becoming more rewarding than agricultural production; and practices imposed or mechanisms introduced by states or the EU, such as set-aside and the McSharry reforms (compensating farmers for non-use of land and low prices) (Van der Ploeg 2008b).

As for repeasantisation, this is in essence the modern expression of the fight for autonomy and existence in the context of dependency and deprivation. Peasant conditions are not static, but display improvements and declines over the course of time. As corporate farming experiences its evolution, peasant farming is changing too, with repeasantisation one of these changes. Essentially, argues Van der Ploeg (2008b), peasants have two options in the face of the developments related to corporate farming:
1. sink deeper into poverty, effectively leading to a depeasantisation; or
2. repeasantisation, a process aimed at transforming these developments into benefits.

A quantitative enlargement and a qualitative strengthening of peasant agriculture, repeasantisation assumes an increased autonomy as fundamental: the basic motive behind the behaviour of the 'new' peasant is control over his/her own destiny. The striving for autonomy impels the desire for self-control over resources; to survive and interact with the

---

[4] Thus Ruivenkamp (1989, 2008) observes the modern development of agriculture as involving four disconnection (and reconnection) processes, viz., biogenetic – separating agriculture from its ecological environment, through seed technology; industrial – separating agriculture from food production (and linking it to foodstuff production); commodifying – a further stage of separation from food production (linking agriculture to non-food production); and ecological – disconnecting agricultural produce from human health, by neglecting nutritional value (quality) in the interest of revenue (quantity).

market; feedback to resources; to enhance communal production and further expand autonomy. Additionally to the end in itself of enhanced autonomy, the benefits aimed at include new added value (of produce), higher income and increased employment.

Looking at large commodity markets restructured and controlled by imperialism, we do indeed see many farmers transforming their production values, systems, techniques, etc. New goods and services are being produced and new firms have mushroomed with new levels of competition. With fertilizing and revitalisation agriculture has again settled on the land; activities have multiplied and new forms of local cooperation coupled with advanced technologies have made a return to artisan production possible (Van der Ploeg 2008b: 2). In emphasizing this response to the new global agricultural environment in the context of neo-liberalism, however, the importance of national political state regulations, taxation and controls should not be overlooked. The trajectory for the (new) peasantry will depend on state interventions as well as economic change (Harrison 2006).

Looking at rural society, the behaviour and fate of the peasant crucially determines the fate of the basic unit of rural settlement, the village. Drawing on the views and arguments outlined, we can start from the position that just as capital accumulation in agriculture may take place in different forms, so also may peasants display varying characteristics and behaviour. In the process of capital accumulation, rural populations (peasants) are transformed into employers or wage labourers, and while some remain domicile and occupied in rural agriculture, the majority are expected to move to urban centres for employment since the demand for labour is more pronounced there (as an effect of the processes of industrialisation, which leads to a combination of increased urban and reduced agricultural labour demand). Those peasants who accumulate capital as smallholders and become employer-farmers have a rather different choice, of whether to keep their assets in farming or move them out of farming (and, probably also, out of rural areas).

Given this overall scheme, four significant sub-categories can be specified – i.e. further to the main category of village farmer (peasant-smallholder) – on the basis of settlement type, ownership of land and occupation sector (agricultural or otherwise) – noting that in comparison to the classical system, which grouped people together in the peasant/farmer class (assuming especially the traditional extended family structure particularly associated with rural life), different family members may now fall into different categories. Those five sub-categories are:

1. people living in a hamlet/village (rural environment) participating in production (agricultural or non-agricultural) as wage labourers or entrepreneurs;
2. farmers living in a town/city (urban environment);
3. people living in a hamlet/village, but out of the production process (living with mainly on public or private origin transfers, who might move in either direction between rural and urban space, i.e. rural-to-urban or urban-to-rural);
4. people living in an urban area and gaining income from outside of agriculture, but who also gain some income from farming;
5. some kind of mix of the above.

The first and second of these cover those people who are occupied in agriculture (as part of the production process, as opposed to peasant-farmers), while the first and third cover those who are domicile in rural environments. The fourth category comprises people who are only part occupied in agriculture, and living in towns or cities. The first sub-category includes farm-workers and 'modern' (enterprise) farmers (who usually employ workers, at least seasonally).[5] In the contemporary situation, derived from decades and more of capital accumulation, much of the mass of the working population that had (and would have) fallen into what from the perspective of historical analysis is (was) the main category of rural peasant-farmers now fall in this first sub-category. The second sub-category refers primarily to those farmers who have accumulated capital and moved away from the rural environment or he/she earns enough income to live in urban. The third sub-category covers mainly pensioners and people who self employed in agriculture or employed by the state administration (local civil servants, road workers, education and health workers/professionals, etc.), as well as groups that previously would not have been distinguished from peasants as a class (prior to the state provision of welfare, especially in the context of extended families), notably the unemployed, the sick and/or disabled, and retired people.

The fourth and fifth categories represent new phenomena. People in this category include, for example, entrepreneur farmers living in a town

---

[5] It also notably includes those who are employed in urban environments but live in the village either for family/community reasons or because their income is too low to afford the outgoings of (independent) town/city life.

with private origin transfers along with city based truck drivers who also manage their own wheat fields, or, again, villagers seasonally employed on local farms during the season but otherwise taking casual jobs in local construction, college students on a scholarship who help out on the family farm during holidays, and mothers and housewives tending the family plot during the week and working in town on Saturdays and whose husbands derive their income from farm machinery repair, etc. To state that these categories represents a new phenomenon is not to imply that agriculture used to be socio-economically one dimensional, but rather that the range and scale of composite options especially has bloomed qualitatively and quantitatively in such a way as to fragment class beyond definition. The possibilities may be more or less historically novel, enabled by things like fast, affordable transport, and niche markets, while sociological developments like family nuclearisation and greater formal female participation in employment sectors have increased the effects of these developments with an exponential increase in permutations. Boundaries between the relationships of individuals and income to different forms of capital have blurred beyond specification in any but the most complex of schema.[6]

The participation of the rural population in non-agricultural production sectors and consequent diversification of their income sources also necessitates modifications in the definition of village, which is traditionally linked to peasants engaged with their own land and instruments of production. This, in turn, requires addressing the village as a space of settlement on the one hand and a space where economic activity (agriculture) takes place on the other, including both their distinct characteristics and interrelationships. With the increase in peasant employment the number of villagers employed in non-agricultural sectors and amount of non-agricultural income in rural environments, agricultural activity continues, but its relative importance declines: people in this position the new peasants now base their subsistence on non-agricultural activities. Recent studies and observations highlight this contemporary form of development, with farmer/peasants surviving through income sources other than farming (Bernstein 2008: 10). According to Bernstein, these incomes signify the reproduction or dissolution as labour when what is earned is wages, and as capital when earned as petty commodity producer.

---

[6] For counting purposes, things like the use of the household as statistical unit and assumption of single, primary and fixed income source have become deeply problematized.

Bernstein also comments on how this new situation relates to the 'death of peasantry' as defined by Hobsbawm; in one dimension, and to developments in the direction of 'de-agriculturisation' in another: 'This type of argument has been formulated with various emphases to address different types of circumstances; for example, and very schematically, the views that non-farm activity and income are pursued by those '*too poor to farm*' or '*too busy to farm*' (*ibid.*: 12). These concepts – too poor or busy to be a farmer, meaning either those non-agricultural activities do not provide sufficient remuneration for farmers, or that farmers do not have sufficient capital or other resources to engage in them – may have positive or negative attributes, according to Bernstein. Looking at the positive aspects, 'too poor to farm' would appear to have a positive attribute when wage work or self-employment outweighs the benefits of full time farming. This may overlap with the second positive aspect of the concept, 'too busy to farm' insofar as both of them cover cases where the farmer seeks better living conditions in waged or self-employment than are to be achieved from farming, and where he pursues (additional) investment and profit opportunities out of agriculture. This coincides with the distinction between diversification in living sphere and its determinants on the one hand and diversification in subsistence and accumulation on the other. It is, of course, a class distinction and one essential for understanding social pattern divergences within a rural population as well as between and within regions (*ibid.*: 12).[7]

With the diversification of economic activities, the behaviour and characteristics of the population will diversify too. Along with diversified modes of work, the characteristics of populations living in villages constitute another reference point giving an idea about the characteristics of diversification in the village. From this point on, both the persistence of smallholding peasants and the reshaping of the village space can be approached by referring to variables related to migration and population, resource transfers from and to the village, and the structure of small farming enterprises in terms of producers and households. The analysis should also cover government policies that affect agricultural production and rural population living conditions, as well as the effects of developments taking place in national and international markets.

---

[7] *Vice versa*, the downside of being too poor to farm suggests a lack of remuneration in agriculture, which is also implied by the inability to make time for farming activities.

Taking all these into account, what kind of rural socio-economic networks emerge and how is the village reshaped upon the transfer of agricultural surplus out through market mechanisms and transfers of non-agricultural assets (incomes) both out and in? The structure of agriculture and (later) changing characteristics of the rural population in Turkey since the 1980s are addressed in the next chapters within the framework of these questions. To understand the 2000s better, a brief historical background will first be given, followed by an examination of recent developments on the basis of available data.

Chapter 3. The development of Turkish agriculture until 1980

Considered in conjunction with the above, we find that in respect of both approaches to agricultural change and developments after 1980 the Turkish case largely resembles most others in the rest of the world (though with some time differences in respect of advancement through the generalised process of development). An explanation of developments in Turkish agriculture after 1980, however, requires the context of an account of state agricultural policies in the country from 1920, in addition to major developments in the sector and their explanations. For an overwiev to physical and economic characteristics of the Turkish agriculture sector see Textbox 3.1

The republic: state input and the development of enterprise agriculture

Upon the foundation of the Republic in 1923, developments in agriculture were determined by the particular circumstances of the time and government policies and targets. Two major problems were paramount: the need to increase output and productivity, and the need to create a domestic market to enhance production and trade. In agricultural policies, populism and a positive-scientific approach formed the basis of government action. The primary policy adopted was that of promoting small producers in agriculture. Policies along this line included the distribution of treasury land and some land taken from landlords, allocated to people entering the country as a result of population exchanges (Köymen 2008).[8]

In the 1920s, agriculture accounted for a large part of the national income. Agriculture was the major component of national employment and a large majority of the population lived in rural areas. What was scarce at that time was not land as a productive factor, but labour and capital (Tekeli and İlkin 1988: 40). During the early years of the Republic, agricultural production was negatively affected by the reduced, variable and shifting

---

[8] Debates on land reform were to continue through the next decades, focusing on ways of giving land to peasants without touching the land of big landowners.

Textbox 3.1. Agriculture in Turkey.

Turkey has a wide range of agricultural produce due to its sub-tropical zone location in the Mediterranean macroclimate combined with a diversity of ecological environments as determined by its peninsular land mass form (extended coastline), with mountain ranges along the northern and southern coasts and in the eastern part of the country, and high central plateau. The northern coastal strip is mild and wet, and the elevated interior and mountainous east generally dry, cold in the winter and hot in summer (Appendices 1-2). Erosion is a major problem, as is the considerable variation in year-to-year rainfall, with widespread droughts every four years or so on average (e.g. in 2006-2007); about 30% of agricultural land is irrigated (Appendix 3).

Turkey can be divided into two agricultural regions, an interior west-to-east corn belt (Central and East Anatolia, with its heart in Konya), and the mostly coastal, peripheral areas, which are identified with specific products or product types (Appendix 4). The main cereal crop covering the greater part of the central land mass is wheat, followed by barley (primarily for animal feed now), and also oats. As well as cereals, the central Anatolian plateau is responsible for most of the country's sugar beet production, and the eastern part of Anatolia known for sheep herding.

Around this central and eastern swathe, the Black Sea (Ordu) coastal strip in the north is famous for hazelnuts, producing 70% of world exports (hazelnuts are native to the region), while the eastern part of this area (Rize) produces the nation's tea. In the northwest, the European Marmara (Edirne) region is known especially for sunflowers, and the fertile western, Aegean (İzmir) region for figs, olives and grapes. In the southern, Mediterranean region, Antalya is known for oranges and lemons, while the irrigated Çukurova plain around Adana, one of the most productive agricultural parts of the country, is the primary cotton growing area. Fishing features in all these coastal regions. To the southeast, in the Tigris-Euphrates watershed mostly, Malatya is known nationally for its apricots, Diyarbakır for watermelons and Gaziantep for pistachio nuts, while this region generally is responsible for most of the country's chickpea and lentil production (also here, an extreme example of cash crop specialization, the single mountain village of Çığşar, in Kahramanmaraş, which, over the last decade, has become responsible for the majority of the country's cherry export).

Around half of the country's land (40 million ha) is used for farming, which puts it at thirteenth in the world in terms of national agricultural land area. In addition to being the world's largest producer of hazelnuts, Turkey is also recorded as the largest apricot, cherry, quince and pommegranite producer, the second largest producer of cucumbers and water melons, the third largest of pistachio, tomatoes, lentils and green peppers, fourth in onions and olives and in the top ten also for wheat, barley and oats, as well as cotton, grapefruit and lemons, and also sunflower seeds (although it is one of the world's biggest importers of sunflower seeds).

In terms of financial value to the country, Turkey's agricultural revenue yield is in the world's top ten. The primary export markets for most products are the EU and USA, but the Middle East is an important destination for fruit and vegetables and meat products. In addition to hazelnuts, Turkey is also the world's leading exporter of dry figs (irrigation being unnecessary for fig trees), and one of the leading dried grape producers/exporters (it is the world's top exporter of raisins, and, with Australia, the major producer of sultanas, which originated in Turkey/Persia). Major exports also include cotton, grapes, pistachio nuts, olives, tobacco, oranges and lemons, apricots and potatoes.

The real value added by the agricultural sector has been increasing steadily, by a total of about 40% over the past 40 years. However, the increase in the value of agricultural exports since the 1980s has been far outstripped that of imports. In terms of productivity, Turkey is about 50th in the world, and in terms of agricultural added value per employee, 60th.

agricultural population as a result of internal strife and migration.[9] In this period three contributions were expected from agriculture:
1. food for the nation;
2. provision of raw materials for industry (support for the industrialisation program);
3. exports (hard currency based foreign income) (Tekeli and İlkin 1988: 39).

All these targets have demanded a rise in agriculture production. The policies focused on increasing productivity and expanding cultivated areas in response to market conditions will not be considered here. In contrast to industry, no protective policy was adopted for agriculture. Farming

---

[9] Including the after effects of WW I, the dissolution of Empire and War of Independence, coupled with the earlier destruction of the Christian population in the East, subsequent 'population exchanges' with the south Balkans, and Kurdish rebellions.

activities were based on world prices, and bridging for the resulting gap (between the open market price and that required by Turkish farmers) was enabled through agricultural credit cooperatives and support purchases. Although with limited impact, productivity increase was achieved. High-yield and resistant seeds were introduced, organised in the sugar beet sector, for example, by the state sugar company. The company trained farmers, provided equipment and established networks, which proved to be successful (*ibid.*: 63). Cash crop cultivation was encouraged, with the state owned and run Agriculture Bank (*Ziraat Bankası*) extending loans to encourage the export of goods such as tobacco, cotton, hazelnuts and figs. Tea plant seeds were imported to Rize accompanied by the establishment of tea processing facilities there, and efforts were made encouraging local farmers to grow the crop. There were also attempts to bring in high yielding breeds in cattle and horse farming. High yielding animals were raised in cattle farming, but extension remained limited.

The first direct fiscal intervention in agriculture by the Republic's single party regime came as early as 1925, when the major agricultural tax, known as '*aşar*' (tythe), was lifted, with obvious benefits for farmers and the agricultural sector. The policy of state-led economic development effected agriculture in other ways, such as through education. The system of Ottoman agricultural schools was expanded with new institutions accompanied by fruit cultivation and nursing stations and olive cultivation organisations. This period also saw the establishment of agricultural research stations (Agricultural Combat Research Institutes, *Zirai Mücadele ve Araştırma Enstitüleri*). Other new initiatives included a poultry institute, a sericulture school and station, breeding stations to breed animals fit to climatic and other circumstances, a breeder bull distribution system, forestry management centres, forestry schools and nurseries to supply saplings (Toprak 1988: 28-29).

The state-centred system of economic development (and social management) was very much influenced by the Soviet model. It was the state monopolies that established food production systems (establishing factories, distribution networks, etc.), and which also led the way in industrialisation on farms themselves. The early imputes this gave proved difficult to maintain. In 1924, for example, there were about 500 tractors in the country. This number had multiplied to 1,200 within four years, by 1928, but did not reach 1,750 until twenty years after that, in 1948. Most of these tractors belonged to state enterprises. Tractors of the time were technologically backward. With iron wheels and limited traction power, they were hard to operate on stony and hard ground (Toprak 1988: 33-34). There was also a problem of maintenance, and broken tractors became useless. This problematic situation prompted new efforts to mechanise agriculture and increase yields, accompanied by the success of state farms established to open new areas to cultivation (Tekeli and İlkin 1988: 87-88). The policies designed to encourage mechanisation included military service exemption for machine operators; exemption from customs, consumption and monopoly taxes on fuel and lease of government owned tractors to farmers on favourable terms (Köymen 2008: 208).

Although there were specific capital investment issues with technology related inputs, the lack of development in this area after the 20s was also a consequence of the overarching generalised problem of the time. The years of the Great Depression and world economic crisis of the 30s that followed obviously had a major negative impact. Rural males were forced to move to urban settlements to maintain support their families and pay their taxes, for example, which led to villages without males. Other peasant-farmers were forced to take up contracted loans at exorbitant rates, and thence into bankruptcy and auctions of their land. These years thus witnessed the onset of the process of erosion of the peasant farmer agricultural base and the beginnings of the concentration of landed into fewer hands (Emrence 2000: 32-33). State measures facilitating the development of capitalism in agriculture during this period included measurement and currency standardisation. The variety of measurement standards and units of currency inherited from the Ottoman era was an obstacle for an integrated and smoothly working domestic market. The Central Bank of the Republic of Turkey (*Türkiye Cumhuriyet Merkez Bankası*, TCMB) was established in 1931 in order to solve these problems, and introduced the (European) metric system (Toprak 1988: 21).

It was during this period that the state accepted the need for intervention to protect farmers. The experience of the Depression thus became fundamental in the (further, Keynesian) development of statism in Turkey, against which the recent liberalizing developments have reacted. Commodity exchanges markets had developed from 1924, with 24 such exchanges emerging by 1943, but since access to credit was very limited, farmers had to sell their products cheaply upon harvesting.[10] Wholesale

---

[10] The agricultural credit system usually organized repayment for the first month or two after harvest time, forcing farmer operating on loans to sell their products at the lowest point of the (annual) price cycle.

traders thus had control over prices and markets, and it was they rather than producers (the farmers) who were the beneficiaries of the steep rises that followed the very low prices during the harvesting season. With the slump in world prices also affecting domestic prices and hurting farmers, the government finally acted. In 1932 the Agriculture Bank was enabled to purchase wheat from farmers, which was financially facilitated through income it gained from a tax placed on wheat purchases (under the provisions of the 1934 Wheat Protection Legislation). The role of the Agricultural Bank in this intervention continued until 1938 when the Soil Products Office (*Toprak Mahsulleri Ofisi*, TMO) was established. This office was supposed to protect cereal prices and transfer crops collected from producing areas to consumption areas.[11] Given the authority to export and import, the Office could be used in foreign trade activities as well. Farmers also received support when agricultural credit and marketing cooperatives were encouraged, starting from 1932. Enabled to market their crops through these cooperatives, farmers were now significantly relieved from the manipulations of private tradesmen (Toprak 1988: 23-24).[12]

Upon the clearing agreement acted with Germany in the 1930s, wheat was exported to Germany at high prices, which boosted wheat cultivation. The Government continued to support cotton and sugar beet as basic industrial inputs. The price of tobacco, however, was determined by domestic and foreign traders; in spite of Government support (Köymen 2008: 128). During the Second World War the price of cereals jumped, which enhanced the incomes of big farmers. A tax in response to this situation enabled large purchases for military consumption. Turkey managed to stay out of WWII, but with significant national resources directed to military spending its economy was still badly affected by the conflict. The general effects of the war on the country were extremely damaging economically, and ordinary people in the countryside suffered as much as anyone. Agricultural production declined.

The period following the Second World War can be regarded as divided into two stages, the first of land usage extension and the second of land usage intensification, with both related to further progressions of capitalisation. After the post-War Marshall Plan, agricultural mechanisation started to

---

[11] Given the authority to export and import, the Office could be also used in foreign trade activities.

[12] Turkey has a rich and complex history of cooperatives in the agricultural sector. Some did – and do – facilitate solidarity and gain power for labour, while others have been statist, top-down organisations and others again inactive, non-functioning shells.

develop with imported tractors. In the 50s, the number of tractors rose sharply and new tracts of land were brought under cultivation. This mechanisation too had its effects on a further concentration of land in fewer hands (Köymen 2008: 136-137). The geographical expansion of agriculture initiated with the Republic slowed down markedly during the 1960s as the limit of new land that could be brought under cultivation was approached. This was the decade when intensive agricultural technologies flourished with the use of fertilisers, medication, high quality (high-yielding) seeds and irrigation. Unlike in the 50s, agriculture was given protection from foreign competition, and agricultural inputs were subsidised by the state. This state support, however, was more beneficial to large enterprises with their much higher marketable produce (Köymen 2008: 144).

The 70s saw yield increases rather than land expansion, upon the phasing-in of the 'green revolution' (in seed and fertiliser/pesticide usage). Fertilisation in this period increased by 47%, tractor usage covered 75% of all cultivated land, and there was also expansion of irrigated land. These developments were influenced by larger coverage of support purchases, favourable terms of trade and world prices, and subsidised fuel prices (Kazgan 1988: 264). For smallholders, however, market conditions were prohibitive. According to a study based on the 1970 Agricultural Census and the 1973 DPT income distribution survey, around three-quarters of all small farms were either unable or barely able to provide a subsistence income for a farming family (Köymen 2008: 291).[13]

---

[13] Enterprises with land smaller than 3 hectares (58%) were, on average, unable to provide a minimum subsistence, and enterprises of 3 to 5 hectares (16%) barely able to.

Chapter 4. Developments in the structure of agriculture in Turkey since 1980

Important changes took place in agriculture during the 1980s. Economic and agricultural policies in general became more directly shaped by capital and through US and Western dominated institutions. According to the development report prepared by a team headed by James Baker – US Treasury Secretary under Ronald Reagan, whose input to the 1985 (primarily US bank funded) IMF debt initiative was key – priority had to be given to agriculture (Köymen 2008: 135).[14] At the very beginning of the decade, in fact, a raft of economic reform measures was introduced in Turkey implementing liberal policies – abolishing subsidies, taking steps to lower interest rates and reducing the role of the state in the economy (including privatisation), etc. Thus was inaugurated the new era of neo-liberalism in the country. Known as the 'January 24th Decisions' (*24 Ocak Kararları*), after the date on which they were first presented by the government, the impact of this development on agriculture manifested in curbed supports and pressure on the prices of agricultural goods, which led to the terms of trade turning swiftly against agriculture. With respect to the latter, if the period 1976-79 is taken as a benchmark 100, then by 1988 it had fallen to 53. In other words, the cost of food (and with it, more or less, the value of farmers' incomes) compared to that of manufactured goods halved in the space of a decade. In the period 1980-90, the agricultural sector contracted significantly (Boratav 2009). The following pages look at agricultural change in Turkey in this context.

The period after 1980: the global background and liberalisation

Crucial to the introduction into agriculture of neo-liberal practice in Turkey were international organisations and agreements. The first of these was the European Common Agriculture Policy (CAP) of the then European Economic Community (EEC). With the reform process within the framework of CAP, a transition was envisaged from agricultural

---

[14] This was when the principles of IMF intervention to support struggling and developing economies on the assumption of a neo-liberal agenda were first worked out.

crop based support policies to others shaped by such criteria as rural development, food safety, animal health, etc. (Aydın 2004: 88). In 1984, taxes and fees on imported food products were reduced and an increase was observed in the volume of food imports. The following year, the public administration in agriculture was reorganised, and the following General Directorates in the Ministry of Agriculture abolished: Agricultural Affairs, Agricultural Combat, Animal Husbandry Development, Food Affairs, Veterinary Affairs and Water Products (with the General Directorate of Soil and Water Affairs being merged with the General Directorate of Roads, Water and Electricity). As a result, while the management capacity of the Ministry declined, other units in public administration gained a say in relation to agricultural affairs. The ambiguity in division of tasks and mandates brought with it authority clashes and a lack of coordination, making agricultural management even less effective (Tarım 2004).

In the mid 1990s, the Agreement on Agriculture (AoA) came into effect with the completion of the Uruguay Round of the General Agreement on Tariffs and Trade (GATT), in which Turkey was a full participating member state, and establishment of the World Trade Organisation (WTO). Upon the completion of the process of domestic ratification, the WTO agreement and its annexes took effect on 25 February 1995. Under the 'Market Access' terms of the agreement, Turkey committed to engage in tariff reductions of (at least) 10% for each agricultural product and 24%, on average, for all agricultural products, within a period of ten years.

The European Union has been involved in Turkey's deregulation process also from the mid 90s, through the Custom's Union. Even though Turkey's agricultural products are exempt from this, its EU Custom's Union agreement together with the WTO agreements has provided the external framework for the sector, as well as the strategy for privatisations. Thus, starting from 1999, the Agricultural Reform Project (*Tarım Reformu Projesi*) was implemented, marking a transition to new agricultural policies. These were thereafter shaped by this policy in combination with agreements and stability programmes developed with the IMF and World Bank in the wake of the 2000-01 financial and economic crisis.[15] Turkey's route to free trade is also guided by the Barcelona Process of the Euro-

---

[15] Turkey experienced a boom-bust cycle through the 90s with crises in 1991, 1994, 1998 and 1999, leading to an agreement with (intervention of) the IMF. This was unable to prevent – and partly triggered – banking led financial collapse, which caused massive currency devaluation, lost the country about a third of its GDP and worked through to a 50% rise in unemployment (Macovei 2009).

Mediterranean Partnership aiming at the European Union-Mediterranean Free Trade Area (EU-MED FTA, EMFTA).[16]

Another development in the 90s taking place in the context of international the penetration of global retail and production monopolies into Turkish agriculture was the spread of on-contract farming. On-contract farming in Turkey had started in sugar beet cultivation from 1926 with the establishment of the Turkish Sugar Corporation (*Türkiye Şeker Fabrikaları Anonim Şirketi*, TŞFAŞ). Later, the General Directorate Agriculture Enterprises (*Tarım İşletmeleri Genel Müdürülüğü*, TİGEM) engaged in on-contract seed production, and in the 1970s on-contract tomato cultivation for industrial processing began, during which period the Development Foundation of Turkey (*Türkiye Kalkınma Vakfı*, TKV) with its *köy-tür* (lit. village-type) system introduced on-contract poultry farming. When this practice of on-contract farming was carried out through public institutions and agencies, farmers generally benefited from standardised agricultural activities, better prices and marketing guarantees. The on-contract farming that started in the 90s, however, had different characteristics. First, the practice was hugely expanded, to include fruit, vegetables, tobacco, seed, pasta wheat, wine grapes, and barley for malt as well as flowers. This spread thus serves also as an indicator showing the 'declining effect of support policies on farmers' incomes' (Keyder and Yenal 2004: 365). Second, in spite of mutual bargaining, prices were now largely determined by marketing chains and the large traders as clients of these products (Ulukan 2009: 130). The new on-contract farming can be thus characterised as a major step in the move from enterprise to corporate agriculture.

Data and terminology

Developments in agriculture are investigated here on the basis of such data as agricultural land, number of enterprises, agricultural equipment and machinery, fertiliser and pesticide use, etc. that directly affect agricultural activities. Further variables with indirect effects on agricultural activities are addressed below. These include the support system, state enterprises active in agricultural production, agricultural marketing cooperatives

---

[16] The country's EU Custom's Union membership, it might be noted, detrimentally commits it to the EU position, aligning it with developed countries rather than developmentally better suited Mediterranean allies for (the new round of) WTO agricultural negotiations (Türkekul 2007).

and unions, the activities and impacts of international fertiliser and seed companies, protection of the sector and terms of trade. Most of the nationwide data related to these variables in Turkey have been gathered by the Turkish Statistics Institute (*Türkiye İstatistik Kurumu*, TÜİK), and its predecessor, the State Institute of Statistics (SIS, *Devlet İstatistik Enstitüsü*, DİE), under whose auspices the General Agricultural Census (GAC, *Genel Tarım Sayımı*, GTS) was carried out. For some areas, very recent data has not been gathered, i.e. since the 2001 census (see Textbox 4.1).[17]

In the relevant literature, the terms 'peasant' (*köylü*) 'farmer' (*çiftçi*) are mostly used interchangeably. Similarly, in the presentation of statistical information regarding agricultural enterprises (farms and smallholdings), and villages, 'agricultural enterprise' or 'holding' (*tarımsal işletmelere*) is taken as equivalent to 'household' (*hane halkı*). With the TÜİK data, moreover, the farmer and household are taken as denoting the same unit. There is thus an equivocation between peasant, farmer, household, holding and enterprise, a terminological blurring that operates conceptually on the treatment (definition, interpretation, etc.) of data. Clearly, this may lead to ambiguity in exploring some important characteristics of a given rural population. Of particular relevance here is the lack of distinction in the usage of the terms 'farmer' and 'household'. In respect of those cases in which there are household members engaged in income generating activities other than agriculture, a household may be categorised as farming (or, a population unit equated with an agricultural enterprise/holding) even when the total of its income derived from farming is actually less than that gained from outside farming (non-agricultural activities). Finally, the category 'agriculture' includes fishing and forestry (and hunting) in addition to crop and livestock farming.

In addition to the issues with socio-economic terminology, there are also some related to geo-political definitions. Firstly, the literature also tends not to distinguish between rural (*kır[sal]*) and village (*köy*), or between urban (*kent[sel]*) and city (*şehir*). In fact, it is the words for village and city ('*köy*' and '*şehir*') that are the most commonly used to designate the

---

[17] The next agricultural census would be due for 2011, but this seems unlikely to manifest since a new, regular system of data collection is operative now, the Farmer Record System (*Çiftci Kayıt Sistemi*).

Textbox 4.1. Turkey's agricultural census.

In addition to its regular activities (average ten-yearly general census), the state body responsible for statistics collection and publication has prepared a total of seven agricultural censuses. The first General Agricultural Census was carried out in 1927, the second in 1950, and others thereafter every decade (with variations in year). As well as the somewhat irregular gaps, the parameters changed from census to census. These involved the information gathering system used, and coverage and numerical specifications. Another problematic area has been that of hamlets (of which there were some 40,000), which were not necessarily included (insofar as they were inaccessible and also not fully included in village districts).

Firstly, information was gathered using questionnaires, filled in either by enterprise owners (the farmers and farming business administrators) directly or through the local *muhtar*s.[1] The *muhtar* system was easier and cheaper, but also less accurate. Censuses used either a complete (census) system, or a sampling system, with varying numbers of respondents from varying numbers of villages. Secondly, some (aspects of) most censuses covered just rural or just urban areas. These were defined by the district population levels which were also used as determining coverage separately to other rural/urban specification. The basic details were as follows:

- 1927: purportedly covered all villages and agricultural enterprises; completed less than four years after the establishment of the new republic, this essentially functioned as a state inventory of the countryside;
- 1950: conducted as a *muhtar* sample, with 270,000 agricultural enterprises selected from 21,521 villages; a separate questionnaire was introduced for enterprises;
- 1963: covered all rural enterprises (i.e. located in districts with population under 5,000, as identified in the 1960 General Population Census), using the *muhtar* system from which was selected a sample of 6,450 respondents from 907 villages; again with a separate questionnaire used for enterprises;
- 1970: as 1963, but using a sample of 180,000 enterprises from 20,000 villages;
- 1980: as 1970; also the enterprises questionnaire was used for a sample (number ungiven) in districts with population of 5,000 to 50,000, and both questionnaires were administered to urban districts, i.e. with populations over 50,000);
- 1991: reverted to the previous system, with a sample of 8 respondents from 4,000 villages;
- 2001: as 1991.[2]

---

[1] Village head – see Textbox 7.1.
2 See Saçlı (2009) and TÜİK (reports).

The main methodological problem of these censuses was their dual system, employing a (General Agricultural Census) Village Information Questionnaire (*Genel Tarim Sayimi Koy Genel Bilgi Anketi*) and (General Agricultural Census of) Agricultural Entreprises and Households (*Tarimsal Işletmeler Hanehalki*). Whereas the first, as the name suggests focused on rural areas, the second did not. In delineating on the basis of location, therefore, an assumption is made that there is no agriculture in urban areas (as defined administratively), an assumption which is then undermined by not doing likewise for farms The basic philosophy of this census, therefore, seems to rest on an equivocation of an equation of rural with agriculture.

Agricultural statistics are now gathered and presented routinely, under the Farmer Record System. This includes some 2.7 million farmers, without specifying location (i.e. there are no rural/urban limitations). It does, however, give a somewhat distorted picture due to farmers opting out for various reasons, e.g. cost/benefit analysis (joining the system is a precondition of access to DIS supports, but there is a charge involved); traditional practices (farmers working their own, hereditary land but which is shared and thus unregistered in their name and outside the system), etc.

rural/urban divide.[18] Then, defined as administrative areas, the district division of borough or (small) township (*belde*, or, sometimes, *kasaba [belidiye]*) may include a small urban area even though it is classed as rural, while, contrariwise, the district centre (*ilçe merkezi*) and even provincial centre, or city (*il merkezi*, or *şehir*) may contain farms, although these are classed as urban. Furthermore, while the general administrative definition of 'village' comprises areas with settlements populated by less than 2,000 persons, the agricultural censuses conducted by TÜİK have collected data with respect to population groups of under 5,000, 5,000 to 50,000 and over 50,000. Hence there is in fact significant discrepancy even within the official usage of 'rural'/'village'.

---

[18] The source of this may be the general terminological conflation of (non-distinction between) settlements and administrative areas, as seen in nomenclature: the name given to an administrative area is the same as that of the main settlement in the area (the administrative centre). This holds almost ubiquitously at all four major levels of administration in Turkey (village, borough/township, city and province – *köy*, *belde*, *ilçe* and *il*).

Finally, the agricultural surveys carried out by the state represent the evolution of a work in progress – which is to say that they have exhibited shortcomings in various respects and certainly not been consistent. Most of the General Agricultural Censuses conducted in Turkey have varied in terms of data parameters (see Textbox 4.1). Combining this methodological variability with questionable data collection methods especially during the earlier period, comparison between them is only helpful at a gross level. The most recent agricultural census was conducted in 2001, like previous censuses, was based on a system that was split between investigation of districts specified as village and borough/township (which stand for rural) and of those that were not (investigating agricultural enterprises and households conflated as above).

Assuming the TÜİK definitions and bearing in mind the difficulties they create, issues will be addressed here in three areas: enterprise and household, agriculture as a sector, and rural population in general. In this respect, it should be noted, the household/enterprise (holding) equivalence results in a bifurcation of the term 'household', which is employed by TÜİK as the unit of analysis for data related to population and, at the same time, counted as a production unit (enterprise). The household as defined thus operates as an intersection point, this dual character assigning it a key role in efforts to explain both economic and demographic rural developments.

Enterprises and land

Whereas the statement of the 'main idea, method and aims' of the agriculture section of the original five-year plans produced by the DPT in the 1960s had included a focus on the social aims of reducing poverty and unemployment (DPT 1963: 145, 1968: 302) – reduced in the 70s to a focus on increasing farmers' living standards (DPT 1973: 208) – the new era of liberalism saw this dropped. Henceforth, the five-year plan agricultural section – like the other (mining, manufacturing, etc.) sector sections – of the five-year plans would focus much more strongly on purely economic criteria, opening with lists of (production increase and privatisation) 'targets' (DPT 1979: 224, 1984: 52, 1989: 48). With the seventh Five-Year Development Plan of 1995, this shift was refined to an introduction that dropped even the previously sanctified aim of 'modernisation', and succinctly presented the new analysis of Turkey's agricultural question as its opening paragraph, thus:

> While the agricultural sector share of the GNP for 1990 stood
> at 17.5%, it has since fallen to 15%. The proportion of the civil
> labour force in agriculture, however, remains at 45%. While
> the importance of agriculture in the economy is declining, a
> major part of the population continues to gain its livelihood
> from agriculture (DPT 1995: 57).

Clearly, a major plank in government agricultural policy was for the
numbers of people involved in farming to (be allowed to) decline. And,
realistically, given the numbers involved, this would have to be an
absolute decline (and in all probability, without government intervention,
leading directly to structural unemployment) – which is precisely what
happened. The proportion ratios that have been presented as the opening
to the agriculture section of the two development plans since 1995 put
agriculture's share of GDP at 15% and employment 45% for 1999, and
10% and 30% respectively for 2006, the drop in the proportion of people
employed in agriculture duly noted (DPT 1989: 31, 2000a: 131). Since
then, the proportion of the total labour force employed in agriculture has
declined further, to 25% in 2010. The decade between 2000 and 2010 saw
an absolute loss of over a quarter of the agricultural work force, or around
two million jobs (DİE/SIS 2004: 152, TÜİK 1989-2011).[19] The following
sections may thus be regarded as an anatomy of the process whereby this
was 'achieved'.

In practical terms, the massive lowering of the number of people
directly dependent on agriculture that was intended by the restructuring
(without loss of production) would require a reduction in the number of
smallholdings (and further industrialisation of the agriculture sector). It
is in this context, therefore, that one of the basic variables to be taken
into account here is the size of agricultural enterprises. Put bluntly, the
new liberalism had no room for the peasant-farmer (smallholder). This
was clearly stated in a report prepared as part of the DPT 'Long Term
Strategy' (the Eighth Five-Year Development Plan) by the body established
to direct the sector in concert with the completion of the Uruguay Round

---

[19] Total number of people employed in agriculture in 2000: 7.8 million, in 2004: 7.4 million,
and in 2010, 5.7 million. Comparing the last quarter of 2004 with that of 2010, parallel to the
23% drop in the total number of people employed in agriculture in this period, the number
of registered unemployed people from the sector rose by 23%, which, as a proportion of
the agricultural workforce represented a relative rise of 60% (compared with an unchanged
unemployment rate outside of agriculture) (TÜİK 2009a,c).

and establishment of the WTO (DPT 1995: 60), the Agricultural Policies and Structural Rearrangements Special Commission:

> While according to the results of the 1980 General Agricultural Census there were 3,650,910 agricultural holdings in Turkey, the 1991 General Agricultural Census gives this figure as 4,068,432.[20] The key to efforts to improve the structure of agriculture in Turkey is sought in the concept of enterprise size. Adjusting for the size of existing agricultural enterprises in Turkey, the minimum size necessary to provide subsistence income to a household... is 200 decares for dry areas and 100 decares for irrigated farming. Approximately 4.5 million hectares of land is under irrigation in Turkey. In the light of this, there should be 450,000 enterprises in irrigated parts and 1,125,000 on dry land, which extend over 22.5 million decares, adding up to 1,575,000 enterprises. Adding to this a figure of 425,000 engaged in greenhouse farming and other agricultural activities, the number of agricultural enterprises relative to the cultivated land in Turkey should be 2 million' (DPT 2000b: 7; using DİE 1994).

According to this analysis, therefore, at the turn of the millennium there was an excess of some two million enterprises. The liquidation of this excess was obviously regarded as essential. It is this which is investigated here, with an evaluation of the trends in the number of enterprises and also an effort made to identify those characteristics of farmers in the category of small producers that distinguish them from the peasant-farmer definitions given above. Here again, a context is given by reference to some past data.

Looking at past information on agricultural enterprises, in spite of the questionable figures of some earlier censuses, it is still possible to gain an idea of changes in the number and size of enterprises over time. The first Agricultural Census, conducted in 1927, does not provide much information on the distribution of proprietorship. It can still be inferred, however, that the average size of agricultural land per farming family at that time was around 25 hectares (Kepenek and Yentürk 2000: 36).[21] The

---

[20] Total of all agricultural enterprises, i.e. including those located in (urban) districts with populations of over 5,000.
[21] In fact, 25 *dönüm*, an old Ottoman unit of land measurement (still commonly used today), corresponding to a square of land measured out at 40 paces, and formalized as 1,600 m^2 (so 25 *dönüm* = about 4 ha).

number of holdings was also recorded in 1938 according to the division of 50 hectares, information which is useful in grasping developments to take place later on (Table 4.1).[22] This enables us to ascertain baseline averages for agricultural land area at that time of 7.6 ha per enterprise as a whole and 6.6 ha for the 99.75% of farming units with less than 50 ha, suggesting that the overwhelming majority of the farming enterprises were smallholdings – or, that peasant-farmers dominated Turkish agriculture at this time.

Covering the period 1950 to 2006, Table 4.2 gives the number and size of agricultural enterprises by size of holding. According to this data, there is no significant difference in the number of enterprises comparing 1963 to 2001. Within this time-frame, in fact, there had been a gradual rise (consistent with the 1927 starting point), which peaked at the 1991 census and then fell thereafter, until by 2001 the number of enterprises was back to the 1961 level again. Bearing in mind the figures used by the DPT and cited above, however, it appears likely that the peak was not reached until around 2000, when there were some four million enterprises.[23] This would mean that the development of neo-liberalism during the 1980s and 1990s had no obvious effect on enterprise number – which is entirely

Table 4.1. Number and land-share of agricultural enterprises by holding size in 1938.

Size of holding (ha)[1]	Enterprises		Total land	
	Number	%	×1000 ha	%
<50	2,492,000	99.75	16,500	86
>50	6,182	0.25	2,600	14
Total	2,498,182	100	19,100	100

Source: TEG n.d.: 134.
[1] This refers to the amount of agricultural land available to the enterprise. The terms 'holding' and 'enterprise' are not strictly distinguished here. Generally 'holding' implies land area (and other assets), and 'enterprise' business venture. Thus, there is a collocation of 'holding' with 'small', and the term 'smallholding' implying a household structure that does not necessarily go beyond pure subsistence and enter the market (to gain surplus); enterprises may also be small, however, and not necessarily 'holding' any land (e.g. Table 4.4).

---

[22] The division of 500 decares was used: 1 decare (da) = 0.1 hectares (ha) = 1000 m². Decares and thousand square meters are the most commonly used units in Turkish agricultural statistics, although usage of hectares is also common. All data here is given in hectares, or thousand hectares.
[23] The obvious root of the problem being the double system used by the GAC – see Chapter 8.

Table 4.2. Proportions (%) of number and land-share of agricultural enterprises by size during 1950-2006.

Size (ha)		1950	1963	1970	1980	1991	2001[a]	2006[b]
1-2	Number	30.6	40.9	44.2	28.4	36.7	33.4	24.8
	Land	4.3	6.9	10.4	4.1	5.6	5.3	3.3
2.1-5	Number	31.6	27.9	28.7	32.7	31.1	31.5	32.7
	Land	14.3	16.9	16.8	15.9	16.6	16.0	12.9
5.1-10	Number	21.8	18.1	15.6	20.8	17.5	18.5	21.4
	Land	20.7	23.3	21.0	21.3	19.9	20.7	18.1
10.1-20	Number	10.3	9.4	7.8	11.8	9.4	10.8	12.7
	Land	19.3	23.2	21.0	23.8	20.9	23.8	21.0
20.1-50	Number	4.2	3.2	3.1	5.5	4.4	5.1	6.6
	Land	16.6	16.6	19.6	22.7	19.8	22.8	23.6
50.1+	Number	1.5	0.5	0.6	0.8	0.9	0.7	1.8
	Land	24.8	13.1	11.2	12.2	17.2	11.3	21.1
Total no. enterprises		2,527,800	3,100,900	3,058,900	3,558,800	3,966,800	3,021,196	-
Total agricultural land (1000 ha)		19,452	17,143	17,065	22,764	23,451	18,432	-
Average farm size (ha)		7.7	5.5	5.6	6.4	5.9	6.1	
Median weighted[c]		-	-	-	-	70	70	93

Source: Miran 2005: 12-13, citing DİE 2003.
[a] Results of village based questionnaire.
[b] TÜİK (2008b).
[c] Gürsel and Karakoç (2009). Figures are weighted averages calculated from median of each sub-group.

likely given that neo-liberal policies were not properly engaged with in the sector until the 1999 Agricultural Reform Project. The second important point is that enterprises cultivating up to 10 ha of land and which can therefore be counted as smallholdings constituted around 80-90% of all agricultural enterprises throughout the period covered. This supports the view that petty production is (has been and continues to be) dominant in agriculture, an interpretation that can also be reached by looking at the average enterprise size, which has always been less than 8 ha (and indeed, varying by no more than 10% from the 6 ha average throughout the last half century).

Given this stable proportion of smallholdings and average enterprise size, along with the ultimately unchanged number of enterprises, one might question whether there actually *has* been any development showing that small enterprises are in the process of liquidation as the share of large enterprises increase. The generalised picture of stability, however, is transformed when smallholdings are contrasted with larger holdings by placing the focus on (1) the most recent period (as compared to the previous decades), when the restructuring of the sector through holding size was specifically targeted, and (2) total land share (within this time framework).

Table 4.3 thus shows more clearly the dominant trends here. The share of enterprises under 10 ha fell 3.5% (in absolute terms) between 1963, and 2001, but then by a further 4.5% between 2001 and 2006 (with the reverse occurring for enterprises over 10 ha). Regarding the share of total agricultural land, the area worked by enterprises under 10 ha fell by 5.1% over the four decades to the millennium and then by another 7.7% in the next five years alone (again, mirrored for enterprises over 10 ha). In other words, numerically there was an 8% shift in the share of enterprises from small to medium and large, of which over half (4.5%) occurred during the last five years of the period, whereas land area saw the reverse movement,

Table 4.3. Proportions (%) of number and land share of agricultural enterprises by size between 1963-2006.

Size (ha)	Number of holdings			Total agricultural land		
	1963	2001	2006[a]	1963	2001	2006[a]
0.1-2	40.9	33.4	24.8	6.9	5.3	3.3
2.1-5	27.9	31.5	32.7	16.9	16.0	12.9
5.1-10	18.1	18.5	21.4	23.3	20.7	18.1
Subtotal	86.9	83.4	78.9	47.1	42.0	34.3
10.1-20	9.4	10.8	12.7	23.2	23.8	21.0
20.1-50	3.2	5.1	6.6	16.6	22.8	23.6
50.1+	0.5	0.7	1.8	13.1	11.3	21.1
Subtotal	13.1	16.6	21.1	52.9	57.9	65.7
Total	100	100	100	100	100	100

Source: Miran 2005: 12-13, citing DİE 2003.
[a] TÜİK (2008b).

to the tune of 12.8%, of which again over half (7.8%) took place after 2000. In terms of timing, the expansion of larger (>10 ha) enterprises in the period 1960-2001 is a historical phenomenon when viewed over the past half century, but has, in fact, overwhelmingly occurred during the last decade. In terms of character, it partly derives from small enterprises that withdrew, while the rest is attributed to expansion.[24] This is revealed in stark terms by examining the extremes of holding/enterprise size. Regarding the numerical drop, it was *only* the smallest holding size number that decreased (all larger size categories increased in number, and for each period, before and after 2001); and regarding land area, the two largest size enterprise categories expanded the most, with the largest (over 50 ha) registering the greatest single rise, of 9.8% in the last five year period. It can be concluded that in the period 2001-2006, land that had been exploited by small enterprises was transferred to medium and large enterprises. Thus the conclusion made in a 2009 report on the changing structure of Turkish agriculture that 'small scale producers are being driven out of the market Gürsel and Karakoç (2009: 1).

With the operation of the process of capital accumulation in agriculture, small peasantry is in the process of liquidation less in terms of their overall numbers but more in terms of land they hold, while both the number and land share of larger enterprises are increasing. Meanwhile the fact that small farmers still constitute 80% majority in terms of the number of enterprises gives the image that this form of production is still dominant. The analysis can be carried further from this point by taking a closer look at small enterprises. Then, introducing rural population, settlement unit and other data related to agricultural production and the characteristics of villages may help to build a picture of the contemporary dynamics in agriculture as defined by the dominance of small farmers. The first questions to address, therefore, involve the kind of enterprises that these present day smallholdings are. What do they produce? How do they survive?

---

[24] The difference between the 2001-2006 numerical fall and land increase figures appears to great for the former alone to account for the latter, a suspicion confirmed by examining the breakdown of the small enterprise change, which shows that loss of the smallest holdings (<2 ha) accounted entirely for the small enterprise numerical loss (and more) but only just over a quarter of the land loss.

Small scale agricultural enterprises

Almost all small scale agricultural enterprises have their own land (Table 4.4). The proportion of holdings with plots of up to 5 hectares working on their own land is above the country average for every category measured in the last three sets of figures through the fifteen years to 2006 (i.e. according all combinations of plot size, numerical and land share proportion, and year). Generally, about 30% of land under cultivation was rented as of 2006. In terms of trends, we see that from 1991 to 2001 renting increased strikingly for all but the smallest plots (proportions more than doubling for holdings cultivating 5 hectares and over), a shift in the ownership to labour/management relationship continued after 2001 for medium and large size enterprises (albeit at a slower pace and not including the 5 to 10 ha size holdings or the very largest enterprise units).[25]

Table 4.4. Proportions (%) of number and land share of enterprises farming own land by size during 1991-2006.

Size (ha)	1991		2001		2006	
	Farm number	Land	Farm number	Land	Farm number	Land
<0.5	95.8	95.3	96.0	95.8	95.2	94.7
0.5-0.9	94.8	94.5	92.9	92.9	96.2	95.9
1.0-1.9	93.1	93.1	90.8	90.5	94.2	94.0
2.0-4.9	93.7	93.4	87.4	86.7	89.9	89.1
5.0-9.9	91.7	91.4	82.3	81.8	82.7	81.2
10-19.9	89.1	88.8	77.1	76.4	72.7	70.9
20-49.9	85.7	84.4	70.4	69.1	64.7	62.2
50-99.9	81.8	81.3	64.1	64.7	55.2	53.1
100-249.9	90.4	91.3	71.8	71.5	59.7	59.3
250-499.9	88.1	87.8	71.2	71.6	65.7	63.7
500++	98.0	98.0	80.7	96.4	83.3	92.1
Average	92.6	89.3	85.9	77.8	85.1	71.4

Source: Gürsel and Karakoç 2009, using TÜİK 2008b.

---

[25] In 1991, 10.7% of holdings over 5 ha (farming 11% of the land worked by that size of farm) were rented, and in 2001, 26.1% of plots (with 24.1% of the land share); in 2006, 29% of plots 10-500 ha (farming 29.3% of the land share) were rented, and in 2006, 36.4% of plots (with 38.2% of land share).

In agricultural enterprises, crop cultivation and animal husbandry can be practised together or separately. In Turkey, the more common type of enterprise is that in which both are practised together. In fact, the proportion of enterprises engaged in both arable and livestock farming in 2001 was 72.1%, as compared to 24.4% engaged exclusively in crop cultivation and 3.4% in animal husbandry (Table 4.5). The numbers of livestock only farms are rather small and thus not particularly significant – except that they are the most striking, since *all* non-land owning enterprise are of this nature, and the total land involved is sufficient to wildly skew the average. This basically represents people in permanent poverty, i.e. with very few assets and surviving through selling their labour as shepherd-traders (grazing sheep usually, and driving them to the market for sale). This category may be regarded as representing an underclass in Turkish agriculture.

As a general rule, the joint practice of arable and livestock farming in Turkey becomes more common as the size of enterprises increases, while the proportion of enterprises engaged exclusively in one or the other falls (Table 4.5). Thus, the proportion of smallholdings (i.e. less than 2 hectares) engaged exclusively in crop farming is higher than the national average, and the proportion practicing both crop farming and animal husbandry lower, while the reverse is the case for enterprises over two hectares (and

Table 4.5. Proportions (%) of farming types practiced, by enterprise size in 2001.

Size (ha)	Mixed	Only arable	Only livestock
Non-land owner	0.0	0.0	100.0
<0.5	54.0	43.2	2.8
0.5-0.9	62.5	36.1	1.4
1-1.9	68.4	30.2	1.4
2-4.9	76.4	22.7	0.8
5-9.9	81.9	17.7	0.4
10-19.9	82.3	17.3	0.3
20-49.9	82.7	17.1	0.1
50-99.9	82.4	17.6	0.0
100-249.9	69.6	29.9	0.5
250-499.9	71.6	28.4	0.0
500+	84.8	15.2	0.0
Turkey	72.1	24.4	3.4

Calculated from GAC 2001 data, using TÜİK 2001.

in the case of animal husbandry, for enterprises over 5 ha).[26] But this only holds for enterprises of up to 100 hectares. Large enterprises – of 100 to 500 hectares – engage relatively less in mixed farming and more in crop cultivation alone, while very large enterprises (of over 500 hectares) have the highest proportion of enterprises engaged in mixed farming and the lowest of crops only. In very round figures, 60% of smallholdings are engaged in mixed farming as against 40% engaged exclusively in crop farming, while for enterprises of between 2 and 10 hectares these figures are 80% and 20% (for large, 10-50 ha, enterprises the ratio is around 70:30, and for the very large, over 50 ha, 85:15, approximately). Focusing on smallholdings, therefore, we can conclude that most employ mixed (animal and crop) farming, but it is a relatively slim majority as compared with larger enterprises.

The joint practice of crop farming and animal husbandry has many advantages in terms of enterprise efficiency. Some crop parts (stalks and leaves, most commonly hay) can be used as animal feed, while animal dung can be used as fertiliser (manure). While animal husbandry requires labour throughout the year, the labour required in crop farming varies seasonally, and, according to the type of crop and level of mechanisation, typically requires less labour time. Labour use becomes more efficient when the two practices are used together. In cases where animal husbandry is fully or partly market oriented, particularly in dairy farming, there can be year round income, but also constant expenditure. In crop farming, on the other hand the cash flow is seasonal and upkeep costs minimal. Furthermore, the production and sale of animals itself is a cash source.

It is observed that small enterprises try to gain from the benefits of mixed farming by engaging in both crop cultivation and animal husbandry, in line with traditional practices, in which subsistence farming implies a range of production for nutritional needs and food security, according to local food culture. The question, then, is why the proportion of smallholders engaged in mixed farming is relatively low, or, conversely, why the proportion of arable only small farms is relatively high, or why so few (relatively) keep animals. There are several explanations. One is a negative factor that the impact of the traditional needs of subsistence farmers has declined as they have entered the market – smallholders, that is, have specialised. Also, some smallholdings may be on land that is unsuitable for crops (on

---

[26] Assuming a category number average with landless farmers excluded (avg. = 0.7% only livestock).

rough, hilly terrain only good for grazing). Larger enterprises are less likely to have all their (parcels of) land unsuitable for cultivation.[27] More importantly perhaps, the labour efficiency savings to be gained from mixed farming apply less to very small enterprises, insofar as smallholders do not, generally, employ people.[28]

The relatively low level of mixed farming smallholdings may also, however, be due to impoverishment and related to the costs of husbandry. Poor farming households may have insufficient capital to invest in animals and a lack of income to cover husbandry outgoings). It may also be linked to personal situation with the break-up of the traditional extended family pattern. Older people especially may practice only crop farming as they find it physically easier – a consideration of heightened importance now also with the phenomenon observed (above) of people going back to their village to retire (they use farming to supplement their pensions and/ or savings). Also – and this is the important point here – because crop farming can be relatively easy from the labour input perspective for most of the year, people can sow small plots in the spring and then basically leave them, returning just to harvest. This leaves them free during the rest of the year to do something else, i.e. gain income from other, probably non-agricultural activities – which can in fact become their main income source and allow them to or may require that they move to the urban centres of trade and employment.[29]

As crops have an important share in all small enterprises (and relatively higher than in larger enterprises), we should focus a little on the crops they produce. In line with EU harmonisation programmes, these are divided into various categories and sub-categories, the most important of which are cereals, vegetables, and fruit (including nuts and olives), of which the most important here is fruit (Table 4.6). In 2006, approaching half of small enterprises were engaged in fruit/nut cultivation. This represents a 50%

---

[27] This could also partly explaining why the animal only farming proportions for smallholdings, low as they are nevertheless double and up to four times the average.
[28] For medium size enterprises also, the labour efficiency may be in using family or communal help during the busy harvest period. These labour considerations are probably part of the reason why the relative farming types proportions change as they do (not using employed labour becomes increasing impractical as enterprises become larger, so using the paid workers to look after animals and thereby gain the benefits of a mixed farming system becomes more attractive). (For large and very large agricultural enterprises, different factors apply, related to the economics of specialisation and supply chains, e.g. providing a single product on contract to a single purchaser, etc.).
[29] This is the group of people comprising the new sub-category 4 (Chapter 3).

Table 4.6. Proportion (%) of cultivated field crops and orchards to total agricultural land, by enterprise size during 1991-2006.

Size (ha)	1991		2001		2006	
	Field crops	Fruit	Field crops	Fruit	Field crops	Fruit
<0.5	43.8	30.9	33.5	39.6	33.1	48.1
0.5-0.9	53.8	27.3	39.5	38.2	36.1	49.7
1-1.9	58.9	23.4	48.5	29.4	46.9	39.1
2-4.9	61.7	16.7	56.1	20.6	58.9	24.4
5-9.9	65.6	10.4	65.0	11.9	66.6	13.7
10-19.9	69.3	5.6	71.1	5.3	74.0	5.6
20-49.9	69.2	3.0	73.1	2.5	75.0	3.0
50-99.9	71.9	2.1	76.4	2.1	76.0	1.6
100-249.9	71.8	1.7	74.6	3.0	76.5	2.1
250-499.9	80.6	1.4	80.1	1.3	71.0	7.0
500+	73.0	0.4	42.3	1.4	43.8	2.9
Turkey	67.3	8.3	66.5	9.5	69.7	9.4

Source: Gürsel and Karakoç 2009, using TÜİK 2008b.

increase over the previous sixteen years. And whereas in 1991 the fruit growing proportion of smallholdings was two to three times the national average, by 2006 it was over five times higher. Relatively large proportions of small enterprises also are involved in vegetable cultivation. Bearing in mind the relatively high proportion of smallholding using their agricultural land for crop cultivation generally, as opposed to animal husbandry, these figures are quite meaningful. They suggest two developments taking place: firstly, a very large share (about 45%)[30] of small enterprises is engaged in fruit cultivation, and. their proportion is gradually rising. Secondly, the survival of small scale enterprises in agriculture becomes possible with fruit cultivation, which can be easily be practiced in small plots of land, bringing in higher returns than field crops.

When it comes to small scale enterprises and technology, the common conviction is that since they are unable to accumulate capital, small enterprises will also be deprived of advanced technology. This view is,

---

[30] 45.6% (average proportion for the three categories of fruit producing smallholdings) of 97.5% (average for non-livestock only (crops only or mixed).

of course, logical and generally valid. However, there may also be cases running counter to this. For example, there may not be much difference between small and larger enterprises in terms of technology applications, as is the case in fruit/nut cultivation (constituting another reason why this represents a major and growing proportion of small enterprises). Also, both small and large enterprises may use the same technology without the former possessing it, as can be seen by examining tractor usage.

Tractor usage increases with the size of enterprises, as a rule. In Turkey, seven out of ten enterprises uses tractors, but not a lot more than half of enterprises with land of up to 2 hectares use tractors,[31] which represents less than 4% of the total land on which tractors are used (Table 4.7). This suggests, at first glance, that small enterprises are unable to use tractors. In response to the obvious question at this point in respect of smallholders' crop farming concerning how they till the soil if there is no tractor, the equally obvious answer would be by recourse to the predecessor of motor

Table 4.7. Proportion (%) of enterprises and amount of land cultivated using tractors, by enterprise size in 2001.

Size (ha)	Total farm number	Cultivated with tractor (%)	
		Farm number	Land share
<0.5	251,686	26.9	0.1
0.5-0.9	381,287	44.0	0.6
1-1.9	752,156	57.1	2.9
2-4.9	1,274,609	71.7	13.5
5-9.9	713,149	85.2	19.1
10-19.9	383,323	92.5	22.6
20-49.9	173,774	94.7	22.2
50-99.9	24,201	97.6	7.3
100-249.9	10,266	95.3	6.1
250-499.9	1,930	99.9	3.4
500+	441	99.3	2.3
Turkey	3,966,822	69.1	100

Calculated from GAC 2001 data, using TÜİK 2001.

---

[31] 664,950 from 1,135,129 enterprises = 58.58%.

power, animals. According to the Census of 2001, however, there were just 104,339 animal-draft ploughs shared among the country's near four million enterprises, with only a small part of these belonging to the million plus small enterprises. Clearly the usage of animals does not account for the low proportion of enterprises using a tractor. The more likely explanation, in fact, is that the question itself is misplaced.

Put simply, a major proportion of small enterprises have no great need of a tractor. Considering the high proportion of small enterprises engaged in fruit cultivation (and also exclusively in animal husbandry), coupled with the fact that they mostly have very tiny plots (almost half of them less than a hectare), then actually the low usage of tractor power is only to be expected. Indeed, comparing the proportions of smallholdings engaged in arable cultivation and using tractors for the three enterprise sizes used (0-0.5, 0.5-1 and 1-2 ha), a rather close match is observed between the numbers for crop farming (33.1%, 36.1% and 46.9%), and those for tractor usage (26.9%, 44.0% and 57.1%). There *is* no significant technology shortfall to account for here. And that the relatively low figures for smallholder tractor use does not necessarily imply a lack of means, is shown by looking at how those enterprises then are using tractor access.

Farmers may possess their own tractors or share ownership, or else they may rent them. In Turkey, only a third of enterprises using tractors own or part own their tractors – principally because smaller holdings rent (Table 4.8). More than six in ten of smaller (less than 10 ha) enterprises using tractors rent their vehicles,[32] while for smallholdings (<2 ha) that figure rises to well over eight in ten.[33] This is a meaningful indicator showing three things: tractors are relatively accessible without capital, i.e. through renting; for small enterprises generally, tractor ownership through accumulation is not possible; and, depending, on the size of the enterprise, it may not be 'economical' to have a tractor. In cases where smallholders can and do benefit from motor power on their land, access to tractors through renting means that small enterprises may use the same technology as larger ones.[34]

---

[32] 1,389,500 from 2,186,448 enterprises = 63.5%.
[33] 571.412 from 664,950 enterprises = 85.9%.
[34] With the exception of very small holdings, in which the shortfall between crop cultivation and tractor usage may be met by low-tech tractor devices (which are not recorded in the statistics), in the Black Sea region especially, with German made Hertz, Italian Ruggerini patented, Turkish manufactured Pancar motors tailor-made as 'garden tractors'. N.b. *'Pancar'* is Turkish for sugar beet, which gives an indication of the historical importance of peasant production in this sector.

Table 4.8. Ownership proportions (%) of enterprises using tractors for enterprises and amount of land cultivated in 2001.

Size (ha)	Owned		Co-owned		Rented	
	Farms	Cultivated land	Farms	Cultivated land	Farms	Cultivated land
<0.5	8.7	8.5	1.1	0.6	90.2	90.8
0.5-0.9	11.4	12.4	2.1	2.2	86.6	85.4
1-1.9	12.4	13.6	2.6	2.8	85.0	83.6
2-4.9	22.4	25.6	3.1	3.4	74.5	71.0
5-9.9	37.1	41.0	3.9	4.0	59.0	55.0
10-19.9	50.1	54.4	4.0	4.3	45.9	41.3
20-49.9	62.7	66.6	4.5	4.5	32.8	28.9
50-99.9	68.7	70.8	4.6	3.7	26.7	25.5
100-249.9	66.0	68.6	6.3	5.8	27.7	25.6
250-499.9	84.9	88.3	2.9	2.3	12.2	9.4
500+	84.2	87.1	0.0	0.0	15.8	12.9
Turkey	29.7	53.1	3.3	4.0	67.0	42.9

Calculated from GAC 2001 data, using TÜİK 2001.

These figures, it might be noted do appear to contradict the statement made at the time by Yaltırık (2002: 35) – insofar as it was intended for smallholders – that the very weak domestic market for tractors being experienced then because of weak purchasing power was temporary, and related to lowered government supports to the agricultural sector (reduced as a precaution to offset inflation due to raised oil prices). The positive expectation declared by Yaltırık, that these supports would return in subsequent years was certainly not born out, as will be described in the following section.

Chapter 5. Agricultural policies, market conditions and transfers

The neo-liberal policies adopted by Turkey since 1980 have had profound implications for its agriculture sector. Bearing in mind the focus on smallholders, it is possible to trace these effects by referring to specific areas. This section looks briefly at policies (adopted in the context of agreements made with the IMF, WTO, WB and EU), SOEs (state production and marketing organisations), prices (terms of trade), supports (state inputs, particularly DIS), loans (agricultural credit), product composition, fertiliser/pesticide usage (application patterns), global developments (international financing and capitalisation), and individual and public income and asset transfers (the internal movement of capital) and agriculture sector GDP and per capita agriculture GDP.

Policies

One of the outcomes of the introduction of neo-liberal policies in Turkey was a decrease in the number of crops supported and the shrinking share of supported purchases in total agricultural output. The WTO Uruguay Round Agreement on Agriculture (URAA), ratified by Turkey, took effect in 1994. The URAA targets the 'liberalisation of agricultural production and commerce on the basis of a world trade developing in line with the principle of comparative advantage' (Günaydın 2009: 176). In order to mitigate factors which divert free trade from its main course, the URAA envisages reduction in domestic support and subsidies along with the facilitation of access to markets. The direct effect of the URAA on Turkish agriculture is debatable. It is argued that with the liberalisation of the trade of agricultural goods, products from countries where fertility and supports allow lower prices could drive domestic farmers out of markets. On the other hand, however, some maintain that 'Turkey does not have a serious commitment to the WTO' (Aksoy 1994 cited in Gülbuçuk 2005: 98-99) and that 'the URAA did not have a direct devastating effect on the Turkish Agriculture' (Günaydın 2009: 177).

Regardless of this specific issue, however, the dynamics of neo-liberalism introduced, or rather accelerated, by the URAA/WTO were propelled anyway by other international bodies under whose auspices macro-economic policy Turkey was largely determined. Chief among these was the IMF. The story is not unfamiliar. When the Turkish economy finally fell victim to a variety of long standing structural problems (high public debt, high inflation, under-financed banks, unstable growth), it was forced to accept IMF terms in return for the liquidity that organisation was able to provide.[35] Made in the context also of Turkey's growing linkage to the EU – spurred by the acceptance of Turkey as candidate state for accessioning 1999 and formalisation by 2001 (and with the end goal for the agricultural sector that the country will be in line with the EU Common Agricultural Policy, CAP – Turkey made many commitments in the context of the IMF stand-by agreement in 1999 and letters of intent that followed including the Economic Reform Credit Agreement with the World Bank in 2000, and the Agricultural Reform Implementation Project (ARIP) instigated in 2001. These commitments included:

- privatisation of the state agricultural monopolies TEKEL (for tobacco and alcohol),[36] TŞFAŞ (sugar), and ÇAYKUR (tea);
- restructuring of the agricultural marketing cooperatives;
- setting prices in supported purchases according to world commodity exchange prices;
- phasing out the current support system, and introducing direct income support;
- abandonment by the Agricultural Bank of the subsidised credit scheme (with which farmers took loans to finance, among other things, the purchase of agricultural machinery, especially tractors).

Wed to international norms and agreements, Turkey is now not as 'free' as she used to be in terms of general agricultural policy and has room to manoeuvre for manipulation of the sector market or support of producers. The remaining policy tools, as clearly laid out by the DPT, consist of the following: infrastructure investments of various types, marketing and R&D activities, rural and regional development plans, and environmental and natural resources management (DPT 2000b: 52). These are quite limited and their use requires specific skills. Price policy interventions are certainly a thing of the past.

---

[35] The stabilisation program took the form of a short-term 'gamble' on inflation reduction, which failed and ultimately led the country into a period of financial meltdown and economic depression (Akyüz and Boratav 2001), resulting in the necessitation of further IMF currency support and policy control over the following years (importantly centred on exposure to the world market – i.e. confirming the neo-liberal program).

[36] TEKEL also included a salt industry, which was left in state hands.

State owned enterprises

One of the major post-1980 liberalisation policies assumed in line with commitments to and agreements with the IMF and World Bank at the turn of the millennium was the liquidation, or at least diminishment, of the state owned enterprises (SOEs) and other organisations engaged in the marketing of agricultural products and credit extension. These institutions were never, of course, in a position to wholly purchase the produce of farmers and completely regulate the market, even in the crop/product sectors over which they had most control. On the other hand, even in sectors in which their influence was weaker, they could still provide a market with subsidised price guarantees through support purchases. Upon the liquidation of these organisations – partial or complete – small scale farmers were left in markets directly facing traders, speculators, retail chains, industrial enterprises using agricultural inputs and international agricultural companies.

The major first phase of privatisation in Turkish agriculture had occurred during the nineties, with the liquidation of SOEs for feed, meat and fish and milk. Founded in 1956, the animal feed production Feed Industries (*Yem Sanayi*) was privatised in stages during the period 1993-1995; the Meat and Fish Corporation (*Et-Balık Kurumu*, EBK), having contributed significantly to the growth and development of stock breeding since its establishment in 1952, was sold in 1995; and set up in 1956 for such purposes as supporting milk producers, marketing hygienic milk and milk products, supporting and pioneering the private sector and generally ensuring the development of the national milk industry, The Milk Industries Foundation (*Süt Endüstrisi Kurumu*, SEK), was privatised in 1995 (Aysu 2002).

Focusing briefly on the dairy sector, we observe the process of capital accumulation at work. In the past there had only been small to medium size producers and traditional (local and street based) marketing forms prevailing. With the 1995 privatisation, however, 50% of the national milk market came under the control of no more than 10 companies, a development only exacerbated by the cessation of government support, in this case the development incentive premiums paid to dairies, which in 1998 had been valued at over USD30 m (Togan *et al.* 2005, op cit.). Nowadays milk is increasingly processed by large concerns, some of them multinational, with marketing tied in to supermarket chains. Of about 10 billion litres of milk produced, a third is now processed and sold by medium size enterprises and the umbrella organisation SETBİR representing the major industrialists and producers (of the rest, three billion litres are now consumed or processed by milk producers themselves, one billion are marketed by street vendors, and two billion litres processed by small dairies (*mandıra*) (FAO 2007: 6).

The largest denationalisations came in the early 2000s with the dismemberment of the sugar and tobacco manufacturing and marketing monopolies, which had huge implications for the hundreds of thousands of small enterprises whose products they used.[37] Between 1998 and 2002, price supports were almost completely eliminated from the tobacco and sugar sectors, to the tune of half a billion (US) dollars (Togan *et al.* 2005: 49).[38] Parallel to this, and in line with commitments to the IMF, legislation for the purposes of the privatisations was enacted, facilitated by the establishment of new regulatory agencies. Law no. 23478 (2001) enabled the breakup of Turkish Sugar Factories Inc. (*Türkiye Şeker Fabrikaları A.Ş.*, TŞFAŞ) and transfer of its regulatory powers to a new management board – or, independent regulatory agency (IRA, *Bağımsız Düzenleyici Kurum*) – the Sugar Agency (*Şeker Kurumu*).[39] TŞFAŞ had been established in 1935, bringing together the sugar plants that had been established from 1926, and over the course of time had grown to comprise a total of thirty sugar plants. As an organisational structure, the Turkish sugar SOE was privatised rather than dissolved – indeed, it remains a huge concern and dominant in the home market – but the down-scaling of its operations did involve a selloff of three of its plants into private hands and, more importantly, enable the suppression of supported prices (and thereby enabling large reductions in line newly reduced EU norms) along with the introduction of production quotas. Regarding the latter, a 10% quota of starch-based sugars was set (narrowing the market for home grown sugar beet), with power granted to the Council of Ministers to change this quota to up to 50% and exercise it so as to introduce favourable terms to genetically modified starch products imported from the USA. In 2001, the total sugar output plummeted by 50% (from 18.8 down to 12.6 million tons). It recovered somewhat thereafter, but in the years since the

---

[37] See note 34.

[38] This was also true of the cereals sector, although since this was (is) a much larger sector financially and more heavily represented by large-size enterprises, the effect of the withdrawal of support there was less acute.

[39] Turkey has a total of nine IRAs, including the two mentioned here (for tobacco and sugar), mostly created as a mechanism to facilitate the scaling down of the public sector between 1999 and 2002.

change (2001-2009), sugar output still has only averaged 14.6 million tons, considerably down from the level that it had attained.[40]

The case of tobacco was even more pronounced. With the price support mechanism for tobacco gone by 2002, TEKEL, the massive SOE originally formed as far back as 1841, was disbanded by Law no. 4733 (2002) and its regulatory powers transferred to an IRA, the Tobacco, Tobacco Products and Alcoholic Beverages Market Regulation Agency (*Tütün, Tütün Mamülleri ve Alkollu İçkiler Piyasası Düzenleme Kurum*, TAPDK). Thereafter, the old TEKEL tobacco products sections of were privatised – bought eventually by British-American Tobacco (the Texas Pacific Group acquiring the beverages section) – and large companies were effectively allowed to import tobacco (Günaydın 2009: 200). As a result, tobacco production plummeted, the area sown and the number of producers falling from 266,000 ha and 568,000 enterprises in 1999, to 140,000 hectares and 180,000 enterprises in 2007. The downward trajectory has continued since, with the area sown down to 116,000 ha by 2009, and production near halved in the five years between 2006 and 2010 (TÜİK 2011a).[41] Thus the conclusion that the establishment of the IRAs for tobacco and sugar 'became functional in restricting supportive policies of state and control[ing] production of Turkish farmers in order to provide advantaged conditions for international firms... even in... competitive market areas... [and thus] to serve the neo-liberal principles in general' (Sönmez 2004: 198-199).

ÇAYKUR was the other major state monopoly to be dealt with during this period. Established in 1971, this tea corporation was engaged in such activities and policies as responding to domestic tea demand, establishing tea processing plants, guiding farmers in tea cultivation, improving the quality of tea and marketing. The corporation is still active, but, having to survive in competitive conditions with the market entry of private tea companies, its domain has narrowed.

In addition to the targeting of the state monopolies engaged in product manufacture and supply, the marketing organisations were also diminished. With origins dating back to 1863, these were formally recognised in 1935 as the Agricultural Marketing Cooperatives and Associations (*Tarım Satış*

---

[40] Even this average is only due to a major (10-20%) increase in productivity, which saw sugar production reach 17.2 million tons in 2009 – but which was still less than a decade previously (TÜİK 2011a).
[41] 2006 – 98,000 tons produced, 2010 – 55,000 tons (TÜİK 2011a).

Kooperatifleri Birlikleri, TSKB). While still operating, these cooperatives and associations now have a limited domain of activity, primarily since credit flow from the government is much reduced. Indicative of the trend here is the EU-supported Agri-Marketing union of cooperatives, active in a wide range of product areas, but in vocational training, and not directly in marketing itself. Indeed, the 1980s origins of the new policy of state (non-)intervention in agriculture can be traced back with changes in the functioning of a marketing organisation, the Soil Products Office (*Toprak Mahsulleri Ofisi*, TMO).

The somewhat oddly named TMO was actually a grain marketing board, established in 1938 with a mandate to purchase grains from farmers for domestic and international markets, provide for state reserves in grains, keep up with related standards, and establish and run flour mills, bakeries and storages. Up until 1988, TMO had prevented over-production and drastic price falls through purchasing goods from farmers, with credit extension from the Central Bank in particular. From 1988, however, it was decided by the government that the TMO should provide for its funds from existing markets, and the corporation started to go into loss. In line with WB/WTO agreements, maize supports were phased out between 1999 and 2002, when TMO was privatised. At present the TMO maintains its purchases, but it gives lower prices and purchases smaller amounts.[42] A recent measure with the potential to reduce the number of small producers in particular is the regulation regarding grain purchases adopted with the TMO Board's decision No. 2/16-6 in January 2008, according to which TMO determined not to buy maize below set quantities, with obvious implications for smallholders.[43] Any significant effects of this policy will be only seen if and as world prices fall and peasant farmers need TMO purchasing support (currently unnecessary with the high prices). The intent, however, to support larger enterprises is clear.

Prices

A crucial plank in the liberalisation strategy is the removal of trade barriers and deregulation of the internal economy so that world prices are effective and open market conditions prevail. For Turkey, that meant

---

[42] http://www.tmo.gov.tr/tr/images/stories/istatistikler/bugdayarpacaet alaryulaf.pdf.
[43] Minimum purchases amounts for wheat, barley, rye, triticale, oats and corn are set from 2009 to 2018, at 3, 5, 10, 15, 25, 40, 60 and 80 tons respectively.

allowing agricultural prices to fall, and thus farmers losing income. This is indicated by the terms of trade. The prices received by the farmer and prices that the farmer pays as a comparative index (index of the agricultural terms of trade) offer a picture of the base economic situation for farmers. Setting this index at 100 in 1968 and looking at the relative movement since (Table 5.1), we see that the index first rises and then drops by 46% in the period 1978-1988, followed by an 80% increase to recover the late 60s parity through the mid 90s,and then another decrease, by 35% in the period 1998-2001. The index value which had attained 126.3 at its recent height in 1998 had dropped a third to 82.6 in 2007. In short, prices paid by the farmer for his agricultural inputs increased at a higher rate than his earnings from selling his products, which depreciated his net income – or, the collapse in the terms of trade based net income around the time of the economic crisis which brought the WTO in (1998-2001) has not since been recovered.

In the same period, an annual decrease by 4.73% in agricultural employment was accompanied by increase in labour productivity approaching 50% (1980=100, 1998=135.5, 2007=202.3) (Boratav 2009: 17). The gain from higher productivity, therefore – the rationale for reform of the sector – has partly been offset by the loss in the terms of trade. And while larger concerns are not adversely affected overall by this equation in terms of their bottom line, for smallholders that do not benefit from the increased labour productivity resulting from economies of scale, only the negative side, the reduced terms of trade, operates. Tellingly, therefore, there was

Table 5.1. Agricultural terms of trade (indices) in the world and Turkey during 1968-1998.

Year	Turkey	World	Year	Turkey	World
1968	100	100	2000	102.3	55.2
1974	127.6	176.9	2001	78.6	55
1978	131	106.3	2002	78.6	57.6
1988	70	69.6	2003	89.9	60.3
1992	77.6	58	2004	91.8	62.6
1997	100.7	72.4	2005	82.7	66.6
1998	126.3	65.3	2006	77.1	70.8
1999	109.3	55.4	2007	82.6	-

Source: Boratav 2009: 11.

a decline in agricultural employment to the tune of some three million people during this period (which was the intention, after all). A significant proportion of these people became unemployed.

Supports

Although the agricultural terms of trade for Turkey have been and continue to be favourable in comparison to the rest of the world, globally the situation has changed little over the last thirty years – fluctuations notwithstanding – whereas in Turkey the 'adjustment' continues to be felt. The drop has been related to the relative level of supports. In addition to the support withdrawals mentioned, pesticide and seed and natural disaster supports were also eliminated, while the system of direct income support was brought in (Table 5.2). The combined effect of this withdrawal of output price support and input subsidisation was to take approaching two billion dollars out of agriculture, or rather, for the state not to put it in.

The introduction of the direct income support (DIS) scheme in line with commitments to the IMF – with a pilot scheme in 2001 and nationwide implementation the following year – was intended to 'cushion the blow' felt by farmers with the withdrawal of other supports, to 'compensate for the drop in intervention prices' (Togan *et al.* 2005: 48). The DIS system was targeted at supporting smaller size enterprises, with a ceiling of fifty hectares applied to the initial $50/ha payments, but its effectiveness has

Table 5.2. Agricultural supports during 1998-2002 in million USD.

Supports	1998	1999	2000	2001	2002
Direct income support	0	0	0	68	1,159
Sector specific[1]	970	671	384	154	77
Input based[2]	516	267	177	76	0
Generalised[3]	30	303	321	281	145
Credit subsidy	1,663	1,675	563	275	0
Total	3,202	2,923	1,460	874	1,358

Source: Togan *et al.* 2005: 49, citing Turkish Ministry of Agriculture and Rural Affairs.
[1] Cereals, tobacco, sugar beet (market price support), milk (incentive premiums), tea (compensation payment), animal husbandry (development).
[2] Fertiliser, pesticide, seed.
[3] Deficiency payments, natural disaster relief.

been strongly criticised. The most significant criticism of the DIS scheme is that it is based on land proprietorship and thus encourages farmers to quit cultivation (Günaydın 2009: 185). This occurs in three ways.

First, since the time of payment is indefinite, it is difficult to use these payments as the financial basis of agricultural activities. DIS payments are made after a time lapse and without any regular schedule, so farmers cannot rely on use this source to finance his inputs. Thus, farmers borrow for their actual activities and service their debts after harvest or when they receive their DIS payment. This means that a part of the DIS budget goes directly to lenders by way of interest payments, thus reducing its benefits to the farmer, and the sector. Second, the scheme is flexible and the DIS can also be given for land that is not sown, in spite of certain conditions intended to prevent this. It is possible for landowners to benefit from the scheme without cultivation and in cases where there is capital shortage or risk of drought, the farmer leaves his land idle. Third, and maybe most importantly, the reduced terms of trade have hurt the income of farmers far below the benefit gained from DIS. This operates as a major motivating factor for the farmer to take advantage of the state income without doing anything on his land. In practice, therefore, DIS payments function rather like the EU set aside system in reducing agricultural production, except that in the Turkish case a loss of output is *not* what is desired.

A 2008 field survey made in Edirne (an area between Istanbul and Greece) yielded interesting observations on this:

> The Edirne Agriculture Directorate states that direct income support and premium payments today constitute 39-40% of total income of farmers growing sunflower. When farmers are asked how much they gain from this cultivation, they give their profit in comparative terms with what they earn from direct income support. According to this information, 11% can barely cover their costs and 9% say they are in loss. The remaining 24% gave no answer to the question. According to this information, if the premium payment is lifted, 51% of farmers will gain nothing and only around 25% will be making any profit (İslamoğlu *et al.* 2008: footnote 61). [44]

---

[44] The cited survey also found that in cases of leasing or sharecropping, the owner of the land keeps the DIS payment without sharing it with the other party: in this case, working leased or shared land becomes less lucrative and more risky.

Thus, the DIS system has signally failed to 'continue to provide adequate support to the agricultural sector in an incentive-neutral way' (Togan *et al* 2005: 48); it has *not* been adequate and it has operated in an incentive-*negative* fashion. This support was lowered, first proportionately – from its initial near 80% of the massively reduced agricultural supports in 2002 to around a half of the recovering supports in 2005-2006 – and then, after 2006, reduced in absolute terms, falling to less than 20% of agricultural supports by 2008 (although returning to 25% the following year) (Table 5.3). Indeed, the old system has since been partially revived, with some return of supports for diesel and fertiliser, and major new animal husbandry supports. Viewed in overall financial terms, the old, sector-specific product-oriented system can be regarded as having been partially replaced by the system of land based direct payments, which has itself been partly superseded by a new sector-specific system. There are two important considerations related to this 'return' though.

First, the phasing out of the old system and phasing in of the new was enacted on a time lapse. In very round terms, agricultural supports which had totalled around 3 billion USD nationally in 1999 dropped to under 1 billion by 2002 and did not recover to the 1998 figure (in absolute terms) until 2006 (Table 5.3).[45] This five-year hiatus of course left farmers themselves in arrears (on loan repayments), a situation that could not be maintained by peasant-smallholders especially, for many of whom it was economically fatal (especially when compounded by the drought years of 2006-2007 that followed).[46] Second, with over a third of the supports now targeting animal husbandry, the system currently operative tends not to benefit small enterprises so much. Over two fifths of the smallest enterprises do not possess any animals, of the order of double the figure for larger enterprises, and peasant smallholders (typically carrying only a couple of animals) do not have the need for the subsidised artificial insemination or qualify for the milk supports (their production being too low for them to meet the precondition of milk cooperative membership), and often they just do not even know about the low cost or free investment credits available.

---

[45] 3.2 billion USD (1998) agricultural supports = approx. TL 4.7 billion (2006), assuming 2006 TL:USD exchange rate at approx 3:2. Adjusted for inflation, we might note, however, the current (2009) value of agricultural supports remains significantly less than the three billion dollars of the 1990s.

[46] Drought relief payments accounted for the major part of the generalized support increases in the following years (2007-2008).

Table 5.3. State agricultural budget realisation during 2002-2009 in million TL.

Supports	2002	2003	2004	2005	2006	2007	2008	2009
Direct income support	1,469	2,019	2,125	1,673	2,653	1,640	1,140	1,255
Animal husbandry	35	107	209	345	661	741	1,095	1,183
Supporting premiums	240	268	334	897	1,292	1,797	1,848	1,870
Sector specific (sub-total)	275	375	545	1,242	1,953	2,538	2,943	3,053
Input based [a]	-	311	355	680	-	925	944	?
Generalised [b]	124	99	61	113	141	497	882	644
Total support payment	1,868,	2,804	3,084	3,707	4,747	5,555	5,809	4,951
Inflation rate (GDP deflater)[e]	(37.4)	23.3	12.4	7.1	9.3	7.5	12	5.2
Agricultural support/GNP	0.53	0.62	0.55	0.57	0.63	0.65	0.58 [c]	0.45 [d]
Agricultural support/budget	1.56	1.99	2.03	2.32	2.66	2.72	2.57 [c]	1.91 [d]

Source: Günaydın (2009: 181, citing BÜMKO and DPT.
[a] Diesel, fertiliser.
[b] Rural development, agriculture insurance, drought, compensation payments, agricultural reform application project, other.
[c] Realisation estimate.
[d] Budget.
[e] http://www.worldbank.org.tr (using TÜİK figures).

Loans

The agricultural credit scheme conducted through Agricultural Credit Cooperatives and the Agricultural Bank was assessed by a WB team visiting Turkey in 1997. According to this team, 'rates of interest are below market rates which shifts the burden of cost to consumers while credit does not reach small farmers; therefore, interest rates by these organisations should be pulled up to market rates' (cited by Günaydın 2009: 186-187). It was also frequently mentioned that agricultural credit support creates a financial 'black hole'. Consequently, the share of the Agricultural Bank in total agricultural lending fell from 98% in 2004 to 47% in 2007 (*ibid.*).

Looking at total agricultural credit since 2004, increases in 2008 and 2009 are noticeable (Table 5.4). At present, more than 60% of agricultural credit is extended by the public sector. More importantly, however, with the lifting of subsidies in credit farmers can now only borrow on market terms, which means higher interest rates and only upon a certain level of collateral, which make it relatively inaccessible. As a result, agricultural credit is flowing more and more to medium and large landholders as confirmed by observations:

> Having the deeds to a small plot of land does not help much in borrowing from privatised sources, especially from banks. Small farmers prefer agricultural cooperatives for borrowing, but seeing that they have now adopted a market mentality, the farmers are turning to usurers. Farmers who have over 100 decares of land benefit much more from both income support and credit facilities' (İslamoğlu *et al.* 2008: 54).

Therefore, shrinking credit facilities and rising costs are both developments threatening the survival of small enterprises, while the fact that credit facilities are used more widely by larger enterprises is indicative of the policy favouring larger enterprises in agricultural production. In other words, credit policies constitute another of the factors explaining the recent decrease in the number and activities of small enterprises

Table 5.4. Agriculture sector credits during 2003-2009 in TL.

Year	Total loans	Public bank share
2003 [a]	5,433,518	41
2004	5,463,217	59
2005	6,653,226	74
2006	7,799,786	65
2007	8,931,913	65
2008	13,203,825	60
2009	15,682,418	66

Source: BDDK 2007.
[a] At month 6.

Product composition

The changes in government policies have direct effects on changed product compositions, basically, that is, on what farmers grow. Product composition in the agriculture sector can be categorised in various ways, including that presented in Table 5.5, as divided between crops and husbandry, with crops sub-divided into grains, vegetables and fruit (and other), and husbandry divided between livestock and dairy/manufactured products. With cereals (primarily wheat) covering around 90% of all cultivated land in Turkey (see Textbox 3.1), the relative drop of the share of the value

Table 5.5. Proportions of crop and animal production[1] (marketable value, %).

Year	Crops			Crops/husbandry		Husbandry	
	Cereals and other grains	Vegetables	Fruits, beverages & spices	Crops	Husbandry	Livestock[2]	Animal products[3]
1995	51.9	21.3	26.8	68.5	31.5	48.1	51.9
1996	45.7	24.5	29.9	71.2	28.8	51.3	48.7
1997	52.4	24.3	23.3	71.8	28.2	41.1	58.9
1998	46.7	24.4	28.9	71.6	28.4	39.8	60.2
1999	45.3	24.7	29.9	67.3	32.7	46.2	53.8
2000	42.0	25.6	32.4	69.4	30.6	46.2	53.8
2001	41.5	28.0	30.5	72.2	27.8	49.2	50.8
2002	42.5	24.9	32.5	73.3	26.7	42.2	57.8
2003	41.1	26.6	32.3	68.3	31.7	34.9	65.1
2004	44.0	26.9	29.1	66.7	33.3	37.1	62.9
2005	38.8	25.2	36.0	67.3	32.7	39.2	60.8
2006	34.0	29.2	36.7	66.4	33.6	38.3	61.7
2007	31.5	31.8	36.7	63.3	36.7	35.4	64.6
2008	33.3	29.2	37.5	66.1	33.9	35.7	64.3
2009	34.8	30.4	34.7	64.1	35.9	35.3	64.7

Source: TÜİK 2007a, 2008-2010.
[1] CPA 2002 Classification, an international product classification standard.
[2] Animals and fresh meat.
[3] Dairy and processed meat.

of grains value among crops is particularly significant. Production values for grains declined from roughly a half to a third of the crop share in the period 1995-2009, leaving this crop group on a par with the value shares for vegetables and for fruits, beverages and spices. Concomitantly, the planting area and quantity production of grains as a whole has dropped by something of the order of 10% over the last ten years (TMO 2010). Meanwhile, in the balance of crop to husbandry value, there was a shift of 4.4% to the latter during the decade and a half from 1995; and with the composition of the total animal production there was another big shift, with the livestock marketable share falling from around a half to a third, and animal products marketable share climbing by an equivalent amount.

Vegetables, fruits beverages and animal products are known as relatively high value added products, certainly higher than cereals. Thus, it would appear, Turkish farmers have been trying to survive by switching crops, moving, overall, from a low value added product composition to a high one. Crucially, these high value products also have a competitive advantage in the international arena, especially in European markets. One characteristic of vegetables and fruits is that they depend less on weather conditions. Almost all these high value added products are grown in irrigated areas reducing immensely the threat posed by drought, which is particularly important for small scale producers who cannot easily diversify for risk management. Indeed, another characteristic of these products is that they can be grown on small plots with labour intensive techniques, again suggesting a product change attempt by smallholders from grains to fruits and vegetables in order to stay solvent (c.f. Tables 5.5 and 5.6).

The change within husbandry is related to structural changes in this sector. In recent years, large-scale livestock farming (including 'factory farming' techniques in the poultry and dairy sectors) and manufactured meat and dairy production have grown very rapidly. Internal and external markets in these areas have boomed, enabled in part by a capitalisation of farming facilitated by state supports (Table 5.3). The neo-liberal approach, we might note, is to provide an environment conducive to competition, which does not rule out state support of capital (business) to this end (i.e. to develop a market and thus build a sector). Finally, the increase in animal products also a positive effect on the livestock sector, which further stimulates total husbandry product value (implying the relative shift away from crops, as shown).

Fertiliser and pesticide usage

A question that arises in the light of the shrinking credit sources, price movements and diminishing support is whether there has there been a change in the pattern of fertilizer and pesticide use as a result. The 2001 General Agricultural Census data point to a wide use of fertiliser applications at the beginning of this period (Table 5.6).

Taking the country as a whole, we observe a rise in fertiliser use from 2003 until 2007 and then a fall. A decline in pesticide use is evident after 2005 (Table 5.7). In 2006-2007 there was a drought, which would appear to have been a factor in the reduced use of applications at that time. The fact that pesticide usage was already falling markedly before this, however, militates against assuming this as a full explanation.

The Edirne field survey mentioned above (in 'Supports') also reported reduced applications usage. İslamoğlu *et al.* (2008) reports wheat farmers as stating that the (then) recent decline in wheat yield was associated with a declining use of seed, pesticides and fertiliser, and with a time reference that noticeably transcends temporary weather issues:

Table 5.6. Number of sites with fertiliser applications in 2001.

Natural fertiliser application sites	Chemical fertiliser application sites	Agricultural combat application sites	Total application sites
30,198	35,052	28,721	37,465

Source: 2001 GAC data, using TÜİK 2001.

Table 5.7. Fertiliser and pesticide usage during 2003-2007 in metric tons.

Year	Fertiliser usage	Pesticide usage
2003	9,762,347	35,665
2004	10,152,705	35,123
2005	10,260,076	44,337
2006	10,455,212	36,155
2007	9,709,654	20,544

Source: TÜİK 2008a.

About 43% of wheat farmers either started to use less fertiliser or switched to lower quality fertilisers within the last five years. This figure, however, is more modest in sunflower farming (28%). As to which farming enterprises reduced their fertiliser input, we see enterprises with 5-100 decares of land reducing their fertiliser usage more than others (İslamoğlu *et al.* 2008: 86).

Although this survey was conducted after the period covered by these data and the rates of fall given are higher than country averages, the two sets of data are consistent in point to a marked trend. Such a trend would, in fact, also be predicted as a slow, enforced change in agricultural practices on the part of farmers in the face of raised prices due to the earlier removal of supports. It appears that in addition to natural circumstances, shrinking financial means and falling output did push down the use of fertilisers and pesticides. In the case of fertilisers, relatively stable gross figures probably mask a change in type (more dung, lower quality chemical applications). In the case of pesticides, however, there are less options for farmers to choose from to save money, and the decline is more apparent.

Global developments

Some outstanding global developments in agriculture over recent decades include the increasing dominance of private companies in the production and marketing of seed and agricultural chemicals, the dominance of international markets in price setting, and increasingly common on-contract farming practices related to marketing chains and agro-industries. These developments are not isolated from overall trends in the world economy, of course, and their roots can be traced back to the 1970s:

> ...looking at the economic dimension of globalisation, the crisis of the world economy in the 70s and the ensuing process of restructuring, the capacity of international companies to control global commodity, cash and capital flows was significantly enhanced. This trend manifested itself fully in agriculture as well and the process of internationalisation led, in all countries including Turkey, to a shrinking role of the state in regulating domestic markets and further integration of national sectors of agriculture to the global agricultural/ industrial complex (Keyder and Yenal 2004: 361).

Associated with this, on-contract farming, the increasing complexity in setting domestic prices and advances in communication technologies all combined to create a smaller world – comprising also the rural sector. Taken as a whole, all these eroded the determining role of farmers and states as main actors in agriculture:

> The world agriculture is now organized in line with demands of multi-national food companies, which has marginalized the role of states in regulating the world economy. In this new order, production is global, but consumption mainly remains at the centre. Secondly, a global class of riches is created and maintained to consume food produced by export oriented agricultural sectors (Friedman and McMichael 1989: 112, cited by Yenal and Yenal 1993: 102-103).

Stedile (2009: 101), explains how this has operated in the now global agricultural sector. First, the increased control of financial monopolies in the world economy has had its implications on agriculture with the following interlinked developments:

- Financial capital moved into agriculture, through the acquisition of the shares of companies engaged in the sector (i.e. agricultural inputs, machinery, agro-industries).
- International capital enhanced its control with the dollarisation of the global economy.
- Trade in agricultural goods was rearranged to the advantage of large companies with the WTO, IMF and multi-lateral agreements.
- Bank loans and the necessity of industrial inputs further deepened dependency.
- Governments abandoned policies geared to protect agricultural markets and rural economies.

As a result of policies pursued over the last two decades, therefore, there are now only thirty large multi-national companies controlling world's agricultural production and trade. Then, global economic crises further enhance the dominance of large multi-national companies over agriculture since:

- companies of the North invest in fixed assets such as land, water and agricultural production;
- oil prices and the impact of global warming and environment leads to large investments in agro fuels;
- big capital heads for agriculture and mining exchanges of the South.

Finally, and associated with all these, the price-cost relationship in agricultural goods is broken and the handful of large companies gains control over and ownership of inputs, prices, scientific findings and technologies, genetics, water and biodiversity.

The world seed market is one of the areas in agriculture where the dominance of multi-nationals is most pronounced. Turkey became a member of the UPOV (International Union for the Protection of New Varieties of Plants), an organisation founded by six European countries led by plant breeding seed companies which were later to become giants in the area. According to the FAO, there has been a 75% loss in biodiversity in those countries where its practices have been adopted (Özkaya 2009: 259). A similar course may be expected for Turkey. By 2007, in fact, companies had cornered a 67% share of world seed production and trade, valued at 22 billion dollars. The total global market in seeds has been valued at 77 billion dollars (Özkaya 2009: 256-257), which gives an indication of the prize that awaits if farmers' trading of their own seed is eliminated. The 2006 Seed Law no. 5553 in Turkey bans the trade of genetic materials identified as local varieties or rural populations, allowing the trade only of recorded varieties and, while allowing farmers to barter seed, prohibiting them from exchanging it commercially (Aysu 2002: 232). This law is not implemented effectively at present, but when it is the market dominance of international monopolies will be further strengthened. In 2007, Turkey became a member of the UPOV (International Union for the Protection of New Varieties of Plants), an influential organisation founded by six European countries led by plant breeding seed companies later to become giants in the area. According to the FAO, there has been a 75% loss in biodiversity in those countries where UPOV practices emphasizing intellectual property protection for the process of plant breeding have been adopted (Özkaya 2009: 259).[47] A similar fate may be expected for Turkey as a result of UPOV.

A similar story is told in the agricultural chemicals sector. As of 2007, just ten companies had captured 89% of the world market (*ibid.*). In Turkey, according to 2001 data, there were a total of fifteen agro-chemical companies employing ten or more workers, and of these, the top four had a market share of 83% and the top eight 95.8% (Koç 2005: 157). The privatisation policies of the recent period have affected agriculture, taking farming in this same direction. With the privatisation of state farms previously run

---

[47] http://www.upov.int/en/about/introduction.htm.

by the SOEs, large-scale private firms expanded: as TEKEL was privatised five foreign companies came to dominate the tobacco market, and with the privatisation of SEK, private companies, many with foreign capital, established a dominant position in the dairy sector (Özkaya 2009: 271).

Individual and public income and asset transfers

A consideration of the overall movement of capital into and out of agriculture and rural areas is also helpful in ascertaining trends in the sector. Income and asset transfers can be from the non-agricultural to the agricultural sector or *vice versa*. Income and asset transfers to agriculture consist of public and private transfers. Regarding the former, apart from transfers through support purchases, there are also transfers of a social nature, such as irrigation infrastructure and special social programs (in Turkey, administered through the green card system). Regarding the latter, the movement of private transfers into agriculture involves individuals not in rural areas transforming their non-agricultural revenues into investments in rural areas or using them for household spending there, as well as the movement within rural areas of non-agricultural incomes into agriculture. The opposite course of transfer, from agriculture to non-agriculture, occurs through taxation, and the pricing of public goods and services. We have touched upon the latter under the heading of prices. Individual transfers from agriculture essentially involve profit-taking (and dividend payments) and (parts of) agricultural incomes or returns from the sale of rural assets being used in non-rural areas for investment, consumption or saving.

Looking first at public transfers to agriculture, we need to consider irrigation and other agricultural investments along with social assistance. Irrigation is vital to Turkey's agriculture. In fact, with a fairly dry climate across much of the territory and a high, heavily sloped topography, much of the land in the country is arid (a third is classified as steppe) and soil erosion and also sedimentation are a major problem (see Appendices 1-3).[48] The total land area in Turkey that would be amenable to irrigation amounts to some 8.5 million hectares, of which a little over a third (three million hectares) is irrigated at present using the facilities of the State Hydraulic Works (*Devlet Su İşleri*, DSI) (DSİ 2009: 41). For the last ten years the DSI investment budget has ranged between extremes of 2.6 to 4 billion TL (Table 5.8). In 2008, the total DSİ investment budget was 3.5 billion TL,

---

[48] http://balwois.com/balwois/administration/full_paper/ffp-522.pdf.

Table 5.8. State Hydraulic Works investment spending during 1999-2008 in million TL.

	1999	2000	2001	2002	2003	2004	2005	2006	2007	2008
Spending	2,730	3,400	2,962	4,025	2,792	2,623	3,221	2,853	2,645	3,422

Source: DSİ 2009: 121.

of which 1.8 billion TL was deployed for agriculture. Naturally, in the case of irrigation, one needs to bear in mind that facilities and investments are not distributed evenly across the country, and agricultural enterprises vary in terms of benefit derived from these facilities. Nevertheless, and various critical reservations notwithstanding, it is clear that major investments for irrigation purposes are made. It should also be born in mind that some investments in drinking water supply and flood prevention are also made in rural areas and thus indirectly beneficial for the agricultural sector, and also, that about 10% of irrigation related investments are made by other agencies (i.e. not the DSI).[49]

Another important component of transfers to the agricultural sector is that effected through the social security system and social policies. Farmers were first covered by the Bağ-Kur social security scheme from 1971. This insured the self employed (on a voluntary basis) as well as state employees (automatically) against illness and old age (i.e. giving access to the state provision of free or reduced cost medical treatment, along with an unemployment allowance and a retirement pension. Farmers were transferred to another security scheme within the Bağ-Kur system in 1983 upon the passing of Law no. 2926 specifically designed for the self-employed in agriculture, the smallholders and agricultural enterprise owners social security law (*tarımda kendi ad ve hesabına çalışanlar sosyal sigortalar kanunu*) – colloquially referred to as the 'farmers' Bağ-Kur' ('*çiftçi Bağ-Kuru*') (Tanrıvermiş 2005: 94-95). Farm workers (employees) continued to be covered by the general social security scheme (*Sosyal Sigortalar Kurumu*, SSK). The change in the social security set-up for the agricultural sector was very successful in terms of the numbers of farmers covered, with uptake of the new Bag-Kur insurance system – and coverage

---

[49] Including the Directorate General of Village Services, Directorate General of State Highways, Ministry of Agriculture, GAP Regional Development Administration, TÜBİTAK and DİE. See http://www.dpt.gov.tr/Portal.aspx?PortalRef=3).

for all people working in agriculture – trebling from the hundred thousand odd in the first year after the change and doubling again in the next two, to reach over six hundred thousand people by 1988 (Table 5.9).

Examining the history of social security coverage a little more closely, a strong, steady rise in SSK numbers is observed from when the system was changed until 1995 (a fourteen-fold increase over the decade). Numbers decreased in the years after 1995 – rather strikingly, when the liberalisation of agriculture first began – until 2002, in fact, when the privatisation program began in earnest. Prima facie this would seem to indicate that so far as social insurance coverage was concerned, the initial economic shift had a negative effect, but the entry of larger enterprises was beneficial for

Table 5.9. Numbers of people actively employed in agriculture covered by social security during 1984-2004.

Year	SSK	Bağkur	Total
1984	71,420	36,715	108,135
1985	18,300	105,563	123,863
1986	29,677	291,943	321,620
1987	36,358	513,055	549,413
1988	41,334	624,528	665,862
1989	74,407	711,049	785,456
1990	74,407	752,075	826,482
1991	93,756	732,525	826,281
1992	115,174	752,863	868,037
1993	177,145	775,563	952,708
1994	212,995	778,547	991,542
1995	253,463	799,132	1,052,595
1996	244,232	796,805	1,041,037
1997	246,401	802,343	1,048,744
1998	228,343	805,005	1,033,348
1999	193,826	875,888	1,069,714
2000	184,675	888,645	1,073,320
2001	142,306	899,999	1,042,305
2002	149,163	900,691	1,049,854
2003	165,268	993,967	1,159,235
2004	176,850	1,009,935	1,186,785

Source: Gülçubuk 2005: 71, using ÇSGB n.d.

workers, a conclusion that would probably confirm most expectations.[50] This speculative assessment, however, is rendered unimportant by the small size of the numbers recorded; it is insignificant in the face of the overwhelming fact of the lack of social security coverage for agricultural workers – most of whom, of course, are employed on a casual basis (temporarily, paid by the day, for the harvest, on a piece rate, etc.).

Meanwhile, the number of people covered in the sector as a whole has also risen fairly constantly, but ever more slowly. After the early jump following the change in the system mentioned, it took six years for the next 50% rise in the total number people working in agriculture to be covered by state insurance, and another decade for this to increase by another 10%. The main reason for this was the much reduced pace of small to medium size farmers joining the Bağ-Kur system.[51] Despite all the gains, therefore, even by 2004 the number of farmers covered by the Bağ-Kur security scheme was only about a million, not a lot more than a quarter of the number of farming enterprises recorded by the 2001 census.

Taking these statistics on SSK and Bağ-Kur insurance coverage into account, it appears evident that neither farmers nor agricultural workers benefit properly from existing social schemes. However, the picture might be a little more complex than this. A survey of rural insurance coverage was made in 1994, which took data from all heads of household in two villages selected from each of the provinces of Aydın, Bursa, Gaziantep, Nevşehir and Rize. Located across Turkey, these are areas that might be described as fairly representative of the country's more prosperous agricultural regions. It was found that 64% of household heads in the ten villages were covered by a security scheme (40% these being covered by SSK, 49% by Bağ-Kur and 11% by other agencies), while of the household heads mainly engaged in farming 29.3% were covered by Bağ-Kur (Aksoy *et al.* 1994). The low coverage for farmers indeed serves to confirm the impression that most farmers are unwilling – or unable – to make the payments for farmers' insurance coverage under Law no. 2926, but the more interesting aspect of these figures is the overall high level of coverage. At almost two thirds

---

[50] Farmers who do not even insure themselves – as most clearly do not judging from these figures – are certainly not likely to insure their workers properly (it should be mentioned that unofficial employment, i.e. on a cash basis and uninsured, is not uncommon in Turkey, in all sectors); companies, on the other hand, are required to show workers on their books (at least a sufficient number of them to be credible).

[51] This notwithstanding a renewed gain in uptake at the end of this period, specifically in the years 1998-1999 and 2002-2003, which might also be linked to privatisations.

of villagers, this is over double that of farmers, suggesting that something of the order of a third of the populations of these villages are not mainly engaged in farming.[52]

In fact, this is evidence of the scale of the phenomenon referred to of the change of social structure. In recent decades people (and families) have become increasingly mobile between urban and rural environments (returning to the village at the weekend, in the summer, or when they retire) and they have increasingly been gaining their income from a mix of activities of which agriculture is only one, and not necessarily the most important. In the more prosperous villages, where formerly almost everyone depended almost exclusively on agriculture, a significant part of the population now does not – at least a third, it would appear. Indeed, if the figure 64% is extrapolated on the basis of the number of agricultural enterprises it can be said that about two and a half million farmers were covered by security schemes at the turn of the millennium,[53] whereas Table 5.9 gives a figure of something around one million. This difference suggests the existence of some one and a half million farmers, out of the scope of social security data for agriculture but in some way covered by a security scheme.[54]

In the period after 1980, two significant developments took place in the field of social security of a general nature but particularly important for agriculture and rural society. The first was the establishment in 1986 of the Social Assistance and Solidarity Fund (*Sosyal Yardımlaşma ve Dayanışmayı Teşvik Fonu*) known as the 'Poor and Destitute Fund' ('*Fakir-Fukara Fonu*'), the second the 1992 introduction of the Green Card for Covering Medical Expenses of the Poor (*Ödeme Gücü Olmayan Vatandaşların Tedavi Giderlerinin Yeşil Kart Verilerek Devlet Tarafından Karşılanması Hakkında Kanun*). Further to these, the World Bank 'Social Risk Mitigation Project' offers regular cash transfers to poor families on

---

[52] Very simply, the calculation is a third (29.3%) of farmers are insured (with Bağ-Kur), a third (100 – 64 = 36%) of the villagers are uninsured (probably mostly in agriculture), leaving a third (100 – 29.3 – 36 = 34.7%).

[53] Assuming the GAC 2001 figure of 3.97 million enterprises.

[54] The 64% figure comes from more prosperous areas and therefore should not be applied to the country as a whole; against that, however, this figure comes only from household heads, and thus takes no account either of dependents or of other family members that might have other social security arrangements. The numbers given here, therefore, can be evaluated as indeed indicative of a major phenomenon, although they cannot be used to ascertain its precise extent.

the proviso that they send their school-age children to schools and have the younger ones immunised.

Covering various basic needs, including food, fuel and clothing, direct cash assistance, scholarships and health expenses, the Social Assistance and Solidarity Fund (SASF) – and the Directorate General set up to administer the system – ensures resource transfers through charitable foundations (Gülbuçuk 2005: 114). The importance that the law assigns to such foundations, including financial incentives (i.e. tax exemptions), leads to a situation in which social assistance is extended by the state on the one hand and by foundations operating through the state on the other. The political dimension of the SASF scheme is also interesting: 'Networks of cash/in-kind assistance by the local branches of the central government as well as local governments led by the ruling party, foundations, associations and companies controlled by them, private firms in business-contracting relations with the former and religious orders reaching many poor households in villages and towns have their increasing effect in shaping the voting patterns of people' (Oyan 2009: 247).

Notwithstanding the unusual administration and questionable politics of the SASF, it clearly operates as a public income transfer to rural areas, especially to smallholders who have stopped farming or who use it to ameliorate their impoverished circumstances. Oyan, for example refers to an 'increase in the number of farmers subsisting on old age pensions and direct income support' (*ibid*). Rural areas also benefit from the Green Card system, which extends free health services to those falling or all time outside the social insurance system. According to 2005 data there are almost nine million green card holders in Turkey, making up 13.2% of the total population, the majority of whom are rural people (Gülbuçuk 2005: 101). The WB Social Risk Mitigation Project, meanwhile, focuses on the heavily rural eastern part of the country. While beneficiaries of this project constitute 3% of the population as a country average, this figure rises to 14% in the East and Southeast Anatolia regions (Buğra 2008: 234). The project is composed of four interconnected components, related to support and development.[55]

---

[55] Mitigating the impact of economic crises on needy people (rapid assistance), building capacity in state agency extension services and social assistance to the poor (institutional development), establishing a social assistance system consisting of improving basic health and education services targeting 6% of the total population (conditional cash transfer), and enhancing income generation and employment opportunities of the poor (local initiatives) (Gülbuçuk 2005: 115).

Also impacting on the life of rural populations, individual or intra-household transfers may take a variety of different forms: in-kind or cash assistance to a relative/household member (both rural-to-urban and urban-to-rural); sales of animals, land and agricultural equipment to finance life and/or business in urban settlements; investments using urban accumulations in agricultural enterprises or buying land; etc. The massive migration from villages seen across Turkey over recent decades has also, of course had a role in transfers into and out of rural areas, both external emigration (to other countries) and internal (generally to one or other of the major cities). There is a need for further detailed studies on the evolution of relations between rural origin people with their relatives in villages, how resources in the rural sector are used and how these uses affect rural populations and farming activities. Nevertheless, there has also been enough work done to indicate some of complexities involved here.

Internal migration transfers are commonly understood to flow out of the rural environment. It has been often observed that having migrated to an urban centre, migrants receive considerable material support from their rural settlements until they become established, and which may continue even after that. Research (Öztürk 2010) has confirmed the assumption that such people constitute a cheaper source of labour power since rural support reduces their costs of living in urban centres. However, this explanation implicitly assumes that rural migrants would starve without support and even when they are fully settled their income would not suffice for urban life without assistance from their villages. Looking at the process of rural to urban migration since the 1950s, the existence of such a group may well be evident. However, migration from rural areas comprises persons from various segments of rural people, not just the economically desperate supported by their home settlements. In fact, following any process of rural-to-urban migration, it is the specific forms of relations between the migrants and those who remain that determine the direction and nature of resource flow and income transfer.

Among the classes of people moving from village to city other than that most commonly assumed, there are households above a specific threshold of income who migrate temporarily or permanently mainly for the education of their children. There are also the impoverished who move to the city but are not supported, for a variety of (personal, economic, etc.) reasons. Another case is those people continuing to be engaged mainly in agriculture but living in an urban settlement (a local town, perhaps), or others again engaged in a non-agricultural business in the town or city where they have settled, but still maintaining their farming activities in the village. In these different forms mentioned above, it is clear that ties with the rural sector may continue intensively for at least some time but without fixed, uni-directional transfer flows, continuing as mutual assistance, investments in agricultural activities or transfer of rural resources to support urban activities. A 1984 study of migrants' urban and rural assets remains instructive in this respect. In the five-year period prior to migration, migrant families' rural assets increase significantly, but they start to decline one to two years before migration; the year of migration they tend to remain fairly unchanged, after which they increase until about ten years later, when rural assets start to decrease (Kartal 1984: 110).

The true picture of transfer here is obviously somewhat complicated and certainly not defined by a simple snapshot of the economically desperate supported by their families in the village until they can make it in the city. Indeed, standing as a testimony to the persistence and intensity of migrants' relations with their rural origin, the traffic congestion on roads leading from urban centres to rural areas during religious holidays (and many accidents occurring during this rush) indicates also a reverse movement of capital. And the solidarity shown by economically successful urban settlers in helping rural families is a factor that particularly needs to be taken account in understanding how rural populations subsist. Furthermore, considering the increase in the number of retired people now living in villages, and many of them retired from non-agricultural jobs, it is manifest that (part of) their urban accumulation is transferred to the rural sector for farming activities or the purchase of real estate (land or property). Meanwhile, these relations weaken as nuclear families become more prevalent, as Ayşe Buğra (2008) points out, and, more importantly perhaps, as second and third generation emigrants fail to maintain close contact with their family roots. However, even if weakening gradually, it is clear that these relations still continue, and that the process of urbanisation is still continuing, with an as yet unending human movement from village to city.

Leaving aside the initial, temporary outflow of capital (for spending made until a family member finds a job and settles), external migration transfers since the sixties are mostly from Western European countries (especially Germany) back to villages. A part of the income obtained by migrant workers either while working or upon returning home is definitely used for the subsistence of other family members in the village or agricultural investments there. This occurs partly through remittances sent from abroad and partly upon permanent return to Turkey, when migrant workers invest their funds in land and animals for agricultural activities, equipment and machinery for manufacturing or trucks or cars for transportation business (Abadan Unat *et al.* 1975: 229-305). Investigating this in more detail, Abadan Unat *et al.* quantify this with the calculated estimation that some 80%[56] of migrant workers sent remittances to their family members remaining in Turkey, with multiple effects (*ibid.*: 209-210).

Migrant workers abroad were found in this study to have implications for agriculture and rural life beyond the immediate financial transfer. For example, by importing tractors in the 1960s and 1970s (making use of a 'permit' that entitled of migrant workers to import) and by investing in irrigation facilities, migrant workers abroad contributed to yield increase and mechanisation, thus increasing productivity. In addition to an increase in incomes of rural population as a result of these transfers, therefore, a surplus emerged (usable in agriculture and/or in the local area, as well as being transferable out). According to the study, deposits during the period investigated (1970-1973) in the Agricultural Bank in the Boğazlıyan District of Yozgat (a far from prosperous province in central Anatolia) were higher in total than lending's, a rather unusual situation for a bank used as a principle source of credit/loans, and explained by increased farming returns in combination with the transfers (*ibid.*: 214). Meanwhile, the withdrawal from agriculture of a part of the working age population improved the rate of unemployment.

Although moving abroad as a migrant worker has become more difficult now, it still continues through some methods such as arranged marriages, with many of these migrants coming from villages. And as in the case of internal migration, migrant workers abroad tend to maintain strong ties with their home villages which weaken but still continue with the second and third generations. Indeed, the continuation of these bonds can be more pronounced in the case of external migrant workers, for whom permanent adjustment to the foreign environment may be more difficult, for which reason also returning to their villages after retirement and sometimes becoming engaged in farming activities may also feature more strongly in this case. However, the economic practicality of transfers in the contemporary financial situation is much weakened.

---

[56] 2,730 of 3,583 migrants covered by their survey.

Earlier, those who accumulated capital in rural areas considered investment in land as a profitable endeavour. In the current era of neo-liberalism, on the other hand, investing in gold, foreign currency or repo – or urban construction, perhaps, Turkey's most vibrant economic sector – has led potential investors in agriculture – like the external migrants to speculative activities. Even more importantly, land is no more considered as a lucrative field of investment, not only for urban dwellers but also returnees and well off farmers. This takes us back too, to Marxist theory and the latest revision in this context, insofar as it also explains the fact that the impoverishment in rural areas appears not to be accompanied by land concentration (Aydın 2001b: 17).

In the current circumstances, land is concentrating (see Tables 5.2 and 5.3) but not excessively (especially not in the context of the loss of rural population). This is primarily a function of market economics and socio-economic specificities. First, Turkey is a large country and not particularly densely populated outside of the main conurbations, so inherently the price of land is not high. Much of it is not easily converted to industrial production (for topographical reasons, for example, because it is steep and not easily susceptible to mechanisation). Not particularly profitable, such land carries more risk which in turn causes the capital investment opportunities to be further limited. Also, now, the capital returns in agriculture generally are relatively poor – as compared with, say, construction or tourism. There are better options open to investors, small (individuals/families) as well as medium and large. As a result of all these factors and more, rural land prices in much of Turkey today do not particularly invite sale. The market is fairly flat, and not overly attractive to potential sellers.

Second, in addition to the lack of incentive to sell land, there are certain motivations working directly against it. For poor people, holding land is a kind of security, offering a psychological and sometimes practical escape route: when or if ever unable to survive in the city, s/he can always head back to the village. Also, as discussed, the land functions also a second income source. An important factor to bear in mind here is the practicality of combining farming with town and even city life. The time required for some forms of farming in particular is very short, and some people do it are able to work there land by commuting out to the country just at weekends and/or (summer) holidays. Examples of farming that need limited labour time input are crop and fruit farming. These considerations all come to bear on the tendency and ability of smallholders and families hold their land and go against the concentration expectations.

If we find we need to look again at the mechanics of land concentration from the combined perspective of a psychological as well as material rationale, then perhaps the economic imperative of migration ought also to be revisited. When we look at the agriculture GDP and per capita agriculture GDP from 1927 to 2010, we see a continuous increase; until 1980, the rural population also rose; and except for the 1927 to 1935 period, the increase in agriculture income was always less than that of the general national rate (Table 5.10). Agricultural income can be analysed from two main perspectives: if there is enough income, farmers can find the investment sources for agriculture; and if the farmers earn enough to live, they can subsist through farming and continue to live in their villages

Table 5.10. Indices for agriculture GDP, rural population, and per capita agriculture and national GDP during 1927-2010 by index period.[a]

Year	Agriculture			Turkey [b]
	GDP	Rural population	Per capita GDP	Per capita GDP
1927	100	100	100	100
1935	156	119	130	74
1940	250	130	192	160
1945	149	136	109	345
1950	100	100	100	100
1955	135	109	124	172
1960	169	120	141	216
1965	177	131	135	163
1970	100	100	100	100
1975	108	107	100	220
1980	117	115	102	286
1985	118	109	108	247
1990	132	106	125	498
2000	148	109	137	550
2010 [c]	165	80	206	1870
2010 [d]	165		144	

Source: TUİK 2010a, 2011c.
[a] Three index base used according to GDP series (there are four GDP series from values fixed at 1948, 1968 and 1987 and 1998).
[b] Turkey per capita GDP calculated from TUİK as US dollar base.
[c] 2010 GDP converted from 1998 to 1987 index.
[d] Calculated assuming that 2010 GDP and 1980 population.

(all other things being equal, like income distribution). We can see from tractor size and other equipment investments that farmers are, in fact, able to find investment sources, albeit, of course, facilitated as necessary with credit system supports.

During the 1927 to 2010 period, rural people always migrated out to urban areas and abroad. Up to 1980 the rural population rose and people migrated, while after 1980 the rural population fell (and migration continued). At this point, it would appear that we can explain migration as based on income level. However, if we look at average annual rises in per capita agriculture income, the growth rate declined after 1980 (Table 5.11). Had the rural population stayed at the 1980 level, the per capita agriculture

Table 5.11. Indices for agriculture GDP, rural population, and per capita agriculture and national GDP during 1927-2010 (by index period for annual changes and averages).[a]

Period	Agriculture index changes			Annual average			National changes	
	Agri. GDP	Rural pop.	Agri. per cap. GDP	Agri. GDP	Rural pop.	Agri. per cap. GDP	Per capita GDP	Per capita agri/Turkey
1927-1945 (18 years)	49	36	9	2.7	2.0	0.5	2.5	20%
1950-1965 (15 years)	77	31	35	5.1	2.1	2.3	4.2	56%
1970-2000 (30 years)	48	9	37	1.6	0.3	1.2	15	8%
1970-2010 (40 years)	65	-20	106	1.6	-0.5	2.7	29.25	9%
2000-2010 [b] (10 years)	17	0	7	1.7	0	0.7	–	–

Source: TÜİK 2010a, 2011c.
[a] Calculated from Table 5.10.
[b] 2010 GDP, 1980 population.

GDP would have shown an annual decline from 2.3 to 0.7, but we see 2.7. This was only enabled through the huge outward migration from rural areas. Therefore, in analysing the relationship between rural income and migration, we need to look at rate of income rises rather than the simple income level. But is this enough to explain these relationships? In fact, it is well known in Turkey that high income level rural people migrate out from rural environments, just like other income groups, if not more. At this point we need compare rates of income increase.

Table 5.11 shows indices for the changes in the agricultural and general national per capita incomes and the comparative rate of change between them. The annual rates of change of agricultural income have always been less than that of the nation as a whole, and after 1970 this rate hit its bottom level for the period. Therefore, the tentative explanation may be proposed that rural people migrated when the non-agriculture income level rate of increase was higher than that of the agricultural. In other words, for life changing decisions like leaving the homeland of generations, a sense of likelihood needs to be introduced into statistical analysis. From the perspective of the would-be migrant, the question is looking at the way things are going, does migration seem to offer the best future? Comparative income level and income change rates may be more meaningful than analysis only of simple income level and per capita income rises.

Chapter 6. Conclusions

Consisting of two sections, this short chapter is added by way of summary and analysis of the processes described thus far. Comments are grouped into two, with seven main points on the recent changes in agriculture in Turkey – generally over the last three decades and specifically during the last ten-year period – which are then followed by five points relating these developments to the agrarian question and overall rural situation, thereby referring back to the theory explicated in the opening chapter and completing a review of the first part of this book.

Changes in the structure of agriculture

In terms of the structure and other features of agricultural enterprises, the major developments described can be listed as follows:

- If five hectares is taken as a basis, small scale enterprises had a 57.5% share of the total number of enterprises as of 2006, which equated to 16.3% of all cultivated land. If the basis is taken as ten hectares, these figures rise to 78.9% of all enterprises and 34.5% of land under culture. If the 2001 GAC 3,012,000 figure for agricultural enterprises is used and taken as, at the same time, the number of households, and combined with the 2006 figures, then the number of farming families working on less than 5 hectares of land was 1,737,000 and the number of households working on less than 10 hectares 2,383,000. Using 4.5 as average household size, these figures give 7,817,000 and 10,726,000 people, respectively, which corresponded to roughly a third and a half of the rural population at that time, again respectively.[57]

  The characteristics of these enterprises and populations are important in understanding the development taking place in agriculture and the rural sector. Importantly, they are based on the conceptual equation of household = farmer, but for a significant share of these households agricultural activities are no longer necessarily the determining factor

---

[57] These, of course, are very much approximations, but most effected less by the likely decline in (rural) enterprise numbers between 2001 and 2006 (which would mean the final estimates may be inflated) than by statistical measurement procedures for the rural population (c.f. the affect of the move to the ADNKS – Address Based Population Count System, e.g. Table 8.4) and, most of all, the ballpark 4.5 factor for household size. This was the official census rate for the whole country in 2000, and was certainly significantly higher in rural areas where families of ten and more were not at all uncommon. In conclusion, the estimates of a third and a half given here are probably quite conservative.

for their subsistence. The number of people engaged in non-agricultural activities, their incomes derived from such activities, the number of retired persons and existence of various forms of solidarity and assistance all point to the conclusion that an important share of the households in this category can no more be considered as farming families per se. That is not to say that economic dependency on non-agricultural income and public or personal transfers implies that these people are not significantly engaged in crop farming or animal husbandry, but rather that although living in rural areas, they people subsist heavily on non-agricultural income and have thus moved out of the status of being 'farmers'. Here it should be kept in mind that there is a category of farmers whose enterprises are not engaged in large-scale activities, but are still engaged in relatively high value added activities such as, tea, hazelnuts and fruit and vegetable cultivation, including the usage of greenhouse and irrigated farming technologies.

- As a result of the combined impacts of market relations and government policies, it is observed that medium and large scale enterprises in agriculture are increasing both in numbers and share of total cultivated land, with a gradual process of land aggregation. There are some striking developments that influence the process by which the share of large-scale enterprises continues to increase their position in the market, related, among other things, to tendencies in the relative prices of agricultural goods, changes in marketing channels and support policies, on-contract farming, large-scale international agricultural investments and access to export markets.

- The privatisation or liquidation of some organisations which had an active role in the marketing of agricultural products and functioned as guarantor for product has left farmers unprotected against (in competition with) professional trading organisations, retail chains and industrial corporations. Upon the withdrawal from market of such organisations as SEK and TEKEL, companies with large market shares and enjoying a monopolistic position are now much more influential in setting prices. Factors such as the determining role of big business, commitment of governments to the IMF and WB philosophy of setting prices parallel to world market prices in support purchases and setting these prices low in the context of WTO agreements has lowered farmers' incomes, reduced marketing guarantees and led to uncertainty and marketing risks. Accompanied by the very real threat of drought in Turkey, farmers who could not afford to take all these risks just withdrew from production.

- The net return to peasant and small scale farmers has been decimated due to a variety of factors including companies dominating the market for agricultural goods; the sector penetration of retail chains, monopolistic structures in agricultural inputs including seed and pesticides that determine input and product prices, and increases in the cost of other inputs such as fuel and fertilisers. Under these circumstances, agricultural enterprises with limited land and other capital means can no longer provide satisfactory returns for their entrepreneurs.

- While market conditions and government policies squeeze farmers as described above, the shifting of agricultural support from crops to land proprietorship and the possibility of using fallow land to benefit from the new (DIS) scheme positively encourages farmers to cultivate less and less. Although the negative consequences of this support policy were eventually realised and there has been a partial return to crop-based support, it is still operative. In sum, the DIS system continues to discourage farming activities. Meanwhile, there is a growing practice of enjoying the benefits of state support through the DIS for plots that are actually leased for income without risk. Since these plots are utilised mainly by medium and large enterprises, the policy is in effect promoting these enterprises and the further capitalisation of the sector (and thus as diametrically opposed to acting as a small producer support, the original stated aim).

- Leaving aside such crops as fruits, vegetables, tea and hazelnut, small farmers engaged in grain culture can continue their activities, but only by procuring services (tilling, sowing and harvesting) from other farmers owning tractors. In terms of technology, that is, all small and large enterprises (have to) use tractors. Equally, farmers (have to) purchase high yielding seed, as necessary (to build/replenish stocks). The more important difference in this field is in the amount and also quality of applications (pesticides and fertilisers) used. Insofar as this is the case, then the argument that small enterprises work on low productivity rates because of a lack of technology is not particularly well founded.

- If not engaged in animal husbandry, farming households in this group have lost their character of (re-)producing their own labour. If they, or at least some part of them are not engaged in agricultural wage labour, probably neither are they engaged in cultivation, with the exception of their own orchards. For this group, the village is primarily a living space rather than a space for economic activity.

The agrarian question

Considering these changes in agriculture in Turkey, considerations in respect of the agrarian question can be made as follows:

- At first glance, rural depopulation, the increasing proportion of wage earners and self-employed in the total rural population, and the concentration of land in the hands of large enterprises are combining in a process that suggest the dissolution of the peasantry, however slowly, and enhanced domination of capitalism in agriculture. One point is clear: all the developments described as well as the almost complete market orientation of production makes it indisputable that capitalistic relations of production are operating in agriculture. Nevertheless, the fact that there has not yet (at least as of the 2006 figures) been a significant decline in the number of agricultural enterprises, suggests a combination of traditional petty farming with income gained from non-agricultural activities and sources, which in turn suggests that the implications of the recent period of global developments for agriculture calls for a somewhat different approach to that of the classical labour/capital critique.
- Examples include the cases of farmers engaged in waged work or small scale initiatives in other areas beyond working their small plots, diversification of crops in response to changing market situations, and the increase in fruit and vegetable cultivation. The introduction of breeds that increase returns in animal husbandry, acquiring better and more informed methods of stock breeding (i.e. increasing productivity – currently, output is not going down although the number of animals is declining) and efforts to maintain land possession while trying to subsist through both interpersonal and public solidarity can all be construed as rural people's striving for resistance and autonomy as conceptualised, for example, by Van der Ploeg.
- On developments observed in agriculture and rural population, the policies pursued after 1980 were particularly influential. It is also clear that these policies were shaped in the context of relations with and commitments to the World Bank, IMF, WTO and EU. Complemented by the ever-increasing dominance of international monopolies manipulating agricultural inputs and the increasing market share of retail chains as well as of domestic and foreign companies using agricultural products as inputs, these developments taken together make it necessary to address the agrarian question not as a national but global issue, as argued by McMichael and Bernstein.

- In the processes of capital accumulation which now operates at global level, it is observed that Turkish farmers have suffered serious losses of income in the context of market relations and support policies and found it increasingly difficult to subsist on agricultural production. As villages lose population, the remaining farmers seek different sources of income and ways of enhancing those already available. However, it cannot be said that these developments drive farmers to different political attitudes and preferences (class consciousness). With the exception of some demonstrations related to the announced minimum prices for some agricultural goods, farmers or the rural population in general have not been moved to become active in new forms of organisation or a different approach to defend their rights. The collective action aspect of class definition is little applicable in rural Turkey today.

- Instead, populations remaining in rural areas resist in the individualistic forms described (forms defined by the very operation of capital), or they and others moving to and settling in the outskirts of towns and cities live on old age pensions, green card and fuel donations as forms of public support, and on personal assistance and cases of solidarity. In conclusion, in spite of the coping mechanisms mentioned, an important part of the peasantry has joined the ranks of the reserve army of labour, a classical concept with a very real, modern expression – in Turkey, hundreds of thousands, perhaps millions, of people living in towns and villages below poverty and hunger thresholds.

Clearly, developments in both the structure and process of agricultural production and the composition and behaviour of the peasantry and rural population in Turkey need to be addressed through theoretical frameworks that take due account of global circumstances and trends. There is also a need for further in-depth analysis taking into account dimensions such as income transfers, multi-occupational peasantry and devillagisation accompanied by detailed data from field studies.

Part II
Neo-liberalism, rural life and poverty in Turkey today

The neo-liberal development of Turkish agriculture constitutes an important force driving rural change and affecting a transformation also in the structure and character of poverty. In order to understand this, it is necessary to look at the relations between these, as well as aspects specific to them in isolation. The second part of this book thus examines rural change and poverty in the context of the current neo-liberal reality.

Chapter 7. Sociological approaches to recent developments in agriculture and rural Turkey

Under the impact of the structural change in agriculture and worsening circumstances, Turkey's rural population has been hard hit. Economic migration largely prompted by the effects of the liberalisation of the agricultural sector has accounted for a major part of what has been a massive population loss from (migration out of) the countryside. Those who stayed have developed various methods of coping including, especially, engagement in non-agricultural activities. Social scientists have tried to account for the situation emerging with these developments. Following a brief historical sketch of Turkish rural sociology, some observations and opinions of social scientists on recent developments as derived from field studies are outlined.

Background

Rural studies in Turkey, almost without exception, are addressed from the 'paradigm of rural transformation' (Sirman 2001: 251). Most studies have focused on changes in village communities upon the entrance of capitalistic relations to the rural sector. The modernisation/development paradigm laid its imprint on agricultural and rural studies in the period 1950-1960, with efforts made to explain agricultural development through such concepts as 'modern mentality', 'enterprising', etc. This development oriented point of view engaged with the investigation of obstacles to market oriented production, and social phenomena were assigned meaning in this context. In general, this approach assumes the legitimacy of the rural/urban divide from an urban centred stance (i.e. assuming the rural-to-urban movement of population in-accordance with modernist/Marxist theory), but maintains that divisions on the basis of gender or class work differently in rural and urban settings. In the 1970s, the modernisation problematic was applied to the rural sector with its Marxist variant, which replaces 'mentality' with capital and, correspondingly, reduces social relations to the logic of capital (Sirman 2001: 252).

The main issues in the 1950s and 1960s concerned the levels of capitalistic development in agriculture and polarisation in land ownership. It was then found that capital accumulation in agriculture did not run parallel to commercialisation, commoditisation, capitalist development and land conglomeration (Akşit 1987: 17). A research conducted in these years predicted the different paths of development. These paths were identified with village types:

- villages engaged in traditional lines of production, resulting in migration to urban centres and abroad;
- small landholding village engaged in commercial production with diversified economic activities;
- medium-size landholding village engaged in accumulation and producing 'kulaks'[58] by using modern equipment and family labour;
- village becoming 'capitalistic' (Keyder 1983, cited by Akşit 1987: 18).

Another approach was to focus on people rather than places. Such an approach does not eschew considerations of place, of course, which would hardly be possible in research related to agriculture. A 2001 survey conducted in the Black Sea region, for example, inevitably included hazel nuts in its specification of people's activities, since income derived from hazel nut cultivation and related activities constitutes 32% of total cash income of households in this area. According to the findings of this survey, pressures for income generation (within or out of agriculture) combined with labour migration (domestic or external) during the 1970s led to the emergence of 3 types of villagers:

- villagers employed in towns/cities (on regular, seasonal or occasional basis) – in the public sector (including transportation, communication, public works), construction sector hazel nut mills or industrial enterprises, and skilled workers and trainees, or salesmen;
- resident in both village and town/city – small entrepreneurs and shopkeepers, civil servants and hazel nut traders;
- villagers with diversified income generating production – beekeeping, dairy farming, poultry farming, greenhouse farming and kiwi cultivation (Sönmez 2001: 97).

This mixed income picture is emphasised by residence, with 74% of 239 rural households having another residence out of the village, a further 3.7% being dual (village/city) residents and 5% living abroad and only

---

[58] Kulak: in pre-revolutionary Russia, the class of (relatively) wealthy independent farmers (from whom the lower level peasant classes were to be liberated).

returning to their villages in the summer[59] (*ibid.*: 92-96). The longitudinal complexity of people moving between 'categories' over time can lead to the generation of new, highly specified categories from observed phenomena – such as above, returning retiree village migrants (who buy local rural land). Another such category was identified by a study conducted in 1966, of 'truck entrepreneurs' who invest capital gained from agriculture in areas outside agriculture (Akşit 1987: 15). These are farmers who use their accumulations from farming activities to buy a truck and start a small transportation business.[60]

A nationwide study conducted in the early 1980s found that a total of 21.7% of the active rural labour force was found to be engaged in non-agricultural activities. Among the other findings of this research, keeping and/or raising cattle and/or sheep was found to be prevalent among around four fifths of farmers (only 17% of small peasants and 23% of wealthy farmers had no livestock, as compared to 51% of agricultural workers and 47% in rent earners). Regarding gender, 22.5% of rural women were found to be engaged in income generating activities (sewing, embroidery, carpet weaving, marketing and formwork [8.5%]) (Boratav 1985: 11, 66).

Recent developments

As the change taking place in the structure of agriculture and rural settlement patterns became increasingly manifest through the 80s, doubts emerged in discussions and debates about the nature of agriculture in Turkey concerning the common diagnosis that petty commodity production was dominant. This led to a new sociological movement focused on the complex new reality of income and residence patterns in the developing agricultural and rural context of liberalism:

> To sustain itself, petty commodity production has diversified, enabled by its flexible nature to transfer to and continue with different economic activities. This heterogeneous situation calls for new concepts. Heterogeneity can be addressed with

---

[59] Largely first generation emigrants typically returning as families for extended holidays, these people are technically listed as resident in their villages (which they consider to be their 'home' and to which they are likely to retire) although generally, in fact, they are not.
[60] The truck entrepreneurs may discontinue their formwork or continue, on a part-time or seasonal basis, as employers, i.e. paying others to work the farm while they run their trucking business; they might also, of course, move home to a nearby town or city.

> such approaches as 'multi-occupational class', 'multi-facetted class' or 'hybrid class'. The contrary [conventional] approach is to define this group as 'semi-labourers' or regard it as prospective labourers... [However, in fact] this group cannot really be regarded as 'prospective labourers' or a form of petty commodity producer (Bozoğlu 1987: 34).

Another idea put forward during this period was that the village and peasantry as unit of analysis had lost its explanatory power:

> Understanding rural structures and the peasantry in the face of a globalizing agriculture requires new theoretical approaches and new paradigms. The traditional-modern dilemma of the school of modernisation which was dominant in social sciences in the period 1940-60 and formed the basis of 'peasantry' analyses especially in sociology and anthropology fails to understand and explain our present day. The 'village' and 'peasantry' as isolated from the wider society and assumed to have its functional integrity can no longer serve as unit of analysis (Aydın 2001a: 5).

A similar opinion is also put forward by Çağlar Keyder and Zafer Yenal, who suggest that 'the range of income generation means has widened' in particular 'as means of transportation and communication have reached villages' (Keyder and Yenal 2004: 370). The lack of integration into the national system of administration of Turkey's myriad rural communities – almost 80,000 rural settlements in 1993 (split roughly 45:55, villages to other smaller or seasonal settlements) – has long occupied Turkey's modernizing nation-builders (Jongerden 2007: 122-134,), and here it is the modern integration of infrastructure that is seen as key to what may termed a process of *post*-modernisation.[61] Interestingly, the widening income generation base in villages in combination with the phenomenon of well-off retirees returning 'home', and also, in some villages, emigrant population exhaustion (everyone able and wanting to leave has done so), is resulting in a new rural demographic dynamic, even to the extent of leading to some instances of population increase (see Chapter 8). Given these emerging patterns and taking the idea of a post-modernisation

---

[61] Although it may be dubbed a process of post-modernisation, it cannot really be considered one of post-industrialisation. The possibilities in this respect – within agriculture – would be better represented by niche production/marketing, tailored biotechnology, etc. (see, e.g. Roep and Wiskerke 2004; www.ijtds.com/).

process seriously, we might even question whether it is very helpful to still call these settlement units 'villages' (see Textbox 7.1).[62]

Retracing the steps of recent rural sociology in Turkey, the development of the notion of 'subsistence strategies' may be cited to exemplify one of the new concepts demanded. Zülküf Aydın conducted field studies in Turkey in the 1980s showing farmers engaged in petty production who had started to seek other means and channels to support their farming

---

Textbox 7.1. The village and rural structure in Turkey.

Rural sociology in Turkey has a rich subject. The Turkish word '*köy*', translated as 'village', is heavily impregnated with a deep cultural value which, though fading now, is still strongly maintained in the national psyche. Prior to the 1980s the village represented a principle constituent of identity for the majority of the population, as emotional 'home'. Turkish music (in various forms), for example, is replete with songs about one's *köy*, such as a yearning to return, or at least to be buried there. Traditionally, villages have been defined by the local agriculture, of course, but there may be differences within this. Villages in some areas are differentiated ethnically, for example, with a Kurdish village near to a Turkish one, or a village of, say, Balkan migrant ancestry.

In addition to its basic meaning of village, the word '*köy*' also has other referential functions to linked concepts: '*köy*' is used for 'rural', and '*köylü*', literally 'villager', also translates into English as 'peasant' and 'rustic', including as a pejorative term. Administratively, it specifies a sparsely populated (rural) district – officially defined as one with a population of less than 2000 – as well as the village settlement itself. All *köy*s are integrated into the hierarchy of the national administrative system, as the bottom layer, and officially headed by the *muhtar*.

Generally translated as 'village headman' (although the *muhtar* system is not limited just to village districts, extending even to the local neighborhoods of metropolitan cities), the *muhtar* is an elected office, an official administrative position. Historically, the *muhtar* has been used as a primary connection between

---

[62] The word for 'village' in Turkish ('*köy*') has an emotive, socio-economic reference to something quite different to the emerging pattern described here, such that its usage for these contemporary settlement types may be quite misleading.

the state and the people, with comunication passed down to village level through him from the nearest district center (essentially, the nearest town), and vice versa. This might also extend down another level (though the *muhtar*), to local hamlets. Smaller settlements (*köy altı yerleşimler*) may be linked to the village in which (in whose territory) they are situated, although historically they have also retained a certain independence.

If the word '*köy*' is multi-functional, at smaller settlement level the reverse is the case, with a few different words used with quite specific meanings. The word '*oba*' translates well as 'hamlet', meaning a small, independent, permanent settlement consisting of (say) five to ten houses. It – the *oba* – also continues to survive in a traditional form linked to the origin of the word. This refers to the place where a small community stays for a temporary period of time – thus related, that is, to the relatively recent nomadic heritage of central Asian Turkic peoples (whose outward, probably drought-driven migration reached Anatolia a thousand years ago). Still occasionally to be found in the south of Turkey are *oba* in the form of a small group of tents (traditionally, rounded tent structures, perhaps a single large communal one, itself the *oba*). The people living in *oba*s are still following a semi-nomadic, husbandry-based form.

Associated with the central and especially eastern and southeastern part of the country is the *mezra*. The (modern) Turkish form of the Arabic word for agricultural area, or farm, this usually refers to an area of very loosely linked farms. Though it may be considered a community, it is only really a settlement structure in the sense of a scattered settlement. It has no particular centre as such. The *mezra* form is also linked to the feudal-type landlord (*ağa* or *bey*) and tribal (*aşiret*) systems, which continue to be relavent today in a variety of (social, economic, etc.) ways.

Common in the mountainous territories skirting the northern Black Sea and southern Mediterranean Sea regions is the '*yayla*'. These are mountain pasture retreats, used by villagers who drive their animals up to escape the summer heat. Seasonal settlements, therefore, and empty during the winter months, these can be quite large with, say, a hundred basic dwellings. Depending on the local topography and climate, a village might have two *yayla*s, the second higher up the mountain, with a traditional two-stage system of retreat. With the decline of smallholder husbandry especially and subsistence farming generally over the last three decades, these settlements have become both less and differently used, less used in the traditional way, that is, but employed now also as summer holiday (i.e. non-agricultural) retreats.

income and thus changed their patterns of behaviour. Reviewing the cases of Tuzburgazı and Kınık, two villages of the relatively prosperous Aegean region, Aydın has coined the term 'subsistence strategies' to refer to the different approaches that villages employ in attempting to deal with the contemporary situation:

- *Strategies for creating new income sources: working on larger plots of land through leasing and share-cropping;* migrating either seasonally or permanently. In the village of Kınık, all households without exception had at least one member working out of village or earning income from some non-agricultural activity. In Tuzburgazı, falling agricultural returns had led some small farmers demote farming to a secondary role. Fishing and animal husbandry come to the fore, while excessive utilisation of natural resources are observed in both villages.
- *Strategies based on spending savings and borrowing:* getting into debt and selling production instruments (mainly tractors and other farming equipment).
- *Strategies based on limiting consumption and lowering costs:* consuming less, substituting help from the community (*imece*) for wage labour (Aydın 2001b: 22-27).

Clearly the asset-realisation and belt-tightening aspects of the second and third of these are can only be stop-gap measures, while the use of loans and community support have equally obvious limitations, and so only the first, mixed income approach offers a long-term viable alternative. Through the notion of subsistence strategies, therefore, the peasant as actor thus becomes central to explanation of observed phenomena in the development of a new theory of rural development for the contemporary situation (rather, that is, than just the object of forces beyond his/her control). Thus, moving into the 2000s, Keyder and Yenal imply the post-modern approach questioning of the very notion of 'village' in viewing the contemporary evolution of agriculture and country life as follows:

> What we argue is that the population subsisting exclusively on farming has decreased and an ever greater part of the rural population is engaged in diversified and complex income generating activities which *place them in different circumstances and invoke those in urban areas'* (Keyder and Yenal 2004: 358, emphasis added).

In fact, the diversification in income generating activities and advances in transportation and communication (above) are seen to be making villages into extensions of cities (a phenomenon more common in the west and south of the country. Contemporary Turkish rural studies is here seen to take up the issue of the rural: urban dichotomy – or rather return to it, for this type of analysis does, in fact, have a well-established, if somewhat neglected history.[63] The same researchers remark also on the following developments, both materially facilitating and theoretically supportive of the analysis developed:

- Internationalisation and regulation have made prices, products and production chains a complex multi-component phenomenon.
- Labour markets in urban areas have become less attractive for newcomers (*ibid.*: 377-378).

İlhan Tekeli says the following in regard to developments taking place in the rural sector in the 1980s:

> Studies on rural transformation unfortunately lost value after the 1980s. During this period there were some significant developments, including the expansion of irrigated farming and growth of greenhouse cultivation, which induced a demand for labour. The numbers of villages with a declining population have become a majority of the total. Many villages are inhabited almost completely by elderly people and retirees alone. In such villages there is almost no market-oriented production. Inhabitants in these villages live on their retirement pensions or remittances from abroad. In some villages inhabited by retirees, population growth can be observed. Living on retirement pensions means there is a return, back to the village. Even the depopulated villages are not the villages of earlier periods, and even those people remaining in their villages have changed. Unfortunately, however, we have no comprehensive study typifying transformations taken place in villages after 1980 (Tekeli 2008: 53).

---

[63] Nusret Kemal Köymen had notably advocated a re-industrialisation of the countryside and re-integration of industry and agriculture in the rural setting during the foundation years of the Republic, for example in the peasantist journal *Ülke*, which he published between 1933 and 1936 (see Jongerden 2007: 195ff). Taking this a step further in the direction of a more contemporary post-modern analysis, questioning the rural/urban divide may be also taken as an incipient a post-ruralism, i.e. questioning the power relations assumed and invoked in the assignment of the category 'rural' (Murdoch and Pratt 1993 cited by Jongerden 2007).

Reiterating most of the points made above with some new observations and adjusted emphasis, this can be read as a single paragraph summary of recent Turkish rural sociology (including, perhaps, its arguably over-negative assessment of the current state of the field). It is clear that important changes took place in agriculture and the rural sector especially after 1980, which have demanded fresh approaches employing a different conceptual base to those previously dominant. And it is on the basis of these alternative concepts and a collation of relevant data that an account of variables related to the developments in the structure of agriculture and rural population is presented in Chapter 8.

Chapter 8. Village loss, village urbanisation and villages as shelters for the weak

Developments in agriculture and the rural sector can be examined more closely by combining an analysis of rural population trends and employment with the overall developments in agriculture addressed on the other. To this end, therefore, the chapter comprises an overview of demographic developments in the rural sector, including population, distribution of employment, migration, retired population, population out of the labour force and employment in non-agricultural areas. It ought to be reiterated that the considerations introduced earlier continue to apply in respect of the principle data source, the state department Turkish Statistics Institute (*Türkiye İstatistik Kurumu*, TÜİK), along with its predecessor, the State Institute of Statistics (*Devlet İstatistik Enstitüsü*, DİE), the most important of which here is the definition of 'rural' and 'urban'.[64]

Rural population, urban population and migration

The proportion of rural population is taken both as data upon which to base development comparisons and as an indicator of the level of capitalist development. In developing countries, rural employment and rural population levels are almost everywhere indicators of paramount import. Keeping this general approach in mind, rural population can be addressed in terms of labour force required for agricultural activities. To begin, we need to establish the basic demographic dynamics of the gross rural and relative rural-to-urban population numbers. Most fundamentally, during the period 1927-2010, the share of Turkey's rural population fell from three quarters of the total population to one quarter – in fact, this occurred just in the period after 1950. In absolute terms, the rural population was at its highest at the census of 1980 when just over twenty-five million people were recorded as living in the countryside (Table 8.1). Over the last thirty years, therefore, the rural population has been in decline both relatively and absolutely. By 2010, the rural population had dropped to seventeen

---

[64] The rural being the settlements, populations, etc. located in administrative territories specified as 'villages' and also '*belde*' (Chapter 5).

Table 8.1. Rural and urban population during 1927-2010.

Year	Urban	%	Rural	%	Total
1927	3,305,879	24.22	10,342,391	75.78	13,648,270
1935	3,802,642	23.53	12,355,376	76.47	16,158,018
1940	4,346,249	24.39	13,474,701	75.61	17,820,950
1950	5,244,337	25.04	15,702,851	74.96	20,947,188
1960	8,859,731	31.92	18,895,089	68.08	27,754,820
1970	13,691,101	38.45	21,914,075	61.55	35,605,176
1980	19,645,007	43.91	25,091,950	56.09	44,736,957
1990	33,326,351	59.01	23,146,684	40.99	56,473,035
2000	44,006,274	64.90	23,797,653	35.10	67,803,927
2010 [a]	56,222,356	76.30	17,500,632	23.70	72,722,988

Source: TÜİK 2000, 2008-2011.

[a] Employing ABPRS (Address Based Population Research System) 2010 – a reformed database methodology introduced in 2006-2007.

and a half million, around 70% of the 1980 figure, and on a par with its level during the 1950s.

This decline of the rural population suggests migration. Three main observations may be drawn from the (domestic) migration statistics covering the period 1975-2000 (Table 8.2).[65] First, there was a significant net migration from rural to urban areas after 1980, but which only accounted for around a third of the fall in the rural population over the subsequent two-decades.[66] Emigration to Europe would thus be assumed to account for the remainder. Second, while rural-to-urban migration during the 1980s led to a decline in rural population, in the periods 1975-1980 and 1995-2000 it was outweighed by movement in the opposite direction, with urban-to-rural migration resulting in a net increase in the rural population. Related to this is the overall rate of increase in urban-to-rural

---

[65] Oddly, the period 1990-1995 appears to be missing from the original figures because of population census was not been conducted. The obvious working assumption would be that migration during this period was in line with (somewhere between) that of the periods immediately preceding and following. Factoring in this would increase final totals by something like a quarter, but most other calculations would be little affected.

[66] Net decrease in rural population due to rural-to-urban migration 1980-2000: 400,000; decrease in rural population: 1.3 m. With the assumed missing period (1990-1995) bordered by net rural-to-urban movements of +289 and -174 thousand, factoring in assumptions for this would not be expected to greatly change the calculation.

Table 8.2. Migration by place of settlement (rural and urban) during 1975-2000 in thousands.

Direction	1975-1980		1980-1985		1985-1990		1995-2000		Total	
	×1000	%	×1000	%	×1000	%	×1000	%	×1000	%
Urban-to-urban	1,753	49	2,146	56	3,359	62	3,868	58	11,126	57
Rual-to-rural	529	16	323	8	393	7	314	5	1,558	8
Rural-to-urban	610	17	860	23	970	17	1,168	17	3,609	19
Change (%)	–		41.0		12.7		20.5		–	
Urban-to-rural	693	19	491	13	681	13	1,343	20	3,207	16
Change (%)	–		-29.2		38.7		97.3		–	
Total	3,584	100	3,820	100	5,403	100	6,692	100	19,499	100
Rural-to-urban net	-83	2	370	10	289	5	-174	3	402	2

Source: TUİK 2000.

migration, recorded as higher than that of rural-to-urban migration for the period covered. In fact, the rate of urban-to-rural migration increased greatly for each period specified, while that of rural-to-urban migration slowed, albeit unevenly. A third point of note about these statistics refers to the level of rural-to-rural and urban-to urban migration. Rural-to-rural migration declined in both absolute terms and as a proportion of total internal migration. Movements between different urban areas, on the other hand, accounted for well over half of all migrations during the period covered. Taken together, these points lead to a final observation, which is to remark on the low level of net urban-to-rural migration as a proportion of all internal migration in Turkey during the last quarter of the twentieth century.

Historically, the Turkish state had directed tens and even hundreds of thousands of enforced migrants from the ex-Ottoman Balkans to rural areas in different parts of the country, partly in an attempt to repopulate areas devastated by war and civil strife (including enforced outward migration), as well as starvation and disease. The nation thus has a history of population movements into and out of rural areas. After the Second World War, Germany's economic recovery of the 1960s saw Turks travelling there to contribute as 'guest workers' to the labour supply required. Prior to the economic downtown in the wake of the 1973 oil crisis, three quarters of a million people had migrated to north western Europe as 'guest workers,' mostly single men. Thereafter, immigration limits were set, but the outflow continued, especially through marriage, with women emigrating to join their husbands (in 'family reunification' and 'family formation'). By the mid eighties, the Turkish national diaspora in Europe had risen in number to almost two million: 'Most of them came from small villages in central Turkey or along the Black Sea coast (Avci and Kırışcı 2008: 126). Another million was added to the figure over the next decade, between the mid eighties and mid nineties, with asylum seekers (increasingly Kurds) adding to the numbers. Today the total Turkish origin population in Europe stands at around four million people, about two thirds of them in Germany: 'The immigrants consist almost exclusively of rural folk, most of whom had never lived in a town for any extended period of time prior to emigrating' (Manço 2002).[67]

Two points might be made on this subject here. First, as indicated (above), this level of migration has had an important effect on the Turkish countryside in the form of capital transfers. During the 1990s, annual remittances averaging some three and a half billion dollars entered Turkey from Europe (calculated from *ibid.*: 141). What proportion of this found its way to agriculture and rural areas is impossible to say, but certainly it entered through more than one route, both directly (e.g. people constructing new houses in their villages) or indirectly (e.g. through trickle down into local economies from remittance monies spent at local markets on farming produce, etc.). Second, as indicated, migration to Europe in particular would seem to be the major reason for the decline in the rural population during the latter part of the century. Not only does it account for some two thirds of the drop, it also, presumably, accounts for the difference between the figures recorded and the figures that would otherwise have been expected given the high birth-rate in the country generally. The last two decades of the century saw a 50% rise in the overall population. Although it is not possible to deduce from the information available how many people actually left rural Turkey (in excess of those moving to it), the real figure was clearly significantly higher than the net drop of 1.3 million

---

[67] Another half a million plus people have emigrated elsewhere in the world (about half of them to North America), but these are not predominantly from rural regions. Equally there have been – are – major migration flows into and out of Turkey involving other countries/areas (such as 'pendulum' movements between Turkey and the CIS states, and influxes related to wars involving Iraq), but again these are not predominantly related to rural areas in Turkey. Other complications include counting issues such as transnationalism of various forms (with people evidencing more or less dual national identities, at one time or over time), and 'irregular migration' (i.e. outside the usual, legal channels, and therefore unrecorded) (Avci and Kırışcı 2008).

prior to 2000, and it must have been migration to Europe that accounted for most of this difference.

In relation to the record of urban-to-rural migration, the high and increasing number of people moving to villages demands comment. The received wisdom is that people move out of agriculture as capital accumulates in urban industry, not that there should be significant movements of people in the opposite direction. There are a variety of reasons why this occurs in Turkey. As mentioned in the context of European migration especially (above), people in urban areas of Turkey also retire back to their homeland ('*memleket*'). This has been a very strong aspect of Turkish culture, emphasised, perhaps, by the cultural distance people were travelling when they went to live in chaotic, overcrowded, modern cities from villages that might not have electricity, for example, as was not uncommon before the 1990s. The reality of retirement in Turkey needs to be explained, however. As a non-rich country with a moderate life expectancy and still relatively well-developed state system inherited from the post-WWII and 1960s political environment, Turks can retire relatively young but with low state transfers. Until recently, when the law was changed in line with the EU harmonisation process, it was quite common for people to be able to claim their state pensions of something around 500 TL (200-250 Euros) a month from their early fourties (after twenty years of work).[68] Retirees to villages are usually not so young, but they are often far from infirm.

Another group of 'returnees' comprises people who go back 'home' after living in towns and cities for their children's education. Again, the practice of supporting offspring by setting up for a decade or two in urban areas where there is secondary (and tertiary) education is not at all uncommon in Turkey. Some people, of course, returned to their villages because they could not survive in the city (economically, psychologically, etc.). Among non-returnees, some people retire to rural environments rather like in the West, as a forward rather than backward move, for quality of life. This, more prosperous group migrate especially to small holiday, summer villages in the coastal Aegean, Marmara (southwest) and Black Sea regions, where their presence has an obvious economic benefit to the local area. Finally, investments in (industrial expansion of) some satellite towns in the environs of the major cities – like Çorlu and Çatalca in Thrace (on the western, European side of Istanbul) – has had a spill over effect of people moving to the surrounding villages.

---

[68] Of course the minority with private pension schemes receive much more than that.

Some of the reasons for urban-to-rural migration listed here are related to prosperity, and thus to this type of migration to villages as a phenomenon which is increasing. Rural-to-rural migration, on the other hand has been falling. It was not long ago that this form of movement was about or almost as common as those involving rural and urban exchanges: people moved between villages (e.g. through marriage, and generally staying dependent on agriculture) almost as frequently as they moved to towns or cities. During the last quarter of the twentieth century, however, while the rural population declined by 5%, rural-to-rural migration fell by 40%. This, it may be conjectured, is in large reason due to people migrating out of rather than moving between rural environments (such as young adults relocating for employment).

Migration between urban areas tells another story again. The large numbers for this category most likely account for the huge influx to the major cities, Istanbul in particular. Until 2000, the swollen ranks of the urban poor came from small towns. Thus, according to the figures recorded, the image of rural masses flocking to the city does not reflect the Turkish experience during the country's early period of rapid capital growth and nascent neo-liberalism. On the contrary, when totalled up, only a very small percentage of all migration involved a net movement out of rural areas. In fact, given that the agricultural workforce was maintained in relative terms until 2000 – leading to the DPT plan to reduce it – this is unsurprising. It is to be expected, however, that this has changed.

With the big thrust towards a deregulated, unprotected and importantly unsupported economy, the plunge in the rural population during the first decade of the new millennium of some six million people, 9% of the entire population – coupled with the stricter immigration policies in Europe – strongly indicates a mass rural-to-urban movement. The mobility characteristics recorded at the end of the twentieth century will still be shown – especially the urban-to-rural movement related to prosperity – but in general, it can be predicted that their relative importance will be much reduced. When the relevant statistical information becomes available, the tidal wave of neo-liberalism will probably be revealed to have had a flattening effect on many of these phenomena.

Households, place of settlement and agricultural activity

Like migration – state enforced, economically impelled or otherwise – employment outside of agriculture in the rural regions is hardly a new phenomenon. On the contrary, the equation of industry with urban is a relatively recent development. In Anatolia, 'cottage industries' in rural settlements related to food and cloth production among others (e.g. spice grounding, carpet weaving) continued into the modern period from centuries past. And mixed work practices borne of economic necessity – and state compunction – with peasant-smallholders combining agriculture with other, non-agricultural activities, were recorded, for example, in the 1940s. Newspapers of the time mention peasants employed in precarious daily jobs, rural people facing severe difficulties were provided temporary wage employment in some public works, while the Government also imposed obligatory paid work on rural people in such endeavours as road construction and mining (Pamuk 1988: 99-100). This led to further non-agricultural engagement (and another migratory movement). In fact, a survey conducted in Central Anatolia towards the end of that decade revealed that 'two-thirds of agricultural enterprises are too small to produce even for the basic needs of their holders and thus an important part of farmers in Central Anatolia need temporary jobs for subsistence in addition to their farming activities' – temporary engagements in small artisanship or industrial employment as well as other agricultural works (Von Flügge 1948/1949: 134).

During the preliminary work for the First Five-Year Development Plan during the mid 1960s, it was found that even for the month July, the busiest time of the year for agricultural activities, the redundant workforce totalled some 400,000 for the year 1955, and 800,000 for 1960. This redundancy was, of course, much higher for other months of the year. In January, for example, the redundant workforce in agriculture was calculated as 7,400,000 and 8,300,000, respectively for the years mentioned above (DPT 1963: 445). The second Five-Year Development Plan put the July rate of disguised unemployment at 9.9% (DPT 1967: 132-163). This redundant workforce derived from landless peasants and peasant smallholders engaged in semi-subsistence production without any means for capital accumulation and technology application.

Various forms of marginal employment – including underemployment, disguised unemployment and unrecorded employment in agriculture –

continue to be characteristic of rural life. This takes a variety of forms, principle among which is the use of unpaid family labour on family farms. In Turkey, as elsewhere, women especially and also children feature strongly in this category. Although less than 30% of workers were employed in agriculture (regularly or otherwise) by the mid 2000s, still this was the sector registering the greatest number of child workers, officially, approaching four hundred thousand (TÜİK 1989-2011). Some official statistics are also available that give an indication of how the gender divide operates in this respect, which, although indeterminate, are quite conclusive (Table 8.3). Although the correlations are not necessarily direct, the statistical overlaps clearly link men to paid employment in the service sector and women to paid and unpaid employment in the agricultural and service sectors. Two and a half times more women than men are employed in agriculture – so women are far more directly impacted by the impact of the structural changes on agriculture. And women are seven times more likely than men to function as unpaid family worker.

Linked to the grey areas around unpaid employment, those of disguised unemployment, under-employment are seasonal workers. In Turkish agriculture prior to the current era, 70-80% of the total rural population experienced seasonal unemployment (Kazgan 1988: 75). Seasonal workers

Table 8.3. Employment status (%) and sector by gender in 2005.

	Men	Women	Total
Employee [1]	61.6	48.5	58.1
Employer or self-employed	32.8	13.3	27.8
Unpaid family worker	5.6	38.2	14.1
Total	100	100	100
Agriculture	19.1	47.3	26.4
Industry [2]	29.3	14.8	25.6
Services	51.6	37.9	48.0
Total	100	100	100

Source: TÜİK 1989-2011.
[1] Regular or casual.
[2] Includes construction.

in Turkey have traditionally been mainly occupied in the cotton, tobacco, sugar beet and nut sectors, along with vegetables and fruit, such as potato, tomatoes and oranges, and also grain crops. The numbers of seasonal workers are declining now, partly because of the decline in the sugar, tobacco and cotton sectors (the first two linked especially to the state pullout from these sectors described), and partly to the mechanisation of cotton and sugar beet harvesting, along with that of grain crops. Nevertheless, and inevitably, seasonal work continues to play a major part in agriculture in Turkey, and thereby to function as a way in which 'classes of labour are fragmented... by capital[ist] production and reproduction' (Bernstein 2008: 5).

Seasonal workers, of course, have less advantageous working conditions than permanent employees (e.g. they have no social insurance). The category of female seasonal workers in agriculture, therefore, exemplifies the intersection of three levels of the operation of capital – fragmenting the fragmented, or, exploiting the exploited. This is shown by remuneration. A simple comparison of men's to women's wages in this group, i.e. seasonal agricultural workers shows the men to be earning a third higher than the women.[69] This ratio is the most extreme in the province of Konya, the heart of Turkey's wheat belt, which is renowned as a very conservative (and religious) area. In this, the country's largest province, male seasonal workers in agriculture earn near double that of their female counterparts.[70] And the lowest absolute rates are paid/received in Hatay, the extreme south-eastern province, where women receive less than 20 TL (9 Euro) for a day's work. In terms of job type, the best paid seasonal work is boxing (over 50 TL a day), which women do not do, while the highest differential is for dipping grapes (into a drying solution, which pays men at almost twice the rate as women.[71] The same kinds of comparisons can be made within job type by product sector, such as the harvesting of barley or olive picking – with similar results. Men are paid more than women in every single category (permanent as well as seasonal work, in every province and every job type for every product sector) (TÜİK 2011b).

Just as Bernstein emphasises gender as the most ubiquitous social difference effected by the 'typically hierarchical, oppressive and exclusionary nature' of the way the labour class is fragmented by capital (*ibid.*) – and evident

---

[69] Women 26.95 TL, men 35.95 TL (daily, = about 12 and 16 euro; average across 28 provinces).
[70] Men 45 TL, women 22.9 TL daily. The conservative, Islamic oriented political party AKP gains its biggest victory margins here.
[71] Men 31.4 TL, women 21.4 TL daily.

through unpaid family labour – so also do other differences become defined thus in Turkey through seasonal work on the land. Here, the obvious specificity is an ethno geographical dimension, with the largest group of seasonal workers in Turkey being Kurds from the southeast. They often work as (extended) families, as groups of ten or twenty people with children as young as six or seven. Vehicles are crammed full and loaded high taking them, for example, north to the Black Sea region for the nut and tea harvests (and to which the regular toll of summertime traffic accidents testifies). Another category of seasonal workers is made up of the generalised marginal workforce of people without permanent employment who find temporary work in agriculture especially in the summer season. These people may live in towns or villages, and tend to work fairly locally.

Although the demand for seasonal work generally is decreasing leading to excess labour, in certain, well-defined specialised areas this is not necessarily the case. The decline of sheep husbandry has seen a shortfall in shepherds, for example, some of whom are seasonal. And although seasonal work is typically poorly paid (less than fifteen dollars or ten euro's a day), in its specialised form the market can determine good returns for skilled labour that is relatively immune to downward pressures on wages. A reaper (harvester) driver/operator, for instance, can secure around 3,000-4,000 Euro's for a two- to three-month season (personal observation). Even in an essentially depressed rural economy, therefore, possibilities exist for capital accumulation among diverse groups of people. These may be invested in agriculture, of course, and – as in the driver/operator example – they may derive from agriculture as a sector (offering possibilities for relatively well-paid work) rather than farming as an activity as such (dependent on crops and animals for consumption and marketing, primarily as food).

In order to quantify and better understand the dynamics of employment in agriculture and rural areas, base figures can be calculated from official statistics. Of the total rural population, the number of those employed is given as around eleven million for the period 1990-2000. After 2000, this figure fell steadily, dropping to eight and a half million by 2007, when the measuring system changed (Table 8.4). This reduction in the working population of something around 25% matches the fall in the rural population as a whole during this period. The share of these rural employed engaged in non-agricultural activities in 2009 was 37.8%. In 2007, prior to the change in data collection methodology, this figure had been 50.9%. Approximating, it appears that around 40 to 50% of rural

Table 8.4. Distribution of rural employment (aged 15+) by agricultural and non-agricultural activities, 1989-2009 in thousands.

Year	Agriculture	Non-agriculture	% (non-agriculture)	Total
1989 [a]	8,308	2,632	24.0	10,930
1990	8,291	2,389	22.4	10,680
1991	8,960	2,411	21.2	11,372
1992	8,289	2,624	24.0	10,914
1993	7,762	2,169	21.8	9,931
1994	8,702	2,347	21.2	11,049
1995	8,518	2,556	23.1	11,076
1996	8,539	2,687	23.9	11,226
1997	8,850	2,616	22.8	11,467
1998	8,230	2,761	25.1	10,991
1999	9,207	2,697	22.7	11,904
2000 [b]	7,338	3,139	30.0	10,471
2001 [c]	7,350	3,099	29.7	10,449
2002	6,371	3,872	37.8	10,243
2003	6,346	3,514	35.6	9,860
2004	5,902	4,046	40.7	9,948
2005	5,148	4,332	45.7	9,480
2006	4,646	4,603	49.8	9,249
2006 [d]	4,360	4,319	49.8	8,679
2007	4,222	4,374	50.9	8,596
2007 [e]	4,269	2,704	38.8	6,973
2008	4,369	2,815	39.2	7,184
2009	4,651	2,787	37.5	7,438
2010	4,981	2,934	37.1	7,915

Calculated from TÜİK 1989-2011.
[a] Pre-2000 figures recorded for the month of April.
[b] From 2000, figures recorded monthly and totalled for the year.
[c] Occupation coding ISCO-88 adopted from 2001.
[d] Revised according to new population projections.
[e] Revised according to the Address Based Population Count System (ADNKS) total population from 2007.

workers are engaged in some kind of non-agricultural activity. During the first half of the 1990s, however, this proportion had ranged between 20 and 25% (using the old system). In other words, within the last fifteen years, the share of non-agricultural employment in total rural employment has doubled. Parallel to this, the gross number of people living in rural areas and engaged in agricultural activities has halved, falling from eight to nine million farmers and agricultural labourers in the early 1990s, to around seven million at the start of the 2000s and five by mid decade, to between four and four and half million at the end of the decade.

Interestingly, the four sets of figures under the new system show an increase in the number of rural employed for 2007-10. At almost a million people and representing a rise of 13.5%, this is far from insignificant. Furthermore, this gain is registered as coming in both agricultural and non-agricultural sectors, but especially from within the agricultural sector, where there has been a 16.7% increase. This would appear, therefore, to indicate stabilisation in the rural employment situation and an end to the rural collapse brought on by implementation of neo-liberal measures and the restructuring of agriculture. This positive indication receives some limited support from the yearly population statistics available now (Table 8.5). According to these, the rural population did continue to decline after 2007 while the urban and national populations both rose. However, at around 400,000 people (2.3%), the rural population loss over the last two years was much reduced, suggesting a bottoming out of the curve. Whether, the longer terms trend will be of continued stability (and even recovery and growth) or else of continued and even renewed decline remains, of course, to be seen.

If these data are considered together with the employment status of the active rural population the situation becomes clearer. In 1989, the share of unpaid family labourers of the total rural workforce was 48.9%, falling to 32.2% by 2010 (Table 8.6). The share of paid workers, on the other hand, increased from 18.9% in 1989 to 31.7% in 2010 (TÜİK 1989-2011). Meanwhile, over the same period, the share of employers increased from 1.2% to 2.7% and self-employed from 31% to 33.4%. The decline in the

Table 8.5. Rural and urban population during 2007-2010.

Year	Urban	Rural	Total
2007	49,747,859	20,838,397	70,586,256
2008	53,611,723	17,905,377	71,517,100
2009	54,807,219	17,754,093	72,561,312
2010	56,222,356	17,500,632	73,722,988

Source: TÜİK 1989-2011.

Table 8.6. Work status of rural employed (aged 15+) as a proportion (%) of total rural employed, 1989-2009.

Year	Paid [a]	Entrepreneur	Self employed	Non-waged household worker	Total
1989 [b]	18.9	1.2	31.0	48.9	100
1990	18.2	1.2	31.8	48.8	100
1991	16.6	1.4	30.8	51.2	100
1992	19.1	1.6	30.4	48.9	100
1993	18.5	1.6	32.6	47.2	100
1994	16.4	1.6	31.4	50.6	100
1995	19.1	1.5	31.3	48.2	100
1996	19.7	1.5	30.2	48.7	100
1997	18.3	1.5	32.2	48.0	100
1998	20.3	2.0	32.6	45.1	100
1999	18.7	1.5	30.1	49.7	100
2000 [c]	23.7	1.9	34.5	39.9	100
2001 [d]	21.0	1.9	35.4	41.6	100
2002	24.7	2.3	34.6	38.5	100
2003	24.5	2.1	36.3	37.1	100
2004	25.5	2.3	34.9	37.4	100
2005	30.0	2.6	35.7	31.7	100
2006	32.4	2.8	34.8	30.0	100
2006 [e]	32.4	2.8	34.8	30.0	100
2007	33.0	2.8	34.5	29.8	100
2007 [f]	30.7	2.6	35.6	31.1	100
2008	31.5	3.0	34.6	31.0	100
2009	30.6	2.7	34.7	32.0	100
2010	31.7	2.7	33.4	32.2	100

Calculated from TÜİK 1989-2011.
[a] Monthly or daily pay.
[b] Pre-2000 figures recorded for the month of April.
[c] From 2000, figures recorded monthly and totalled for the year.
[d] Occupation coding ISCO-88 adopted from 2001.
[e] Revised according to new population projections.
[f] Revised according to the Address Based Population Count System (ADNKS) total population from 2007.

agricultural workforce matched by a proportionate decline in unpaid family work and parallel increase of paid work in rural areas indicates the beginnings of the change of production mode in agriculture, from peasant smallholder and subsistence-based to capital intensive and market oriented. This is reflected also in the doubling of entrepreneur numbers.

Rather than focusing on rural areas and considering agriculture within that, as we have been doing, we might instead prioritise a perspective on agriculture to reveal better the situation of agricultural work, farming enterprises, and related employment as well as some of the location type (rural or urban) permutations of these. First, referring back to the quantitative and interpretive issues mentioned above in the introductory section on data and terminology (Chapter 5), the 2001 agricultural census in Turkey was composed of two parts, the Village Information Questionnaire and the survey of Agricultural Enterprises and Households, the former focusing on rural areas but the latter not (Textbox 4.1). Whereas the village questionnaire ascertained a total of 3,021,196 agricultural enterprises, the enterprises and households part of the census for 2001 recorded 4,046,236 (TÜİK 2001) – or, recorded in the Eighth Five-Year Development Plan and cited above (Chapter 5) 4,068,432. This implies that there something around a quarter of all agricultural enterprises, about one million in total, were in settlements with a population 5,000 and over (urban areas). In fact, this appears rather surprising, given that such settlements (district centres, mostly) numbered under a thousand, as compared to the over 35 thousand villages. There would have to be nine times more farms listed in each district centre than each village district. On the other hand, this would be entirely believable – and interesting – if a major proportion of the urban enterprises were listed as such according to owners who were resident in the towns, while the land itself was in villages.

Second, looking at the urban employment data (for four years later), we see 673,000 urban people recorded as employed in agriculture (self-employed or waged/salaried), representing some 10% of all agricultural employment (Table 8.7). The 25%/10% difference would appear to suggest a large number of enterprises situated (or enterprise owners resident) in towns and using a workforce from the villages. This, it would appear, is one way in which entrepreneurship became extended in Turkish agriculture through the 1980s and 1990s, in informal (officially unregistered and unrecorded) labour employment of villagers by small or smallish landowners who whose enterprises were situated in local districts centres. Indeed, employment – viewed through the prisms of sector (agriculture or other) and location – offers a third perspective on the situation.

Table 8.7. Employment status numbers, and proportions by sector and location type in 2005.

Job status	Number (thousands)			Percentage		
	Agriculture	Non-agriculture [a]	Total	Agriculture	Non-agriculture [a]	Total
Turkey						
Paid worker [b]	521	11,428	11,949	4.4	95.6	100
Self-employed or entrepreneur	2,965	3,605	6,570	45.1	54.9	100
Unpaid [c]	3,007	520	3,527	85.3	14.7	100
Total	6,493	15,553	22,046	29.5	70.5	100
Urban						
Paid worker [b]	158	8,948	9,106	1.7	98.3	100
Self-employed or entrepreneur	332	2,602	2,934	11.3	88.7	100
Unpaid [c]	182	344	526	34.6	65.4	100
Total	673	11,893	12,566	5.4	94.6	100
Rural						
Paid worker [b]	363	2,479	2,842	12.8	77.2	100
Self-employed or entrepreneur	2,632	1,005	3,637	72.4	37.6	100
Unpaid [c]	2,825	176	3,001	94.1	5.9	100
Total	5,820	3,660	9,480	61.4	38.6	100

Source: TÜİK 1989-2011.
[a] Industry, trade and service.
[b] Waged, salaried or daily waged.
[c] Unwaged household worker.

Compiled from 2005 figures, Table 8.7 confirms agriculture as the link between gender and unpaid family work indicated above with 85% of this form of labour (and 94% in rural areas) recorded in farming. The near half of the number of self-employed being in agriculture (and three quarters in rural areas) is also confirmatory of the continuing importance of small family enterprises – peasant smallholders – in agriculture. These figures are only emphasised by the fact that less than 5% (and less than 13% in rural areas) of paid workers is in farming. Particularly striking is the fact that industry, trade and services together account for 38.6% of total rural employment, and that, contrary to the situation with agriculture in rural areas, this population consists mainly of wage workers. On the other hand, 5.4% of total urban employment is in agriculture, including over one in ten of the urban self-employed or entrepreneurs, and over a third of the urban unpaid. These data also point out to three lines of development:

1. There is a significant population living in rural areas but employed in non-agricultural sectors, mainly as wage workers. Some of these people are grocers and some run tea houses, while others are teachers or village midwives. Nevertheless, the country's total of 35,000 village settlements still provides only a relatively small share of those employed in non-agricultural sectors nationwide.

2. Taken together with the existence of around one million agricultural enterprises in districts defined by the presence of settlements with population 5,000 and over, the employment in agriculture of between half and three quarters of a million people living in these urban areas suggests that a significant part of total agricultural employment is not actually rural. There are two main explanations that account for this. Firstly, those who have their land in the outskirts of towns/cities commonly prefer to conduct their agricultural activities while living in these urban settlements where they can enjoy the various advantages of civil life. Secondly, there are others living in cities who have agricultural enterprises in the (surrounding) rural areas run in their names or, again while living in towns/cities, working in the fields (or fruit orchards, olive groves, tea gardens, etc.), either for wages or as unpaid family labourers. Indeed, this category might well be rather larger than that recorded, given the numbers of farmers, farm workers and farming families listed according to their permanent address as officially resident in villages (their family home, site of their land) while in reality living in nearby towns (personal observation).

3. Even after migrating to urban centres, households sustain their agricultural activities, either directly or by buying agricultural services, leasing and/or sharecropping.

Taking all these together, the established understanding that agricultural activity is basically equal to the activity of rural population or, alternatively, that the rural population can be equated with the population engaged in and dependent on agriculture – and the implications of the flip side to this with reference to the urban – is shown to be essentially untenable. The equation of agriculture with rural is deeply problematised, demanding a radical reappraisal of assumed conventions (in a way, for example, that completely undermines the validity of the assumptions made in the way that the census statistics were gathered). In terms of dynamics, it is easy to draw over hasty conclusions from the reconceptualisation required here to unwarranted generalisations about long term trends. Although there appears not to have been a huge rural-to-urban migration in Turkey during the second half of the twentieth century, that has not been the case for the past decade, which saw the restructuring of agriculture and resulting collapse of rural population, to the tune of some six million people – so far. The question is, then, will it continue? And how far? It is not easy to determine this, and answers may have to wait until the situation has settled (assuming it will). Perhaps this is already happening, however, a possibility indicated (above), in which case the most recent figures may offer a small clue to the direction of change, if any (Table 8.8).

This rather slight information is quite instructive. Firstly, regarding what it does not show, the change in the data collection methodology mitigate against comparison with the earlier figures in respect of the rural/urban divide, and, really, even with the total (Turkey) figures. It is best just to view these figures within their own frame of reference. In general, there is an obvious homogeneity: the trend for all figures is up, confirming the previously mentioned indications of agricultural stabilisation, if not recovery. Crucially, however, although this is clearly more important for the rural sector, it is just actually more pronounced in urban areas. Proportionately, the five-point rise in the urban figure represents an increase that is over four times that of the seventeen-point rise in the rural, and 30% higher than that seen in the nation as a whole.[72] This difference is certainly strong enough to suggest the dynamic of an increasing urbanisation of agriculture in terms of employment.

Table 8.8. Labour force employed in agriculture by location type during 2007-2010.

Year	Urban		Rural		Turkey	
	×1000	%	×1000	%	×1000	%
2007	597	4.3	4,269	61.2	4,867	23.5
2008	647	4.6	4,369	60.8	5,016	23.7
2009	589	4.3	4,659	62.5	5,240	24.6
2010	701	4.8	4,981	62.9	5,683	25.2

Source: TÜİK 1989-2011.

---

[72] Rural: 1.7 rise = 2.8%; urban: 0.5 rise = 11.6%; national: 1.9 = 8.1%

Another snapshot of the changing socio environment is provided by the urban/rural differentiated variables reported in relation to the characteristics of the population out of the labour force. Taking a look at the non-participating numbers of the labour force for 2005, we see an absolute majority among the rural population over the urban in the categories of seasonal workers – (unsurprisingly), of those willing to work but not actively looking (an interesting category that seems to speak of a rural lethargy), and of the disabled, old and sick (Table 8.9). Given that the numbers of the urban population out of the labour force were near double those of the rural, these rural majorities constitute particularly telling numbers. In absolute terms, of 4.5 million rural households, around 1.7 million had sick, elderly and disabled members, while approaching three quarters of a million had members who were retired with a pension and the same again had members ready to work but not seeking it.[73]

Two points need to be addressed here. Firstly, one in every six rural households has at least one legally retired member (there may be more, but this possibility is omitted from the statistics) – households, therefore,

Table 8.9. Population out of the labour force by causes and location type in 2005.

	Urban		Rural		Total
	×1000	%	×1000	%	×1000
Non-job seeker but ready to work	993	57.9	721	42.1	1,714
Seasonal employed	119	24.7	362	75.3	481
Home worker	8,956	68.8	4,069	31.2	13,025
Student	2,489	73.4	905	26.7	3,393
Pension	2,208	75.9	700	24.1	2,908
Disabled, elderly or sick	1,383	44.6	1,715	55.4	3,098
Family, personal reasons	688	68.9	311	31.1	999
Other	444	69.2	198	30.8	642
Total	17,279	65.8	8,981	34.2	26,260

Source: TÜİK 1989-2011.

---

[73] These may have been overlapping, of course.

with earnings other than agricultural activities. In rural conditions and in an environment where a registered urban employment even at the (low) minimum wage is considered as 'bonus', retirement pensions constitute an important input for subsistence. Secondly, households with disabled, old and sick members make up over half of total rural households. Given the national population demographics, this converts to a proportion that is approaching four times that of urban areas. The same is also observed in the proportion of elderly people. About a quarter of the country's total population lived in rural areas in 2008, but a third of the population age 55 and over (i.e. a disproportionate excess of some 25%). Considered together with the relatively high population not seeking jobs but ready to work, this constitutes a huge swathe of the rural population, the subsistence of which is much below minimum standards, and only possible by supplementing household income and produce from rural activities with (combinations of) transfers from the sate, income transfers from elsewhere and household/community solidarity.

With the able-bodied increasingly going to the centres of employment, capital fragments labour into winners and losers, or, those who sell their time and those who do not, who cannot or will not. That this is an increasing phenomenon is shown again by the slight figures of the very recent past, here for age. The proportion of the aged (over 60) among those living in rural areas has now grown to 15% (Table 8.10). This is a massive 40% higher than the urban rate, and represents a relative rise within the rural proportion of approaching a fifth in just three years. Of course it is not just an effect of economics. It also results from positive lifestyle choices by older people, as described, with many staying or returning or even setting out for a variety of personal however much the temporary influx of the transfers that accompanies inward rural migration (from urban areas

Table 8.10. Population of over 60 age group by location type in 2007 and 2010 in millions.

Year	Urban			Rural		
	Total population	Over 60	%	Total population	Over 60	%
2007	49.7	4.4	8.9	20.8	2.6	12.7
2010	56.2	5.1	9	17.5	2.7	15

Source: TÜİK 2008-11.

or abroad) the long term effect for rural life is, in all likelihood, not so far different.

With an image developing of the effects over time for agriculture and rural life, the question of converge arises. To what extent are these developments observable across the country? A general picture of rural Turkey is presented by its division into eight (province-based) regions zones (Table 8.11; see Appendix 5). Across Turkey in 2001, for every two households not engaged in agricultural activities in rural areas five households were engaged in agricultural activities. Interesting points here include the fact that in the Marmara region (where Istanbul is situated) the number of rural households engaged in non-agricultural activities actually outnumbered those engaged in these activities. In the Aegean region there were about double the number of households involved in agriculture as those not and somewhat less than double in the Mediterranean.

There were wide differences within the country in all the measurements presented here, as well within regions in the different time periods

Table 8.11. Numbers and increases of rural households active in agriculture and non-agriculture in 1980, 1991 and 2001 in thousands.

Region	Agricultural activities					Non-agricultural activities					Dif.
	1980	1991	Rise (%)	2001 (I)	Rise (%)	1980	1991	Rise (%)	2001 (II)	Rise (%)	I/II (%)
Marmara	284	338	18.9	294	-13.1	35	198	473.5	345	73.8	117.3
Agean	629	804	27.8	684	-14.8	107	106	-1.4	338	220.2	49.3
Blacksea	582	643	10.5	615	-4.5	39	60	53.9	119	97.7	19.4
Mid-north	444	486	9.5	423	-13.1	44	72	63.3	136	89.4	32.2
Mid-south	343	415	20.9	378	-9.0	31	60	92.3	104	73.1	27.5
Mediterranean	335	480	43.5	467	-2.8	51	88	73.5	274	210.8	58.7
Northeast	238	240	0.8	222	-7.6	9	24	177.4	31	28.8	13.9
Mid-east	227	317	39.8	288	-9.2	16	27	63.7	49	81.1	16.9
Southeast	352	368	4.4	328	-10.9	28	38	33.6	67	79.3	20.6
Turkey	3,434	4,092	19.1	3,698	-9.6	360	672	86.8	1,463	117.5	39.6

Source: DİE 2003.

covered. The absolute numbers of rural households active in agriculture generally increased a little over the last two decades of the century, for example, but climbed by 40% in the Mediterranean region. Combining this with that region's growth in households engaged in non-agricultural activities also, by a factor of well over five suggests a generally vibrant rural environment. The mid-North and Northeast, however, saw an absolute reduction in the households engaged in agriculture, areas which were also among the least impressive in terms of non-agricultural growth, suggesting relative stagnation.[74] The tea-growing and mountainous Northeast also had the smallest ratio of households occupied outside of agriculture to those in agriculture (just under 14%). Developmental change across the country, of both agricultural and non-agricultural sectors as reflected in the household occupation numbers, was uneven. The obvious conclusion from this would seem to be that socio-economic generalisations about the country as a whole need to be made with a strong emphasis on the regional specificities.[75]

A more nuanced picture is afforded by looking at rural population changes at district and province level. For the period 1990-2000, we observe that in 57% of rural districts the population decreased, in 15% district population increased but at a rate slower than that of the relatively slow rural population increase during that period, leaving 28% of districts where the rural population can be said to have increased in all ways (Tables 8.12 and 8.13). In the period 2000-2008, with the rural population dropping by 35,500 annually, the population declined in absolute terms in 81% of all districts. In this period, districts where rural population increased (18.4%) included a significant number of districts in eastern and south-eastern provinces where there was return to villages previously evacuated by Turkish government. Even so, it is striking that in a period of what may be termed rural calamity, the remaining – and still significant number – villages should actually record a positive movement. Again this speaks of the need not to over generalise.

At province level, the rural population increased in the period 1990-2000 in 28% of provinces. In the provinces of Istanbul, Kocaeli and Yalova, the

---

[74] The Southeast also comes into this category, but stands as a special case due to the PKK insurgency being fought during the latter part of this period.

[75] Of course, in the case of these particular data, even the very notion of defining a household by economic activity assumes rather traditional patterns (head of household, family farming, single occupation type), which are becoming less useful as reflections of socio-economic behaviour (and more quickly and widely so in some regions than others).

Table 8.12. Population growth (annual average) rate by location type during 1990-2000 and 2000-2008 in thousands.

Population growth	1990-2000	2000-2008
Rural	4.23	-35.56
Urban	26.81	24.67
Turkey	18.28	6.66

Table 8.13. Rural district population change during 1990-2000 and 2000-2008.

Population change of rural districts	1990-2000		2000-2008	
	Number of districts	%	Number of districts	%
Population declining	528	57	752	81.5
Population growing but less than general rate	140	15	–	–
Sub-total	668	72	752	81.5
Rural population rising	255	28	170	18.4
Total	923	100	923	100

Source: TÜİK 2000, 2008a.

rate of growth in rural population in this period was higher than the rate of urban population growth. These can be taken together as exhibiting the effects of the growth of the metropolis, which continues to spread out rapidly into adjoining rural districts with satellite growth also into neighbouring provinces. This was not specific to Istanbul; however, since the rate of rural population growth was higher than that of the urban population also in the provinces of Ankara, Izmir and Bursa, against the national trend. These provinces, notably, include (are named after) the next largest cities in the country after Istanbul. Other provinces with relatively fast increasing rural populations included Adana, Antalya, Konya, İçel, Muğla, Trabzon, Malatya and Denizli along with Hatay, Muş, Urfa and Van, all of which have large provincial cities or at least cities which are relatively large in their respective regions. From this it can be concluded that urban-to-rural migration (and also rural-to-rural) tended to involve people heading for rural settlements adjacent to cities, particularly in Marmara and Aegean regions.

In the period 2000-2008, the total rural population in Turkey decreased by a third. At district level, rural population decreased in 81.5% of districts and increased in 18.4%. These figures suggest the assumption of observations made; that rural populations moved to cities and that movement to rural areas occurred in the environs of large conurbations. Indeed, beside the special case of eastern and south-eastern districts (whose rural population increased as people who had earlier been forced out started returning), districts with increasing rural population repeat the pattern recounted for 1990-2000. A picture develops of vibrant rural areas around the major urban hubs, especially in the regions of Marmara, Aegean and Mediterranean where the proportion of people living in villages but engaged in non-agricultural activities is relatively high. This suggests that it is not only retired people who are moving to rural settlements in these areas, but also working people (as is confirmed by the regional labour force data). This, in turn, points to a development in which non-agricultural activities expand towards rural areas and people living in rural settlements work in urban areas in what might be termed a process of 'village suburbanisation'.

The population living in villages is still declining. As of 2002, there were a total of 80,890 *rural settlement units*, composed of 2,265 townships (*kasaba belediyesi*), 36,527 villages and 42,098 hamlets or sub-village settlements (*köy altı yerleşimi*). The demographics of rural settlements afford another perspective on recent and ongoing trends. Table 8.14 gives the number of villages by their population and percentage distribution for the period since 1980.[76]

The number of villages inhabited by 200 or less people in 1980 accounted for 15% of all villages in the country, a share which has risen to 38% by 2008. In all other scales with the exception of this the percentage share of village number has decreased, with the exception of the top end, of villages with populations of 1,600 of greater, which have maintained their small proportion (6%). The story is similar for population share, with the largest (over 2,000) and the smallest (under 400 people) increasing their share of the total. In other words, while the share of the total rural population of medium-size villages has declined, that of small and larger villages has increased. In line with the shape of change presented, this suggests a twin process of, on the one hand, depeasantisation and devillagisation – villages are prone to just whither and die without the backbone of small

---

[76] As is usual, villages in Turkey are designated politico-administrative units; changing over time, they may become quite small or quite large while retaining their village status.

Table 8.14. Number of villages and village populations by village size as proportions (%) during 1980-2008.

Village size	1980		1990		2000		2008	
	Number of villages	Village populations	Number of villages	Village populations	Number of villages	Village populations	Number of villages	Village populations
0-199	15	3	23	5	32	6	39	8
200-399	29	13	29	16	27	12	26	15
400-599	21	16	19	17	15	11	13	13
600-799	12	13	11	15	8	8	7	10
800-999	7	10	7	11	4	6	4	7
1000-1,199	5	8	4	8	3	4	2	5
1,200-1,399	3	6	2	6	2	3	2	4
1,400-1,599	2	4	2	4	1	3	1	3
1,600-1,999	2	6	2	6	2	5	2	6
2,000-2,999	3	9	2	8	3	12	2	10
3,000-4,999	1	6	0	2	2	11	1	8
5,000+	0	7	0	1	1	18	1	9
	100	100	100	100	100	100	100	100

Source: TÜİK 2000, 2008a.

scale farming – and, on the other, villages urbanizing and integrating with urban centres – as relatively prosperous communities of rural urbanity.

Finally, one last indication of village depopulation is obtained from statistics on the School Bus services of the Ministry of National Education (MoNE). With the MoNE programme launched in the school year 1989-90, students at local schools where the total number of students is under 60 are bussed to a nearby central school for their education. Under this programme in the school year 2007-2008, 692,369 primary school students from 31,874 schools were bussed daily to 6,164 central schools in 81 provinces across the country (MEB 2007). This means that the there are over thirty thousand settlements less than sixty 7- to 13-year olds, a number which is probably much larger if hamlets that are not served by the programme are counted, and a number that is increasing all the time.

Conclusion: villages

Developments in agriculture and the rural population impact on village settlements. When villages are taken as units of analysis, we observe the following developments.

- Combining such population groups as the elderly and unemployed with others engaged in non-agricultural activities, we can conclude that for a considerable share of the population the country is a living space rather than a space for production activities and income generation. The relatively high proportion of such people outside of the workforce among the total rural population suggests that this space is more favourable for those who need support – or, it is the low cost living space that they can survive best in, or, it is the only space available to them. Taking these in reverse order, many people who need support might harbour desires to move to urban areas but are unable to so and therefore remain in the country. In this sense, villages can become a site for those 'left behind'. Others may be able to live in urban areas but find village a better option for a variety of practical reasons, most obviously financial. Without adequate means of income, the more expensive urban centres can become hostile environments. Third, for those with village support networks – families and neighbours especially (the importance of family and neighbour based relations in villages in Turkey cannot be over estimated) – moving to urban areas might be out of the question.[77]
- It is known that a part of the village elderly population group comprises retirees of whom some settle in coastal areas after having accumulated a certain degree of wealth. This population movement also finds some confirmation in the fact that the few districts whose rural population is increasing are mostly located on coastal zones. This represents a clear (unforced) positive decision to live in a rural environment.
- Meanwhile, there are also districts administratively attached to urban growth centres and economically more developed provinces, particularly in the western Marmara and Aegean regions. As the major metropolises stimulate new developments in their surrounding areas – generally expansions of pre-existing towns – and economic activities at provincial centres likewise spread, peripheral rural populations

---

[77] In this respect, Turkey's poorly developed social service provision should be mentioned as an important factor. There are few provisions of the type now taken for granted in rich countries, as provided by formal local community schemes and charitable organisations as well as state systems, so people have to fend for themselves and rely on those with whom they have a personal relationship in ways that highlight the support needs of the weaker and more vulnerable.

increase in tandem. Such rural settlements tend to be more like suburbs, or, *suburban*. Although the unit of settlement is officially defined as 'rural', economic activities consist of manufacturing and services rather than farming. In some of such settlements, more than half of total employment is non-agricultural, with an important part of the remaining, non-employed population being the elderly.

- While suburban villages are emerging in the countryside, the process of village depopulation and devillagisation is gaining pace. The massive decline in the total rural population has meant the total evacuation of some villages and rapid fall in population of others. This, in turn, has led, on the one hand, to the emergence of uncultivated land (beyond, that is, that reserved for purposes such as housing, road and dam construction), and, on the other, to an increase in land lease and the farming of rented land (since village decline has spurred landholders to leave their land). This process is accompanied by another whereby some agricultural enterprises expand their scale by buying land from those who are destined for urban centres.

- The extent of the school bussing program indicates another reason for village decline. It is known that one motive for rural-to-urban migration is education. The lack of village schools has the effect of encouraging rural families to move out to urban areas. This is a factor which should not be underestimated while investigating the causes of the recent speed of rural depopulation, nor the likelihood of its continuation.

The flip side of agricultural and rural development is related to poverty. Looking at the rises in per capita income (gdp/population) in agriculture and in the country as a whole, we see that that income rise in agriculture are below the national level generally. This is one reason for comparative poverty in the current rural socio-economic conditions. Neo-liberal policies have negatively affected agriculture and thus also the rural/urban poverty balance. On the other hand global, poverty has its own, somewhat different specifies. The following chapter looks at these specifics and analyses poverty in the contemporary period.

Chapter 9. The neo-liberal approach to poverty

The worldwide development of neo-liberal policies has been very efficient for the labour market realisation of the 'Post-Fordist regulation method' of capitalism and flexible specialisation, a distinctive feature of this method. At the same time, policies of liberalisation in the agricultural products trade such as relaxed regulations policies and withdrawals of state support have replaced the developmental approach to agriculture. Neo-liberal policies have been powerful, therefore, in both these areas. On the one hand, they have caused the growth of unorganised and unemployed mass labour, and on the other, they have impoverished rural populations, resulting in a rapid migration from rural to urban areas, and contributing in turn to the emergence of mass poor populations in big cities. This has not been only a quantitative, numerical explosion of poverty, but also a qualitative one: the poor masses have different characteristics to those of past. Thus it is that poverty has been able to find a place for itself on research agendas and in World Bank programs.

The policies have been developed by new institutions, governments, initiative frameworks and the like in the atmosphere of the new socio-economic philosophy towards the aim of poverty reduction are quiet different to those of the past. Importantly, this is precisely because the new poverty is qualitatively different to that of the past. Indeed, the new poverty reduction policies have are, in important ways, neo-liberal solutions to neo-liberal problems. The logic of an approach that tries to solve problems arising from the way that that approach operates by using that very approach is, to say the least, counter intuitive. It seems more rational to state openly that the creation of an underclass is the price paid by for economic growth. Questions thus invited include how this is distributed and what is the balance of winners to losers. In other words, how big is the price and who pays it? In Turkey, as we have seen, the ranks of the peasantry comprise one of the payees, the smallholder farmers of a once agriculturally based economy on the periphery of capital.

In Turkey, similarly to most other countries, neo-liberal economic policies have been introduced and maintained during recent years. Developed through the governments of Turgut Özal from the beginning 1980s, these were experienced by many in the context of a liberation, an unshackling of the grip of military rule in the country following the 1980 coup. Various fiscal and market reforms were instituted and the dismantlement commenced of much of the centralised economic system that had been in place for decades as the state had attempted to propel the nation forward on the development path. The progress of neo-liberalisation thereafter was inexorable, and once the political and economic climate had shifted with the turn of the new millennium with a serial new applications.

This final part will look first at neo-liberal policies generally in respect of poverty reduction, with particular regard for the experience of developing countries, before going on in the final chapter to discuss the case of Turkey. In discussing the way that Turkey has been implementing neo-liberal policies, particular regard will be paid to the nature of the new poverty, the area of employment and the new regime of social aid policies.

The neo-liberal approach

With the implementation of neo-liberal polices, the idea went, the removal of price intervention would create efficiency in the allocation of resources and trade liberalisation would lead to increases in foreign trade – and therefore in production – on the basis of comparative advantages. Direct and indirect foreign investments would enable both productive capacity increase and support to current deficit financing. Also, via the privatisation of public enterprises, services would be provided more effectively and efficiently (and importantly, they would not be a burden to the budget). The combined effects of the new measures, it was argued, would benefit all sections of society, including the poor. In essence, poverty would be reduced as an effect of increased total prosperity resulting from increased economic activity. The implementation of neo-liberal policies would reduce poverty directly, most obviously through higher employment resulting from the raised demand of economies liberated both internally (removal of state controls) and externally (removal of trade barriers). Poverty would also be reduced more indirectly, through the various mechanisms of the 'trickle down' effect. The poor, furthermore, would also be major beneficiaries of the improved (privatised) services. Last, but not necessarily least, a culture of enterprise would be fostered whereby the public would not be demotivated by the State's over provision of supports.

The results, however, have rather failed to meet these expectations. Recognition of the general problem of extreme world poverty led to its positioning as the very first of the United Nations Millennium Development Goals, developed roughly during the effective time period of neo-liberalism. Specified by a simple definition (the number of people earning less than a dollar a day, adjusted in 2008 to $1.25, Purchasing Power Party (PPP)) in a time-relational context (to halve that number by 2015, as compared to the 1990 figure), the first Millennium Development Target on poverty (MDG 1.A) is expected to be attained, just about. This success is somewhat superficial, however, due in main measure to the explosive development of China, previously a particularly impoverished country with an immensely restricted economy (Table 9.1). In Eastern Asia generally, the first MDG has been or will be achieved, but elsewhere, the picture is less bright, with more limited reductions in regional poverty, despite – or because of – the neo-liberal approach.

A recent report made by the UN Development Project comes to a similar conclusion. In a sample assessment of thirty developing countries, eleven are recorded as having achieved the MDG goals on extreme poverty and hunger or being on course to do so, five are 'off track' and the remaining sixteen showing 'mixed progress' (UNDP 2010: xiii). The relationship of growth to poverty is key here. The 30 countries assessed show an average total GDP growth for the 1990s into the 2000s of 63% but an extreme poverty reduction of only 25 (Table 9.2). Thus, as the report emphasizes,

Table 9.1. Regional reduction in proportion of people living in (extreme) poverty ($1.25 a day, PPP) during 1990-2005.[1]

Region	Poverty reduction (%)	
	Of total population	Of people in poverty
Eastern Asia	44	73
Southeastern Asia	20	51
Northern Africa	2	40
Southern Asia (ex. India)	14	31
Latin America/Carib.	3	27
Southern Asia	10	20
Sub-Saharan Africa	7	12
Western Asia	-4	-200
CIS Asia	-13	-217

Source: UN 2010.
[1] For regions with change at ≥2%.

Table 9.2. Growth, (extreme) poverty and inequality during 1995-2007 in selected countries.[1]

Country	Total GDP growth 1995-2007 (%)	(Extreme) poverty rate (%)		Poverty reduction late 1990s – mid 2000s (%)
		late 1990s	mid 2000s	
Albania	71	25	19	27
Armenia	110	50	25	50
Cambodia	102	36	35	3
Colombia	42	60	46	23
El Salvador	38	51	37	27
Kyrgyzstan	49	25	7	72
Laos PDR	78	39	33	15
Mongolia	66	36	35	1
Morocco	46	15	9	40
Nepal	46	42	31	26
Sierra Leone	54	70	66	6
Tajikistan	48	87	41	53
Average [2]	63	48	36	25

Calculated from UNDP 2010: 26, using World Bank, National MDG Reports.
[1] Selected: the two countries with highest and with lowest values for each category.
[2] Averages calculated from all (20) countries listed with full data.

'The evidence is clear... economic gains are not automatically translated into development outcomes or registered MDG achievements' (*ibid.*: 35).

The first Millennium Development Goal has three components, related to employment and hunger as well as to financially measured poverty. While progress toward the poverty goal (1.A) can be given a positive spin, this is rather difficult in the case of employment (1.B) and hunger (1.C). Regarding the latter, the FAO reports the worldwide proportion of 'undernourished persons' for 2010 at 16%, the same figure as in 1990.[78] Figures for this had begun to look promising through the first half of the 1990s, but the story since then has been one of a steady rise in world hunger, a loss of the earlier gains made. The story regarding employment is similarly bleak, with near zero progress over the last decade (UNDP 2010: 8).

---

[78] http://www.fao.org/hunger/en/.

Employment – or rather unemployment, under-employment and poorly paid and unprotected employment – has always been the stepchild of development, and the elephant in the room of poverty. Introduced as an MDG only in 2008, employment continues to be under-represented (it receives just one mention in the 2010 UNDP report, for example).[79] The three UN MDG reports produced since the inclusion of employment *have* given proportionate space to the subject, and the coverage (outlook, analysis, etc.) has been universally negative. Ignoring specific reference to the recent (2008) crisis, various aspects reported on are of note here. First, in terms of macro-economics, employment figures may mean little without reasonable productivity, of course – and in developing countries this remains low, 'a bad sign for future job-creation'. Second, from the perspective of the poor, income may be gained from work, but employment does not necessarily mean an escape for poverty: low-paying jobs lead to the concept of the 'working poor'. Third, working conditions may not be good, leading to concepts of 'vulnerable employment' ('unstable, insecure jobs'). Finally, future prospects are depressing: 'Full employment remains a distant possibility' (UN 2008: 8-9; UN 2009: 8-10; UN 2010: 9-10).

Problems with the neo-liberal approach

There are various reasons why neo-liberal policies have failed to deliver as hoped on the problem of poverty. Firstly, according to Stiglizt stability policies supported by tight fiscal and monetary controls have provided neither growth nor stabilisation. In fact, high volume capital movements has caused frequent crises, exposing countries (especially developing ones) to new risks. Secondly, the liberalisation of foreign trade, in practice has tended to mean the removal of barriers in developing countries but maintenance of these barriers in developed countries, which has given birth to an (even more) unfair international market. Then, these new fiscal and market conditions have led to unemployment and unrecorded work. Finally, privatisation has caused price rises in public services and reduced competitivity. In short, neo-liberal structures and policies have tended to operate to the benefit of developed as opposed to developing countries, and, broadly speaking, at the expense of the poor. Giving the

---

[79] The original UN Millennium Declaration did not even mention employment in its third chapter on 'Development and Poverty Eradication' (UN 2000), and the subsequent emergence of the eight MDGs from the UN Millennium Project did not initially include employment: 'Goal 1', to 'Eradicate Poverty and Hunger' (as it continues to be known), just had these two specified Targets (UNDP 2005: xiii).

lie to any pretension that the reduction of poverty was ever intended as a primary aim of neo-liberalism, the IMF and Washington Consensus has consistently ignored these social and political dimensions of the new approach (Shafaeddin 2010, Stiglitz 2009: 283-286).

Setting aside the East Asian countries that have been narrated as success stories as a result of neo-liberal policies, other concrete achievements arising from neo-liberalism are difficult to find. In terms of raw numbers, a quarter century and more of ever-increasing global neo-liberalism has left us with figures that continue to show huge numbers of people and still horrendously high population proportions living in extreme poverty (Table 9.3). And even where statistically clear improvements are evident – in the so-called success stories, for example, or in the overall reduction of the depth of poverty (the average income level of the near billion people still officially below the world poverty line) – arguments contending that these have resulted specifically from neo-liberal policies are hard to accept – if for no other reason than because of the enactment of other, sometimes plainly non-neo-liberal, policies.[80]

Neo-liberal economists emphasise that rises in public expenditure increase budget deficits, and this leads to high inflation, currency devaluation and high interest rates. Therefore, they desire to reduce public expenditures. The literature, however, offers very little in the way of evidence showing

Table 9.3. Regional (extreme) poverty headcount, by ratio of population (%) at $1.25 and $2 a day in 2005 (PPP).

Region	$1.25 a day	$2 a day
East Asia & Pacific	16.8	38.7
Europe & Central Asia	3.7	8.9
Latin America & Caribbean	8.2	17.1
Middle East & North Africa	3.6	16.9
South Asia	40.3	73.9
Sub-Saharan Africa	50.9	72.9

Source: World Bank, 2009.

---

[80] Most obviously (at the macro level for economic development), the Chinese under-valuation of the Yuan, facilitating its export-driven growth.

that public expenditure raises increase interest rates and exclude the public sector thereby achieving, or that excluding the public sector achieves efficiency with respect to exchange rates (McKinley 2003). Similarly, neo-liberals defend the contention that productivity in the public sector is low and can be increased through privatisation, again in spite of only slight empirical evidence in support of this (Boratav 1993).

On the other hand, these policies clearly have had a negative impact on poor, weak and marginal populations, because they bring increased economic inequality. With the foreign trade and financial reforms, national industries have deteriorated and employment opportunities and the number of small producers decreased; small farmers, poor rural populations and food security have been influenced negatively; and privatisation, budgetary cuts and labour market destabilisation have led to low wages, losses of workers' rights and reductions in their bargaining power. Indeed, it is the very problem of increasing inequalities that the biggest, most quickly developing economies of China and India are having to face now (Angang *et al.* 2003, Ghosh 2010). Thus, in addition to making access to basic services more difficult, rising prices associated with the neo-liberal policies of privatisation, budgetary cuts and other regulations are argued to have actually increased poverty in countries as diverse as Hungary, Mexico, the Philippines, etc. (SAPRIN 2004).

This current era, in which the employment of neo-liberal policies has become the dominant approach, has seen also a surge in the tendency to globalisation. And in this globalised economy, the use of alternative or replacement (substitute) production factors has increased exponentially, relative, that is, to technological development and the characteristics of demand. Thus, even though there certainly has been an increase in overall investments and growth, the labour market has not been able to benefit from the development. On the contrary, the increase of possibilities for substitution can lead to a reduction of workers' income and static, even decreasing employment (EAF 2010). Briefly, stabilisation policies have not managed to maintain growth and stability, the work-force has not flowed through trade liberalisation from low-productivity to high productivity as anticipated, and unemployment in developing countries worldwide has grown (Shafaeddin 2010, Stiglitz 2009: 283-86).

The most important effects of neo-liberal policies relevant to agriculture have come with WTO agreements accompanying these policies. With these agreements aiming at foreign trade liberalisation in the area of agricultural products, the levels of tariffs for these have gradually been decreasing. Concordantly, agriculture support systems in developing countries have been modified: specific (nationally determined) product support has been decreased and direct income support systems have become prominent, funded in some countries by the World Bank. The time-phased dismantlement of tariff walls and reduction of product supports have made the agriculture of developing countries vulnerable to that of developed countries and led to uncertain futures for farmers' incomes.

In developed countries (especially the USA and EU), on the other hand, such trade liberalisation measures have not been taken in the area of agricultural products. Their protection of their own agriculture producers has consequently continued at a much higher rate than that of developing countries, leading the developing countries' protection reduction policies to cause their own farmers' produce to be over-priced in world markets. These conditions also have caused developing countries' farmers to reduce production in areas where they cannot be competitive, or to change products. And when circumstances like the ambiguity of natural conditions, decreasing loan opportunities due to public fund reduction and increasing input costs – especially energy costs – are added to the liberalisation policy of leaving the price determination of agricultural products to the market which is itself combined, moreover, with the effects of international monopolies and supermarket chains in foodstuff price determination, then it is quite manifest why traditional small agriculture producers have had difficulties in maintaining economic viability and their capacity to operate.

Unsurprisingly, these conditions have caused small farmers to seek for new alternatives for survival, with a significant proportion (hundreds of millions of people worldwide) leaving their villages and migrating to cities. The concepts of 'deruralisation' and 'depeasantisation' have emerged. Waiting for the mass of poor people flowing from village to city has been, again, more poverty: the already sizeable and expanding urban poor populations have been further increased with the influx of these migrant peasants.

Through neo-liberal policies process, which may lead to growth but do not tend not to provide employment, poor peasants have been added to the increasing population of the unemployed, and in social contexts of damaged (local, family) support networks. In this way, while poverty had already existed in rural areas, a new, large mass, poor population emerged in urban areas. This has been the birth of a poor urban community with its own, novel characteristics. The dependency on unskilled labour for economic growth decreased as the (increasingly automated) production system no longer needed such a mass, tending instead to require a (semi-) skilled workforce. Thus arose the idea that economic growth alone could not save this community from poverty. This concept was termed 'New Poverty', although other names were also given to it, such as 'marginalisation' and 'underclass' (Buğra and Keyder 2003: 19-20, Işık and Pınarcıoğlu 2001: 70, 72).

The new understanding of poverty has brought with it new strategies to the problem. Promoting neo-liberal policies through and from the 1980s, the World Bank now started to pay special attention to poverty. It is remarkable at a time when the relationships between poverty and labour markets and labour productivity and the redistribution of wealth were being stressed less, poverty itself was entering global discussion and policy forums in radical new ways. And it is also remarkable that these included qualitative issues in the social and political fields of development discourse. For example, it is quiet striking that in the second half of the 1990's the World Bank laid stress on good governance, equality, gender discrimination and social development. Doubts are raised concerning the persuasiveness of this World Bank discourse, however, in the light of its efforts to adopt a neo-liberal economic model and failure in respect of pro-poor projects (Şenses 2009: 687-88). Ultimately, this approach works to absolve state and society from responsibility and ascribe the causes of poverty instead to the poor themselves – from which it follows that the solution to poverty must be found by those individuals and groups trapped in it (with assistance from non-governmental organisations that receive little state support).

The prevailing method by which to reduce poverty of increasing income generally through rapid growth is supported with monetary assistance. State cash aids have been made dependent on various pre-determined conditions, such as registering children for school, or regular physical examination for new-born babies, small children and pregnant women. Clearly, such programs cannot be regarded in terms of citizenship rights, especially insofar as the application procedures to determine who will gain assistance sometimes themselves deter people from seeking it.

Another, privately funded example of monetary assistance supporting the current poverty reduction approach of neo-liberalism is the much vaunted practice of microcredit, which has been successful in Bangladesh (and for which its creator, Muhammed Yunus, was awarded with Nobel Peace Prize). Even this, however, has not been implemented as a system of interest-free loans, but rather, as high interest rate loans. Moreover, it is a credit system which assumes the presence of entrepreneurs in the poor community, again, like the world's economies, waiting to be liberated (in this case by access to small scale venture capital). In fact, entrepreneurs are relatively scarce as a resource in poor community, and the success of such an approach remains rather peripheral to the main picture that poverty presents. The neo-liberal approach here, in fact, amounts to little more than simply saying, 'Here, we have granted you opportunity, go save yourselves!'

In the struggle against poverty, an approach that expects results only from economic policies, regards poverty as a temporary result of economic conjuncture and identifies it merely with lack of employment seems now to be quite invalid (Buğra and Keyder 2003: 12). On the other hand, neo-liberal globalisation has imposed major restrictions on governments' implementing pro-poor national economic policies precisely in conditions where these policies are most needed (S.A.M. 2004). Economic development alone is not adequate for poverty reduction, as has been determined by international development institutions, and for a decade now (UNDP 2000: 42). Even experts at the World Bank are stressing that new social protection understanding needs to be introduced in place of pro-poor growth policies and the approach of making the poor well-supported supplemented by direct support to those in need.

One of the distinctive characteristics of permanent poverty, and a major reason for it, is its intergenerational transmission, a characteristic that cannot be reduced by economic policies. Researchers agree that a leading carrier of intergenerationally transmitted poverty is inadequacy of human capital (Carm et al. 2003, Hulme et al. 2001, Yaqub 2000, cited by S.A.M. 2004). If a family is poor, naturally they cannot allocate sufficient resources for their children's nutrition, health and education needs, so the next generation will be disadvantaged in the fight to escape poverty (even to the extent that they can conceive of and attempt this). If the quality of labour force cannot be improved and if the society cannot make use of manpower resources, lasting poverty is inevitable.

One of the distinctive qualities of new poverty is that this poverty mass exists within a multi-dimensional framework of exclusion (social, economic, political, spatial, cultural; Textbox 9.1). Exclusion has become widespread under a variety of forms to which not only are the poor in developing countries exposed, but also those in developed countries. The groups at most risk of being exposed to social exclusion are children, old people, women, disabled people, migrants and those with alternative sexual and religious preferences (Adaman and Keyder 2006). And it is, of course, the poor among these groups that are most excluded, and these groups who are most disproportionately represented among the poor and excluded. 'The excluded' has come to represent a class of people, like the 'underclass', except that the reference here is to development. Sections of society are excluded in the developmental rush.

Textbox 9.1. Forms of exclusion.

Exclusion as a sociological concept may be defined in terms of the barriers place on and perceived by individuals/groups because of poverty, resulting in further deprivation and generalized discrimination. Various identifiable forms may be distinguished, which include the following:

- *Social exclusion:* the impossibility of joining communal life. Reduced or no access to education opportunities and activities from which to earn a living, and prevention from inclusion in social and environmental networks (other than those of other excluded).
- *Economic exclusion:* Lack of access to the labor market, unemployment and/or poor access to loan/credit opportunities and other financial services. Inability to join the world of consumerism (not targeted as consumers). No insurance.
- *Political exclusion:* the inability to exercise citizenship rights, especially political and legal ones, and prevention of direct or indirect participation in political life. Little or no participation in decision-making processes. Inadequate representation.
- *Cultural exclusion:* the inability to participate in communal and cultural life as desired. Non- or under-representation in all forms of media, leading to cultural invisibility.
- *Spatial exclusion:* the problematic or lack of access to certain places or inability to make proper use of them. The physical expression of the various forms of social, economic, political and cultural exclusion in daily life.
- *Psychological exclusion:* communication failure, low expectations, feelings of weakness and lack of self worth, resulting in rage or depression and leading to anti-social behaviors and psychiatric disorders. The psychological manifestation of other forms of exclusion.

Poverty is, of course, as much a relative as absolute concept, assuming as fundamental the very notion of wealth, or surplus capital (i.e. poverty logically implies wealth). And although in its extreme form it has absolutist implications, generally poverty does operate comparatively. People have more or less access to goods, and the things these can bring, such as health. Poverty is intimately bound up with notions of social justice and equality. Thus it is that even in the among what are, in material terms, the richest societies in all human history, still the statistics of poverty can tell a depressing story. Neo-liberalism does not seem to have made the telling of this particular tale any more palatable. In fact, the situation in the rich countries has worsened on its watch. Reviewing the relevant OECD statistics from the 1980s – which can be understood as the indicators of neo-liberal social justice among the well off – it is still apparent that overall inequalities in income distribution have increased (Table 9.4). The average real income of poorest fifth of the populations of these countries rose by about a quarter in over the period, but the median rise was a quarter of that higher again, and for the richest fifth of the population it was two thirds.[81]

Poverty as a relative concept applies to the community of nations, of course. From colonial empire building to contemporary outsourcing, the practice – and discourse – in this field is well advanced. Thus it comes as no surprise that Turkey, significantly the only OECD economy (other than Mexico) for which relevant figures are available here which is regarded as not developed, is also the country that has been affected most negatively by this inequality growth. Turkey is the only country on this list that – at least until mid decade – had seen an overall reduction of incomes during the neo-liberal period, with the lowest third loss being over half as much again as the median. The irony in Turkey's case was that because of its stock market crash, banking failure and currency collapse (financial crisis) of 2001, the richest fifth actually lost also – fractionally more than the poor even.[82] Of course a loss of income for the relatively rich is of a different order of magnitude to a loss of income for the poor – the former it is an inconvenience, the latter a grinding pain. Or worse.

---

[81] Compounded increase from index 100: poorest, 124; median, 130; richest 140.
[82] Compounded decrease from index 100: poorest, 98.3; median, 98.9; richest 98.2.

Table 9.4. Average annual real income increase, OECD households during the mid 1980s-1990s and mid1990s-2000s (%), ordered by lowest income group.

Mid 1980s – mid 1990s				Mid 1990s – mid 2000s			
Country	Lowest[1]	Median	Highest[1]	Country	Lowest[1]	Median	Highest[1]
Italy	-1.3	0.6	1.5	Austria	-2.1	-0.6	-0.4
New Zealand	-1.1	-0.6	1.6	Japan	-1.4	-1.0	-1.3
Turkey	-0.6	-0.8	1.4	Turkey	-1.1	-0.3	-3.2
Norway	-0.3	0.4	1.0	Germany	-0.3	0.6	1.3
Canada	0.3	-0.2	-0.1	USA	-0.2	0.4	1.1
Greece	0.3	0.3	0.1	Mexico	-0.1	0.2	-0.6
Germany	0.4	1.2	1.6	Canada	0.2	1.1	2.1
Sweden	0.5	0.9	1.2	Czech Repub.	0.4	0.5	0.7
Britain	0.7	1.9	4.3	Denmark	0.6	0.9	1.5
Mexico	0.7	1.1	3.8	France	0.9	0.8	1.0
Japan	0.8	1.8	2.1	Hungary	0.9	1.1	1.0
Finland	0.9	0.8	1.0	New Zealand	1.1	2.3	1.6
France	1.0	0.5	0.1	Belgium	1.4	0.2	1.7
The Netherlands	1.1	2.8	3.9	Sweden	1.4	2.2	2.8
Belgium	1.2	0.4	1.2	Luxemburg	1.5	1.5	1.7
USA	1.2	1.0	1.9	Finland	1.6	2.5	4.6
Denmark	1.3	0.9	0.8	The Netherlands	1.8	2.0	1.4
Luxemburg	2.3	2.4	3.0	Italy	2.2	1.0	1.6
Austria	2.5	2.8	2.8	Britain	2.4	2.1	1.5
Ireland	4.0	3.2	2.9	Greece	3.6	2.9	2.7
Spain	4.4	3.2	2.4	Norway	4.4	3.8	5.1
Portugal	5.7	6.2	8.7	Portugal	5.0	4.2	4.4
Total (avg.)	1.2	1.5	2.1	Total (avg.)	1.1	1.3	1.5

Source: OECD 2008.
[1] Lowest = bottom 20%; highest = top 20%.

Chapter 10. Turkey's experience

It is generally accepted that poverty emerged as a fact in the world with the industrial revolution, since which it has taken various specific forms, such as poverty in countries with newly gained independence. In Turkey, until the 1980s when neo-liberal policies were adopted, there were various problems of poverty like regional differences, the poverty of working people, unequal working conditions for women, helpless old people, orphans, the poverty of disabled people, etc.

Until the 1980s, family/community solidarity – through connections based on extended family and locality networks (between relatives, and among people migrating from the same village) – was the resource from which poor people most benefitted. Poverty was largely rural, and it was out of sight. It became visible in cities during the 1980s with the boom of the city population, which was fuelled by economic migration – i.e. generally of poor people – from provincial districts (Chapter 8). If the specific situations of the old, disabled and orphaned are disregarded, then poverty was seen as a temporary situation. During and after the 1980s, neo-liberal policies, as summarised, were instigated in Turkey. The conditions shaped through the implementation of these policies gave new, different characteristics to poverty in Turkey. Policies for poverty reduction showed parallelism with neo-liberal policies aimed at preventing poverty.

Introduction of measures

The first step in the introduction of neo-liberal policies in Turkey was taken with the stabilisation measures declared on 24 January 1980. A few months later, a three year stand-by agreement was signed with the IMF, and these measures begun to be put into practice. However, there was a strong trade union movement and public opposition which prevented the proper implementation of the neo-liberal policies. On 12 September 1980, the army organised a military coup and took power. Opposition movements were suppressed through force, and political parties and trade unions closed. This led to the easy implementation of neo-liberal policies. These policies were enacted step by step in the following years, when firstly generals and then the political parties active in this military constitutional order were in power. In 1981, the fixed exchange rate system was gradually abandoned and the daily exchange rate set by the Central Bank. In 1983, import restrictions were loosened and restrictions on currency exchange establishments freed up. After a while, the foreign exchange regime was altered and citizens allowed to obtain foreign currency for personal use. Various arrangements were made giving incentives for foreign investments. Meanwhile, conjunctural fluctuations increased, in both frequency and intensity.

In 1988, new stabilisation measures were declared because of the speculative fluctuations in exchange rates and high inflation. More radical regulations were made including free exchange rates in the markets, foreigner operations in Istanbul Stock Exchange in end of month and short term capital movements. In 1992, new economic measures were declared, including widespread privatisation of public enterprises. In 1994, an economic crisis occurred, a stand-by agreement was signed with the IMF and new stabilisation measures were taken. In 1996, the Customs Union Agreement was signed with EU. In 2001, Turkey again went through a financial crisis and took stabilisation measures. Following its recovery from this severe crisis, Turkey's economy grew in a stable way until 2008, when it was hit by the global financial crisis and subsequent economic slowdown. During this period of economic neo-liberalisation, financial crises and stabilisation measures were witnessed, along with robust economic growth outside the crisis periods.

General effects

In first part of the period during which neo-liberal policies have been followed, for the 17 years until 1997, Turkey's GDP increased by a total of 125.8% and its per capita income by 60.6%. During following 12 years, while the total increase in national income was another 38.3%, per capita income could only manage a 9.6% increase, less than 1% annually according to the State Statistical Institute (Table 10.1). In other words, while there have been major income gains over the last thirty years or so, the relative benefits of economic growth for per capita income rises declined dramatically, roughly halving, in fact. While the earlier period (until 1997) saw relative annual average gains in which the per capita income rise that was almost half the total income rise (3.2/6.6), the latter period (until 2009) saw this ratio drop to near a quarter (0.8/3). The prima facie implication would be that the income benefit from the increased total income has declined over time. (Even) the generalised gains (assumed as) resulting from neo-liberal policies seem to be diminishing.

Table 10.1. Change (%) in GDP and per capita GDP during 1980-2010.

Period	GDP change (%)		Per capita GDP change (%)	
	Total	Annual average	Total	Annual average
1980-1997	125.8	6.6	60.6	3.2
1998-2006	37.8	4.2	12.5	1.4
1998-2009	38.3	3.2	9.6	0.8
2009-2010	9.2	9.2	7.5	7.5

Calculated from TÜİK 1987-2011.

At a first glance the slower growth of per capita income appears negative, but a positive development can still be observed.[83] Combining these developments with developments in employment (Table 10.2), however, gives a clearer insight into the neo-liberal growth process.

Reading both Tables 10.2 and 10.3 together, it can be seen that the total increase in national income during the first period (to 1997) of 125.8% (and per capita increase of 60.6%) coincided with an increase in employment at just 28.3%. Since 2007, figures have been adversely affected due to the global economic crisis, so it will be more meaningful to refer just to the period before this. Accordingly, while national income showed a 37.8% increase (per capita, 12.5%) in the adjusted second period, i.e. between 1998 and 2006, the increase in employment was only 2.5% (this increase

Table 10.2. Change (%) in employment during 1980-2010.

Period	Change (%)
1980-1997	28.3
1998-2006	2.5
1998-2009	2.0
2009-2010	6.1

Calculated from TÜİK 1989-2011.

---

[83] It is instructive, if hardly clarifying, to compare these results with those obtained through the PPP instrument, which shows absolute decline (above, Table 9.4).

Table 10.3. GDP and unemployment rates (%) during 2000-2010.

Year	GDP growth rate[a] (%)	Change (%)	Unemployment rate (%)	Change (%)
2002	6.2	-	10.3	-
2003	5.3	-14.5	10.5	1.9
2004	9.4	77.4	10.3	-1.9
2005	8.4	-10.7	10.3	0
2006	6.9	-17.9	9.9	-3.9
2007	4.5	-34.8	10.3	4.0
2008	0.7	-84.4	11.0	6.8
2009	-4.8	-785.7	14.0	27.3
2010	8.9	285.4	11.9	-15
Average	6.1	-	10.9	2.4[b]

Source: TÜİK 1989-2011, 1987-2011.
[a] GDP: constant prices index.
[b] Total change (2002-2010).

in employment turned negative with the crisis, and by 2009 the level of employment had fallen to below that of 2006). Any change in employment, of course, needs to be offset against changes in population. This rose by some 15 million (over 25%) during the period, forcing the conclusion that economic growth has signally failed to create anything like sufficient jobs. The official unemployment rate, meanwhile, stood at around 8% during the 1990s and rose to 10% between 2000 and 2005 (reaching 14% as the economic crisis hit).[84] Focusing just on the current decade (between the 2001 Turkish and more recent world crises), we see little overall change in the official unemployment or growth rates, although there are marked annual disparities between them (Table 10.3).

As these data indicate, employment in Turkey during the recent decades of neo-liberalism has not benefited proportionately from economic growth. Sometimes, dramatic year-on-year changes in growth have contrasted with relative constancy in unemployment, and it is this persistence of unemployment and its long term rise even, alongside the very healthy

---

[84] It needs to be emphasized that for an economy such as Turkey's with so much unregistered work, official unemployment figures are essentially reflexive – that is, they give more informative when compared to themselves, over time, than they do to the real rate of unemployment.

economic growth that suggests some of the longer term, deeper factors at play in the failure of economic growth to poverty reduction equation.

One reason for the persistent and increasing levels of unemployment is that because of technological improvements, labour-saving technologies have been playing an increasingly important role in production. Another reason is that certain inputs have become obtained from other countries. This has been realised in two ways: firstly, more foreign inputs are bought from foreign countries (primarily because they are cheaper, (e.g. foodstuffs from China and India), and secondly, with the increase of foreign capital investments in industry, production systems have increased input levels from companies/plants outside of Turkey (primarily from shared suppliers, either the same institutions or a third party, e.g. European and East Asian engineering technology imported by the Turkish franchises of international companies). In both cases, domestic employment for input provision is lost, or ungained.

According to Table 10.3, economic growth and unemployment declined during the 2008 world economic crisis. Then, a year later GDP growth shifted to positive territory, but unemployment lagged and rose still higher than before the crisis. This is a familiar pattern, but no less significant for that in human terms – it is just the type of situation that calls for specific intervention, a 'qualitative easing', of the type that the neo-liberal environment does not really permit, even if the pill of a massive quantitative easing may be swallowed (as we have recently witnessed). Considering the income side of the subject, there has been a small per capita income increase relative to fixed prices. However this figure may be misleading taken in isolation as it is necessary to consider the distribution of income (Table 10.4). This indicates no significant change between 1987 and 2006. Turkey has the most imbalanced income distribution amongst OECD countries. In the 20-year period of neo-liberalism, therefore, there has been no significant improvement of income distribution while national income, population and unemployment have all increased. And this paints the real picture of the poverty of low-income groups.

The unchanging income distribution means that households in the bottom 20% income group have continued to live below the poverty line, officially (according to the Turkish Statistical Institute), 18.08% the population in 2009.[85] Actually, the official figures do indicate huge gains in poverty,

---

[85] The figure given for families in poverty is 14%.

Table 10.4. Income distribution as share of national income (%), by household income group.

Household income group	1987	1994	2002	2003	2004	2005	2006	2008	2009
Lowest 20%	5.2	4.9	5.29	6.0	6.04	5.1	5.8	5.8	5.6
Second 20%	9.6	8.6	9.81	10.28	10.69	9.9	10.6	10.4	10.3
Third 20%	14.1	12.6	14.02	14.47	15.22	14.8	15.2	15.2	15.1
Fourth 20%	21.2	19.0	20.83	20.93	21.88	21.9	21.5	21.9	21.5
Highest 20%	49.9	54.9	50.05	48.32	46.17	48.4	46.9	46.7	47.6
Total	100	100	100	100	100	100	100	100	100
Gini parameter	0.43	0.49	0.44	0.42	0.40	0.43	0.41	0.40	0.41

Source: for 1987-2004: Turk-İş 2007; for 2005-2006: TUIK 2009c.

with the numbers of the poor as a proportion of the population shown as having dropped by over a third in the six years to 2008 alone 2006 (Table 10.5). The figures do give cause for concern, however. The poverty figures are based on 4-person families, a measurement system probably open to more complications than a simple one-person system; low income figures (for below US $1, US $2.15 and US $4.3) are based on PPP equivalences which rose at a rate of less than half that of inflation, suggesting the low income figures might be an under-calculation (the poverty figures seem to be fixed at lira rates that do not follow the PPP equivalences, that is, making the figures for poverty act differently than those for low income). In terms of inequality, the prime monetary indicator for this has, like income distribution, remained essentially unchanged during the 2002-2009 period. Measured at 50% of the national median consumption expenditure,[86] the figure for 'relative poverty' has been steady at around 15% of the population. And, in reality, the average available income of these people has indeed turned out to be insufficient for their needs, as families to have run into debt or sold their properties just to finance themselves (Yükseler and Türkan 2008: 105-106).

---

[86] Following the first of the Laeken Indicators as adopted by the EU, 2001.

Table 10.5. Individual poverty rate (national, %), by purchase base poverty line during 2002-2009.

Methods	2002	2003	2004	2005	2006	2007[a]	2008	2009
Food poverty (hunger)	1.35	1.29	1.29	0.87	0.74	0.48	0.54	0.48
Poverty (food + non food)	26.96	28.12	26.60	20.50	17.81	17.79	17.11	18.08
Per capita < 1$ daily [b]	0.20	0.01	0.02	0.01	–	–	–	–
Per capita < $2.15 daily [b]	3.04	2.39	2.49	1.55	1.42	0.52	0.47	0.22
Per capita < $4.3 daily [b]	30.30	23.75	20.89	16.36	13.33	8.41	6.83	4.35
Relative poverty based on spending [c]	14.74	15.51	14.18	16.16	14.50	14.70	15.06	15.12

Source: TÜİK 2009b,c.
[a] Revised according to new population projections.
[b] PPP. PPP $1 = (Y)TL equivalence rates – 2002: 618,281; 2003: 732,480; 2004: 780,121; 2005: 0.830; 2006: 0.921; 2007: 0.926; 2008: 0.983; 2009: 0.917. (In 2005, the currency was changed – or revalued – with 1 million Turkish lira (TL) becoming one new Turkish lira (*Yeni Türk Lira*, YTL).
[c] Predicted 50% of median value of the equiv. per cap. consumption expenditure.

Rural effects

As explained, the targeting of agriculture through neo-liberal policies and the effects of this on the rural structure of Turkey involved a concerted attempt to reduce the number of people employed in the sector as a strategy for national economic development. The result was an impoverishment of the countryside and mass exodus from village to city.

Summarizing, uncertainty in agricultural product prices has increased because of privatisation, the sale and commercialisation of public enterprises that have processed agricultural products, solved the problem for farmers of marketing these products, and supplied inputs to agriculture. The resulting uncertainty has created problems that cannot be controlled by farmers. The prices of agricultural products have been increasing much more slowly than those of agricultural inputs over the last couple of decades. The previous agriculture support system has effectively been transformed into direct cash support with the help of the neo-liberal foreign trade policy, WTO agreements and support from the World Bank. These supports have meant a ready income for farmers who did not or could not want to take risks. In this way, the support system has not achieved its goal and even contributed to the rural-to-urban migration.

Outward migration has led to a changed – and probably still changing – demographic structure of the village, with an excess of elderly and population sections out of the labour force and thus contributing to production (or at least, making reduced contributions). The combination of outward migration and altered village demographics led to diminishing local markets (in all senses of the term), which, in a viscous circle, increased the difficulty for farmers to maintain themselves in rural areas through their agricultural income. The upshot has been a continuing high level of rural poverty. In contrast to the positive trend in poverty reduction reported overall, rural poverty has remained consistently high during the current decade, steady at about 35% of the (rural) population. This comparative increase is shown also by a 50% rise in relative poverty for rural areas between 2002 and 2008 (Table 10.6). Comparison with the identical figures for Turkey as a whole (Table 10.5) demonstrates clearly the grim reality of rural poverty in terms also of socio-geographical distribution, with most numbers for the countryside being double or treble those of the whole nation. This difference, of course, becomes even more pronounced when the rural figures are deducted from the whole to give a more accurate picture of the rural/urban divide.

Table 10.6. Individual poverty rate (rural, %), by purchase base poverty line during 2002-2009.

Method	2002	2003	2004	2005	2006	2007[a]	2008	2009
Food poverty	2.01	2.15	2.36	1.24	1.91	1.41	1.18	1.42
General poverty (food + non-food)	34.48	37.13	39.97	32.95	31.98	34.80	34.62	38.69
Per capita < 1$ daily [b]	0.46	0.01	0.02	0.04	–	–	–	–
Per capita < $2.15 daily [b]	4.06	3.71	4.51	2.49	3.36	1.49	1.11	0.63
Per capita < $4.3 daily [b]	38.82	32.18	32.62	26.59	25.35	17.59	15.33	11.92
Relative poverty based on spending [c]	19.86	22.08	23.48	26.35	27.06	29.16	31.00	34.20

Source: TÜİK 2009b,c.
[a] Revised according to new population projections.
[b] PPP. PPP $1 = (Y)TL equivalence rates – 2002: 618,281; 2003: 732,480; 2004: 780,121; 2005: 0.830; 2006: 0.921; 2007: 0.926; 2008: 0.983; 2009: 0.917. (In 2005, the currency was changed – or revalued – with 1 million Turkish lira (TL) becoming one new Turkish lira (*Yeni Türk Lira*, YTL).
[c] Predicted 50% of median value of the equiv. per cap. consumption expenditure.

Meanwhile, the population moving to the cities from a collapsing agriculture base has contributed directly to urban poverty reaching massive proportions. In order to assess the scale of this contribution, it is instructive to consider the population figures for the period following the introduction of neo-liberal policies. Taking the six million reduction in the rural population over the past decade, and assuming that they mostly migrated to the cities and that the poverty rate for this body of people was the same as the national rate generally (30%) translates to what is probably an extremely conservative ballpark figure of two million poor people entering the urban centres from the countryside. To this should be added the unknown number of urban-to-urban migrants leaving agricultural towns and heading for the city for similar reasons (i.e. related primarily to the lack of local employment in or directly or indirectly dependent on agriculture). To this should be added any hidden (unrecorded) numbers of city-bound migrants during this period (who can be presumed to have mostly been poor). And to this should be added the children of these people, most likely born into urban poverty. And in assessing the numbers of the rural poor migrating to the cities for other reasons during this time, then to this should also be added a hundreds of thousands of Kurds (see Textbox 10.1).

For a final estimate, of the scale of the influx of the rural poor to Turkey' major cities, however, we need to return to the start of the neo-liberal period. The rural population in 1980 was about 25 million. Since that time, the population of the country as a whole has risen by about two thirds, implying a rural population of over 40 million. The difference between this hypothetical projection and the current reality is well over 20 million, and if a third of this number were poor then we arrive at a figure of, say, seven million people. This is over 10% of the current urban population. Ignoring the role of government policy in this dynamic and just focusing on the outcome, we are left with the state administration having to respond to the effective institution of urban poverty on a scale hitherto unknown – with policy instruments drawn largely from the neo-liberal toolbox.

Textbox 10.1. Kurds and the Southeast.

The southeastern corner of Turkey is predominantly Kurdish (Appendix 5). Linguistically and culturally distinct from the dominant Turks, ethnic Kurds have been at odds with the Republic since its inception, with a history of rebellions that resulted in state repression. Population expulsions were followed by prolonged periods of emergency rule and a strategy aiming at a ethno-cultural assimilation of Kurds and Kurdishness into the Turkish state heterodoxy. The Southeast is also the poorest and least developed part of the country, with per capita income still less than half that of the national rate, the labour force participation rate 25% below the national average, secondary education levels about a third below (and half for girls) and fertility rates 50 to 75% higher. This is a mostly mountainous territory, with the Euphrates and Tigris rivers rising in the north and flowing down through the region to Syria and Iraq, and it was largely in response to the economic aspects of the socio-political problem – or, as an attempt to solve the socio-political problem through economics – that the massive Southeast Anatolia Project (*Güneydoğu Anadolu Projesi*, GAP) was instigated, making use of the Tigris and Euphrates for hydro-electric power and irrigation (Appendix 3).

Historically, Kurds have a strong base in the semi-nomadic tribal (*aşiret*) system which continues today, albeit in sedentary form. People still have allegiance to their tribal leaders and other landlords (beys or aghas), who wield considerable, if diminishing, power at local level. As a 'divide and rule' aspect of the assimilation approach to the 'Kurdish problem', this large landowning Kurdish elite was largely copted through patronage into the nation-state system (Turgut Özal, incidentally, the prime minister responsible for introducing neo-liberal reforms, was Kurdish). It was partly in response to this that the Marxist-based Kurdish movement the PKK emerged. Widely known for waging war against the state in the 1980s (still unresolved), the PKK equally targeted the region's feudal landlord structure. Indeed, its first operation was an attempted assassination of a Kurdish MP who owned thousands of hectares of land and had control of a district with over twenty villages. The Kurdish armed resistance – the 'guerrilla', as they are termed by most Kurds, or 'terrorists', in the national (now international) discourse – thus operated from a twin aspect of leftist and nationalist (separatist) politics This was instrumental in profound changes to the region, including the following two of interest here.

First, there was a move away from the feudal nature of the region's socio-economic structure. As the PKK employed a Maoist guerilla strategy to take effective of a large part of the countryside, pressure mounted on the old order and a major part of the agha system dissolved. This led, in effect, to a land distribution as local people and tenant farmers bought (their) land from the aghas. Contrary to the capitalist imperative towards consolidation, therefore, in Southeastern Turkey – or, northern Kurdistan, as separatists would have it – there was actually a development of small scale (farming) enterprises. At the same time, however, some aghas (or land owning families) transformed themselves and their land, becoming capitalist entrepreneurs and abandoning the old plotting system.

Second, there was an exodus from the countryside, in part due to the fighting but more importantly through forced migration. In order to retake control of rural areas from the insurgent PKK, the Turkish military effectively emptied large parts of the Southeast during the mid 1990s to mid 2000s. Local villages had to either join the state-sponsored quasi para-military system or else evacuate their settlements. Some 3000 villages were cleared, with buildings, crops and orchards burnt, and the number of the internally displaced estimated at a million or more (Dağ 2006, Tezcan and Koç 2006). These people generally lost their property as well as their livelihoods, mostly without compensation, the severance of their ties to their rural homelands becoming the cause of further poverty. Typically, they evacuated to the nearest town, which of course could not support them, especially with the local agricultural base decimated, and thus operated as a staging post for a second stage migration to the major cities. Consequently, this represented a particularly impoverished, poorly organized and highly excluded large scale influx of people into urban areas. The last few years have seen a partial return and rebuilding of local agriculture, but the effects of the rural impoverishment in the region are likely to be long lasting, or permanent.

From rotation poverty to permanent poverty

Until the 1980s, people migrating to the cities in Turkey mostly met their housing needs by building shanty houses (*gecekondu*).[87] This approach to the problem of accommodation made a contribution to the accumulation of capital through a lowering of labour costs. Generally built illegally on public land, these houses are typically quickly erected, low quality dwellings creating impoverished neighbourhoods of a temporary yet

---

[87] *Gecekondu*: lit. 'nighthouse', implying that these dwellings would spring up overnight, as it were, and also that they were constructed during the dark, when there was less risk of intervention in their activities on non-legally claimed land.

indefinite nature with poor infrastructure and services, like the French African *Bidonville* or Brazilian *favela*.

As time passed, the *gecekondu* population increased which made the occupants an important swing voter group. This group was also able to penetrate political parties and municipalities to some extent through various connections. A significant number managed to improve their standard of living with the help of the increase in employment and job opportunities in the growing, urban economy. Until 1980, extended family loyalties and locality (hometown/village) solidarity could provide sheltering, job and aid when needed to newcomers, who were thus able to improve their conditions in a shorter period than would otherwise have been the case. This both gave the idea that poverty was temporary and offered hope to those following. And as the earlier arrivals started to prosper, or at least maintain themselves, and be replaced at the bottom of the ladder by the newcomers, to whom they passed on their poverty, as it were, a new term was coined, 'rotation poverty'.

By the 1980s, *gecekondu* land had attained value and the owners of these houses had acquired, in essence, property. The *gecekondu* house-owners were receiving urban land rents. These rentable areas started to attract more attention than in the past, from municipalities, private construction companies and investment companies, and the state developed policies which would prevent further building there. Business centres, shopping centres and housing estates began to be built on these lands. Now, accommodation became a high cost problem for newcomers, the latest in the tidal wave of rural-to-urban migrants. As a result of these developments, the *gecekondu* concept began to change in the first years of the 1980s, and distinctions like '*gecekondu* landlord' and '*gecekondu* tenant' began to emerge. New migrants to cities could not find any land to build on. Newcomers lacked the increased financial capacity necessary to construct a dwelling, or acquaintances who could help them on this road. No longer would it be possible for newcomers to construct or easily access new shanty house building in the big cities.

The second important problem awaiting newcomers after that of accommodation was that of employment. The urban poor who had previously worked for the state or local authority in official jobs with low wage salaries but job security began gradually to disappear. In the framework of neo-liberal policies, the downsizing of the state in the economy has been one of the reasons for the increase in unemployment since the 1980s. When the state has downsized, employment in the public sector has been restricted and real wages have decreased, causing general economic slowdowns, often with crises, resulting in rises in unemployment. Those that did manage to find employment have been disadvantaged by low wages. One of the main reasons for the lower wages was the impairment of the labour unions, again in line with the basic tenets of neo-liberalism. In 2006, just 13.3% of the Turkish workforce was employed according to collective labour agreements – as compare with over 70% in most EU countries (Candaş *et al.* 2010: 70)

In this period, the prominent growth sectors in the expanding Turkish economy mostly operated in the exports market, meeting demand fluctuations with flexible production systems. Employment practices in these sectors depended on the use of informal labour, Women and children especially were employed in temporary jobs and for scab work on a casual, often piece-rate basis, without insurance or contracts or any recognised rights. Other factors accounting for the inadequate increase in employment include the extension of working hours enabled by the employer's market in labour relations itself contextualised by the free market ethos of neo-liberalism, as well as the privatisation of nationalised industries, as a neo-liberal policy. So, even though the economy grew, it did not offer sufficient opportunities for people to escape poverty.

As well as contributing directly to worsening the workers' conditions and limiting employment expansion, the development of foreign trade also increased the level of technology in the country through easing the import of machinery and new manufacturing methods as never before. Thus, the proportionate value of labour in production systems declined. The capital-labour combination changed in favour of capital, a change that indicates reduced labour usage relative to economic growth. Again, economic growth has not equated with human gain in a simple way – in this case, it has far outstripped the need to create employment.

This poor community also has to deal with difficulties related to exclusion. The poor are subject to discrimination when employed, given wages and regarding promotion. They work as unpaid family workers, and informally as unwaged labour. Inequalities stemming from gender relationships are another problem to which poor people are subject: gender inequality has made the poverty of women greater.

The expansion of the informal labour market, de-unionisation and sub-contracting encouraged unregistered employment and the shadow economy. The proportion of workers unregistered and uncovered by social security institutions currently stands at nearly 30% in cities and over 45% overall. A large part of the current unregistered worker population is composed of adults who have recently migrated to cities and have lower level of education. Playing a critical role in poverty, the sector of employment is also important in its reduction. Employment opportunity rises in the industry and service sectors have been more effective than the agriculture sector in reducing poverty. Poverty rates for working people are around 33% in the agricultural sector, compared to 10 and 7% respectively in the industrial and service sectors (Table 10.7). Finding a job and deriving revenue from it do not always translate to an escape from poverty. With wage levels going down, social services commercialised and prices going up, even working groups fall into poverty. Especially those in the agricultural sector.

Nevertheless, groups who do not receive pay for labour such as the unemployed, many or most of the old, the disabled, children, women, young tend to rank in the lowest levels of poverty. The highest rates of poverty are found among unpaid family workers, unemployed people, population outside working age and the chronically ill and permanently disabled. The displaced (forced migrant) Kurds also have been particularly badly hit. Poverty has begun to become a permanent fact of life for many households. Those in a state of permanent poverty have to deal with difficulties related to exclusion. They are subject to discrimination when employed, promoted and given wages. They work as unpaid family workers, and informally as unwaged labour, especially women.

Table 10.7. Poverty rates (%) by sector.

Sector	2002	2003	2004	2005	2006	2007	2008	2009
Agriculture	36.4	39.9	40.9	37.2	33.9	32.1	38.0	33.0
Industry	21.0	21.3	15.6	9.9	10.1	9.7	9.7	9.6
Service	25.8	16.8	12.4	8.7	7.2	7.4	6.8	7.2
Working population	25.2	25.9	23.2	19.0	15.8	14.2	14.8	15.4

Source: TÜİK 2009b,c.

Inequalities stemming from gender relationships are a problem to which poor people are particularly subject: rising gender inequality during the neo-liberal period has made the poverty of women greater. For example, while official employment rates for the second half of the 1990s put women's labour force participation consistently at 55-60%, the figures given for the mid-2000s are mostly in the 45-50% range. Education, a possible key to escaping from poverty, is less accessible to girls, as shown by the latest employment figures for uneducated females. While the labour force participation rate for males with higher education is 83.6%, for females it is 70.5%, almost identical to the rate for males not educated to high school 70.7% – but for females in this category, it is just 25.1% (TÜİK 1989-2011). In fact, half of the girls in the 15-19 age group are neither studying nor working (Candaş *et al.* 2010).

The transformation process begun in the 1980s created a huge mass of socially excluded people, and by the 1990s these excluded people were beginning to be defined socio-culturally, as 'slum dwellers' (Etöz 2000: 49, cited in the Council of Urbanisation: 10). The 'ghetto' or 'slum' (*gecekondu*) areas where they had established their urban lives became seen as a threat to the political system, social culture and the existing system as a whole, causing the inhabitants, and especially the most 'vulnerable' among them, to be further exposed to social exclusion (Adaman *et al.* 2006). As emphasised in various researches, with these developments going on since the beginning of 1990s, 'poverty' had become a lifelong concept for some poor groups (Textbox 10.2). And this meant poverty in rotation had ended, and permanent poverty settled.

Social aid policies: practices and effects

The effects of neo-liberal policies introduced during and following the 1980s have operated against the poorer sections of society. A new social policy understanding emerged after 1990 in harmony with the Washington Consensus, but after the 2001 financial crisis in Turkey, the economic growth that recommenced from 2003 did not see unemployment and poverty reduce by similar proportions (Buğra 2008: 199). It was understood that poverty and social exclusion were not problems solvable just through trusting in the labour market and conveying messages about people's personal responsibility to find work. It was clear that the real issue was not at the level of the individual but of the social, and that the solution

---

Textbox 10.2. From rotation poverty to permanent poverty.

The change in the nature of poverty over the last quarter century can be shown in grid form highlighting simple topics:

	Rotation poverty	Permanent poverty
Housing	Building own *gecekondu*	Tenants of *gecekondu*
Likely job possibilities	Official jobs (low wages but job security) or informal work, gender discrimination, child labour	Temporary, long working hours, very low wages, more gender discrimination, child labour
Job contract type	Mostly social security, 50% collective contracted	No social security or collective contract, subcontracting
Family solidarity	Strong	Weak
State/municipality social aid	Weak, rare	SYDTF, SHÇEK[1] – extended but weak
NGO solidarity	Rare	Increased
Importance of aids	For some, some times	For many, continuous
Social services access	Some difficulties, low	Some difficulties, low
Future expectations	Will escape poverty	Will be in continuous poverty
Social exclusion	Limited	Strong

[1] SYDTF: the Social Aid and Solidarity Fund (*Sosyal Yardımlaşma ve DayanışmayıTeşivk Fonu*); SHÇEK: the Social Services and Child Welfare Foundation (*Sosyal Hizmetler ve Çocuk Esirgeme Kurumu*).

---

therefore required an approach based on state policies to be pursued with public funding.

Successive (Ak Party) Turkish governments, initially focusing on economic matters and rather unconcerned about the problem of poverty (like the World Bank), developed various policies that aimed more at the effects than the roots of the problem, reducing the intensity of the symptoms and thus representing an ineffective, essentially false approach. After 2002 two trends became prominent in social policy: (1) a tendency to leaving social issues to charities, combined with (2) an acknowledgement of the need for the state to play a serious role in social support, with measures intended to expand the social security system to all citizens including new arrangements for healthcare (like the green card, entitling people to free state health services) and for old age salaries, etc. This new approach was affected through the following mechanisms in the social support environment:

- informal civil support networks (family, friends, neighbours);
- municipality assistance;
- various non-governmental and religious organisations;
- government institutions (SYDTF/SYDVs and SHÇEK).

Family support continues to play a pivotal (traditional) role in Turkish society and be activated especially in times of crises. This does require extended family networks and individuals with the means to support others, however, and a large proportion of the new poor simply lack these family and community ties. Besides, when poverty is permanent, these supports are typically found wanting as the continuity of inter-family support reduces over time. As the recent 2003 UNDP research on poverty underlined, the new poverty, known in Turkey now as 'permanent poverty' is extremely difficult to tackle with communal/family based support alone (Buğra and Keyder 2003).

The emphasis of the moderate Islamic governments on religious themes and religious charity approaches to poverty has been regarded as quite compatible with the neo-liberal approach to poverty. Historically, municipalities, non-governmental organisations and religious foundations have been active in social life and supported the poor, and the mission of these institutions to struggle against poverty only gained in importance during the 2000s. Applied through the SYDF and various foundations, however, these policies have been used politically by the government and charitable institutions to try to win over the poor and those connected to them through the aid given and thereby gain support for the ruling party. The limited resources of the municipalities and charities, along with the prominence of political interests in municipalities and corruption in some charities weakened expectations of these institutions. And, furthermore, despite the best efforts and continued good work by these local and religious institutions in fighting poverty, they have been hampered by their hierarchical and conservative structures. These kinds of institutions have tended to lack the vision, range and scope and the sheer power which the state can bring to bear in order to embark on an extensive struggle against poverty.

Two state institutions founded during the 1980s became more prominent in the struggle against poverty, The Social Assistance and Solidarity Fund (*Sosyal Yardımlaşma ve Dayanışmayı Teşivk Fonu, SYDTF*), and the Social Services and Child Welfare Foundation (*Sosyal Hizmetler ve Çocuk Esirgeme Kurumu, SHÇEK*). Founded in 1986 under the Social Aid and Solidarity General Directorate (*Sosyal Yardımlaşma ve Dayanışma Genel Müdürlüğü, SYDGM*), a department established two years earlier under the provisions of the wide-ranging and powerful office of the Prime Ministryship (*Başbakanlık*), the SYDTF is funded directly from government revenues (e.g. receiving fixed percentage sums from specified taxes),[88] and works through several hundred local level Social Aid and Solidarity Foundations (*Sosyal Yardımlaşma ve Dayanışmayı Vakıfları, SYDVs*). The objective of the Fund and its related organisational structure was to realise traditional social protection components as well as fortify target groups against social and financial risks. Major tools adopted for this objective are:

- *ad hoc* financial aid and public relief (one-off grants and in-kind benefits) to those entitled to SYDTF support (for fuel, food, education, health, and for victims of terror and of natural disasters);
- project aid to support individuals and families without economic means and unable to participate in production processes, and thus unable to maintain themselves.

The SYDTF and SHÇEK also aim to lessen the effects of social and economic crises and structural adjustment programs on the poor, to reduce poverty and the risk of poverty, to provide employment and to develop infrastructure. These institutions are supported by the World Bank, and, within employment projects, the Fund has allowed microcredit implementations, establishing a connection between microcredit implementations and social aid entitlements, and thus used state resources so as to support the microcredit programs. It is not unusual in Turkey, as elsewhere, for interest loans provided through microcredit to be used for urgent needs as well as establishing businesses. People using borrowed money for their urgent needs in this way are then burdened with interest on their loans.

The SYDTF Solidarity Fund also supports a financial social aid project (a welfare system) for low income families, made dependent on regular

---

[88] The SYDTF budget for 2008 was some two billion Turkish liras, around USD 1.3 billion, although it underspent by some 10% (http://www.sydgm.gov.tr/tr/html/224/SYDTF/).

checkups for children and regular attendance at school (Conditional Cash Transfer). Detailed information, such as how much support is allocated to how many families/individuals by the Fund under this provision, is unavailable. According to the limited figures given, the Fund spent some 375 million dollars between 1997 and 2001.[89] This relief clearly has great importance in the struggle against poverty; regardless of exactly how it is spent (assuming it is spent on poverty relief, that is).[90] It is, nevertheless, extremely low compared to Turkey's European neighbours (the obvious comparison for a country desiring to accede to the EU), comprising just 0.5% of gross domestic product as against 2.8% in the EU-15, 2% in Greece, and 2.5% in Portugal and Spain. The share of these welfare payments made by the public sector on the basis of family income as a proportion of the total SYDTF spending increased by 4.4 points in 2002-2005, to 36.8% (Buğra and Adar 2007: 4).

These data do show that transfer incomes are important for poor families, but what is essential is not top-up income or occasional payments, but major, regular public transfers, which in Turkey only take the form of retirement pensions. Welcome as any help may be, the welfare system here is not essential for poor families when viewed from this angle. The social security system in Turkey is highly criticised in the 2003 county report made to the EU, for being ad hoc, underfunded, inefficient and corrupt. Particular importance is attached to the lack of child benefit as a tool to fight poverty. As the country report concludes, the need is 'to address the utmost necessity of reforming the public sphere and to consider macro policies that will help reduce inequalities' (Adaman 2003: 64).

Families and individuals in the lowest 20% income group of society face the highest risk of poverty. The consumption spending levels of this group increased by an average of 18.4% during the 2002-2006 period, with average consumption spending rising above the poverty level by 2005. On the other hand, the share of imperative spending for the lowest income group in 2006 had reached 70.1% (Yükseler and Türkan 2008: 105-106). This indicates that even if the households in low income groups are deprived of income, they finance themselves through going into debt.

---

[89] See http://www.sydgm.gov.tr/tr/html/224/SYDTF/.
[90] In the context of Turkey's generally unimpressive level of administrative efficiency and reputation for high levels of corruption, this is not a small assumption.

The share of households obtaining complimentary transfer receipts rose from 23.4% to 26.7% between 2002 and 2006. With this increase, the proportion of poor individuals declined from 28.1% in 2003 to 17.1% in 2008, before losing some ground in the wake of the world crisis related downturn (Table 10.5). As mentioned, however, this positive tendency was not reflected in the relative poverty rate, which was 15.5% in 2003 rose to 16.2% in 2005 but declined to 14.5% in 2006, and still remains in negative territory for the period. While relative individual poverty rate based on consumption was 14.7% in 2002, it rose to 16.2% in 2005 and declined to 14.5 in 2006. When these figures are viewed together it is evident that, contrary to what political economists have emphasised generally, neo-liberal policies in Turkey have not caused any reduction in social welfare expenses (or pensions for that matter), as is evident from the absolute spending figures provided by the SYDTF. Therefore, it is stressed, what has really happened is that a fresh 'welfare governance' regime has emerged, i.e. that the present provisions effectively represent the development of an adequate system (Buğra and Keyder 2006). This may appear to be the case when absolute figures are viewed, but this argument must be questioned, from two points of view.

Firstly, in spite of the fact that social aid expenses have increased, poverty is still high. The so-called fresh welfare regime is still missing huge swathes of the population. According to the State Planning Organisation, 80.2% of the adult population is currently covered by institutional social insurance, which means, obviously, that 19.8% are not (DPT 2010). That means some ten million people without any security. For the poor who need social protection most, the deficiency of public social expenses is clearly revealed here. Further detail is supplied by a brief focus on vulnerable, at-risk groups.

The lack of a child benefit system has already been noted, which is particularly important in a country with poverty demographics like Turkey. Some 8.5% of 3-4 person families live below the complete poverty line, whereas for households comprised of seven or more the rate is 38.2% (TÜİK 2009c). Put simply, the bigger the household, the greater the risk of poverty. As a result, the proportion of children at risk of poverty in Turkey today is 34%, as opposed to the general average of 26%, and so thousands of children are working, regardless of its illegality. According to the most recent available official figures (for 2006), 5.9% of 6-17 year olds, and 318,000 of 6-14 year olds nearly a third of a million under children between the ages of six and fourteen are employed (TÜİK 2007b). In 1995-2002, nearly 440,000 children began earning a living even before completing their primary school education. Half of the girls in 15-19 age group in Turkey are neither studying nor working (Candaş *et al.* 2010).The problem of child labour is linked to education provision and uptake, of course, as a part of social provision. The average education period of Turkish society is six years, compared to ten years in Greece and thirteen in Germany.

Regarding the elderly, the 6% of population age 65 and over depend primarily on their families for care and support. In 2005, 37% of the population over 65 lacked a pension of any kind, state or private, notwithstanding the state's statutory obligation here (under Law 2022). Regarding the physically disabled, a TSI (TÜİK) survey has put the proportion of disabled people in the country at 12%. While the illiteracy rate for the general population is 12.9%, it is 36.3% among disabled citizens. Only 20% of disabled people are active in labour force.

A secondly consideration undermining of the idea of that a fresh welfare regime is operative in Turkey today is that part of the social welfare supports are taken back through taxation. The share which the state has reclaimed from household incomes with taxes is not to be underestimated. In 2005, consumption taxes paid amounted to 70% of the total tax income. When the burden of consumption tax on income groups is examined, we find that 23% of the lowest 20% income group's income is paid to the state in consumption taxes (Gökçen *et al.* 2008: 42).

In order to appreciate the subject more deeply, it is helpful to consider the proportion of the public resources that is identified for the purposes of poverty reduction and social welfare enhancement. Among the EU-25, nearly 69% of social protection expenses is composed of old age health expenses, a figure equivalent to 19.5% of GDP. In Turkey, this rate is approximately 90% and equal to 8.4% of GDP. This indicates that in Turkey, social protection expenses (1% of GDP) other than old age and health expenses are pretty much lower than the EU average (8.2% of GDP).

If increases in taxes and contributions and increase in public social expenses are compared, it can be seen that the tax premium per GDP increased 3.4 points in 2002-2006, but the share of education expenses went down 0.3 points and the (combined) share of health and social protection expenses only increased 2.1 points (Table 10.8). While the total social expenses increased by just 1.7 points (relative rises of 11.4% and 10% respectively). Provision for education as a share of expenses actually went

Table 10.8. Share of taxation, social insurance contributions and public social expenditure (%) by GDP.

Tax/contributions/expenditure	2002	2003	2004	2005	2006
Indirect tax	15.5	16.5	17.1	18.0	17.7
Direct tax	8.2	8.5	7.9	8.2	7.8
Social insurance contributions	5.9	6.5	6.9	6.8	7.6
Total taxes and contributions	29.7	31.5	31.9	33.0	33.1
Education	4.4	4.1	4.0	4.0	4.1
Health	4.7	4.8	5.1	5.2	5.2
Social protection	7.9	9.1	9.1	9.7	9.5
Retirement pensions and other expenditure	7.1	8.1	8.2	8.7	8.4
Social relief and non-contribution payment	0.3	0.4	0.3	0.5	0.6
Direct income support to agriculture	0.5	0.6	0.6	0.5	0.5
Total social expenditure	17.1	18.0	18.2	18.9	18.8

Source: DPT 2010.

down, by 0.3 points. The (combined) share of health and social protection expenses increased 2.1 points, but even this rise was only negligibly more proportionately than the general increase in taxes and contributions (an 11.5% increase for income as opposed to 12.3% for health and social protection expenses. These figures demonstrate that public social expenses increased less than taxes and contributions the claim that a new social support regime has been introduced is unsupported by the overall financial data (Yükseler and Türkan 2008).

In addition, given that the income share that put aside for social expenses has declined a little on previous figures for an already heavily criticised system, it is only to be expected that services provided in fields like education and medical are poor quality, less than those of other services. Also, a series of organisational/governmental problems in the delivery and presentation of public services has brought about various efficiency losses.

Criticisms of solidarity fund activities

These following issues are detected in researches on poverty and the activities of the Solidarity Fund system of welfare and social aids (in no particular order):

* social aids are practiced with favouritism and opportunism; therefore, there is political support seeking of administrations and expectations for sustaining these support;
* the Fund is used as a tool of political patronage;
* foundation activities are not based on the concept of 'social right';
* support policy does not include an idea of 'citizenship income' (Buğra and Keyder 2003);
* the conditions attached to securing public relief are often humiliating;
* solidarity fund activities are not based on detailed knowledge relevant to research on the dimensions and profile of poverty (Şenses 1999, 2003);
* these activities are prone to error. For example, supports may be inaccessible to poor people while people who are not poor can access them (METU 2002, World Bank 2002);
* there is no standardisation in the allocation of these supports (Buğra and Keyder 2003, METU 2002, Şenses 1999, 2003);
* the Solidarity Fund is not transparent and accountable (Şenses 2003);
* when applications are evaluated, staff can behave arbitrarily (Buğra and Keyder 2003);
* *muhtar*s (village headmen) play a central role, the Fund is seen as a source of favouritism and partiality in the system (METU 2002);
* it is clearly experienced as shameful for young men who are fit for work to demand support from this fund (Buğra and Keyder 2003);
* the Solidarity Funds do not properly oversee the efficiency of these supports (Şenses 1999, 2003);
* supports are not set up to prevent ambiguities of exclusion;
* education supports do not seem to be able to generate the conditions for eight-year universal, free education (Buğra and Keyder 2003).

Summary

In the context of poverty and neo-liberalism, it is necessary to establish the issues well. Obviously poverty existed before the recent period, with income distribution imbalances, regional imbalances, gender and poverty of minorities, and so on, but with neo-liberalism, however, poverty has become more serious and gained permanent characteristics.

Second, when viewed from the historical developmental perspective, employment increased and poverty decreased with economic growth, but now, economic growth does not create employment which will reduce poverty. If poverty and unemployment allowed and even caused by economic growth with advanced technological developments is the focus, it is clear that emphasis must be laid on growth options creating employment and/or a fairer distribution of rewards from the contribution of advanced technology to society.

Third, in the period before neo-liberalism, social welfare regimes in Europe especially were sufficiently wide covering and well-funded to insure individuals against future uncertainties. On the other hand, neo-liberal policies now support people who do not have income earning opportunities or capacities only to the extent that they will not die from hunger, or offer ultimately romantic (marginal) solutions to today's profound structural problems, like the Gramen system.

Fourth, even though, it is possible to dispute that there has been an increase in resources used for social support policies in Turkey when looking at the absolute figures, a significant part of these supports are taken back from people through indirect taxes, the dominant taxation approach of neo-liberalism. Furthermore, the criterion of efficiency of these supports should not be amount of money spent, but whether and to what extent they reduce poverty.

Fifth, although studies aimed at things like trying to find definitions of poverty or methods of measurement have contributed a lot to the struggle against poverty, it must not be overlooked that one of the main reasons for the poverty is itself built into the solutions, the development approach, that is, assumed by these analyses. This concern cannot ignore when it goes hand in hand with current approaches that relate the reason for being poor to the poor, and leave the struggle against poverty and poverty reduction to non-governmental organisations. Instead of this, Keynesian social welfare policies, at least, attaching importance in the economy to the state, are to be preferred; policies that regard social aid as a citizenship right should be adopted, as opposed to those which treat aid in terms of charity, or, in Islam, *sadaka*.

It is entirely unconvincing that the World Bank, which tries to spread and deepen neo-liberal reforms, should now lead the way in poverty reduction and the development of poverty approaches. The current model of progress that includes concerns like human improvement, involves social exclusion in tandem with poverty measurements based on income and consumption. This raises the suspicion that even that the World Bank is really trying to save and deepen neo-liberal reforms. In this framework, the poverty expression of the World Bank deserves to be discussed critically, particularly in the light of stalling and semi-failing initiatives like the United Nations MDGs.

The essential impasses in the neo-liberal approach to poverty becomes quite apparent when a range of interrelated variables and contradictory pairs are considered together, such as employment increase and labour market flexibility, access to services like education and medical services and the privatisation of these services, inclusion of the poor in the financial system with interest payable microcredit schemes, reduction in tax rates and increase in social aid, reduction in agricultural support and allowing agricultural product prices to be set by the market, etc. When arguing against the neo-liberal discourse, it must be accepted that it does have some positive aspects, which must be appreciated when taking its entirety into consideration, including all these contradictions. The positive aspects of neo-liberalism are contextualised by ideals, policies, measures and counter-effects that work to prevent genuine poverty reduction.

An alternative, broad development strategy which focuses on issues like the structural transformation of foreign trade, industrialisation, employment and poverty reduction must go beyond temporary arguments about poverty and palliative solutions. In this framework, if the rapidly decreasing rural population and fading agricultural system are viewed again from the perspective of rural development, there may be potential poverty reduction solutions. Options include, for example, supporting functions for rural areas not only for cultivation but also as living area spaces for the old and retired; the reconfiguration of agriculture in ways and products which will create employment without giving up the goal of new methods and fertility; the establishment of industries based on agriculture in rural areas; and the development of urban agriculture.

The Turkish state needs to play a central role in addressing regional imbalances, fiscal policy for income shares, the delivery of education, medical, etc. services, and solutions to poverty. While developing policies in this field, it will be helpful to consider the entire range of possibilities, from European social welfare systems to specific national and local conditions, from family ties to non-governmental organisations, in order to make full use of all resources.

Chapter 11. Conclusions on agriculture, rural life and poverty in Turkey during the age of neo-liberalism

The interaction between Turkish agriculture and the rural sector on the one hand with global development on the other is not new. One of the noteworthy examples of this from history was the introduction of cotton farming in the Çukurova region following a commercial agreement between the Ottoman Empire and United Kingdom in 1838. Some other cases can shown assistances from the past of the international relationships of Turkish agriculture include the organisation of handmade carpet weaving by UK entrepreneurs, and the building of large scale farms by entrepreneurs from various European countries and trade with them in agriculture products from the Aegean region like cotton and figs. Although these relationships were advantageous to the Western countries, they were not after the mould of classical colonial relationships. Accordingly Anatolian lands have not hosted production and property structures shaped by colonial needs or colonizing economies. Rather, it is the usage of the state power in shaping the conflict between social classes and global historical and economic developmental trends that has most determined the structure and progress of Anatolian agriculture.

Agriculture was a major part of the Turkish economy in 1923 when the Turkish Republic was founded. The new republic espoused development policies supporting for agriculture, which included, for example, the purchasing of agricultural production, improvement of the transportation infrastructure, provision of subsidised credits and prices, education of an expert class in agronomy, and the development of incentives to produce for the market. Consequently, agriculture production and production for the market increased. Agriculture production and incomes both rose in the 1950s with a combination of widespread tractor usage, productivity improvements, farmland extension, adequate world prices and supported national prices. In the 1960s, the green revolution further supported raised production and income levels. During this time also were observed the positive effects in agriculture and rural affluence of people migrating abroad. Agriculture product and inputs prices were relatively stable, and uncertainty in marketing and price conditions manageable.

Through this history of positive development, there were no great alterations in the structure of agriculture. This had essentially been absorbed, unchanged from the Ottoman Empire. In this structure, small size land property was dominant and the farming done by the peasant people settled in rural Anatolia, in its tens of thousands of villages and hamlets of various kinds. There were two exceptions to this basic structure: big farms established mainly in the Aegean region, and the 'Agha System' in the East and Southeast. The number of big farms increased a little following the foundation of the Republic, with some people taking the initiative of using the state power of public lands and the lands held from which non-Muslim peoples had fled. These large farms comprised a fairly small share of the total farm lands, however, as today remains the case, as even the small share that these farms diminished over time. Some of the big farms dissolved due to heritage sharing and some were transformed to capitalist entrepreneurship in differentiated from past. In the east and southeast Anatolia a large part of the agha system dissolved, either as a result of PKK actions or the entrepreneurial actions of individual aghas. In short, small scale farming has always dominated the structure of agriculture in Turkey, and this continues to be the case. In recent years, the small farm land share has been in decline and that of larger scale farming enterprises rising. Nevertheless, small or smallish holdings (less than 10 ha) still numbered some 80% of all the agricultural enterprises in the country as of 2006, farming almost a third of the land cultivated.

The continued survival of the small farm or petty commodity producer dominance structure can be understand in relation to the development of agriculture activities, global economics and social structures of Turkey. Significant factors are not limited to farm scale. Rather, this combines with a complex interlink age of, among others, total land availability, weather patterns, topographical features and technological innovations, agricultural product composition, export markets and government policies, along with the characteristics of farmers' households and other demographic developments, all taking their place as explanatory variables in the survival – or otherwise – of small scale farmers.

Cultivation area limits were being reached in Turkey by 1960. Before then, there had still been potentially suitable, unfarmed lands in Anatolia. The rise of the total agricultural land area gained speed with the introduction of the tractor and also irrigation. On the other hand, a part of the land share available to agriculture is also being lost now – to road, housing and dam construction as well as to erosion.[91] Currently, there are more than one million modern tractors in the country and practically all crop farming is mechanised. This means that in the 70 to 80% of the total cultivated area where crop farming is done, human labour has been largely replaced by machines that plough and sow, apply insecticide and manure, and then harvest. This, obviously, is not without its consequences.

Firstly, tractor rental enables small as well as big farmers to use mechanised cultivation techniques on their land. That is to say, scale is not a major issue in the application of this technology, and income levels in crop farming are thus little differentiated by enterprise size. Secondly, some the mechanisation that disenfranchised labourers has also liberated a part of the work force – enabling, that is, the youngsters in peasant smallholder households the free time to investigate opportunities for new types of development, meaning, primarily, waged work or entrepreneurship outside of farming as another source of household income, or else longer periods of (perhaps tertiary) education (which, of course, can feed back into the non-agricultural employment option). Alternatively, these youngsters might join the ranks of the 'ready for work but not actively looking'.

Another contemporary peasant pattern to be found is the smallholder that combines crop farming with vegetable/fruits and/or animal husbandry. In this type of case, the income from animal husbandry might be enabled be husbandry cost reduction through the use other agricultural products and secondary products, like hay. This mode of business offers possibilities for the type of additional income that may make the difference between survival or going under for a small farmer. Up until the recent past, home-grown vegetable/fruits and animal products played a major role in support of the grain staple for farmer family nutrition. This is no longer the case, as, with Bernstein's 'commodisation of the living means' at a higher level, the farmer household tends to purchase rather than produce the means for subsistence (financed – more or less – by the sale of the means for subsistence that s/he has produced). This is true now even for bread, which once used to be made by every farmer.[92] Equally, in the case of

---

[91] The loss to construction and similar human activities including that of low intensity agricultural forestry, with development linked deforestation a major ecological phenomenon of the recent past, and ongoing.

[92] In fact, variations between consumption and marketing practices for wheat and flour products may occasionally vary even on a village to village basis in a given locality. While the farmers in one place may mostly sell their produce, in a neighbouring village they may tend to make all their own bread, and in a third mix the two in roughly equal measure. The local culture aspects of market relations can be settlement specific (Öztürk 2011).

milk, an increased share of the milk produce is going to market, and farmer households consume a smaller share of their own milk.

A third survival technique of the modern day small farmer in Turkey is to focus on high value added products (so as to purchase the means for subsistence, among other things). In the past, crops was the biggest agricultural product group for commercially marketed products and its share of total farmer income therefore also the biggest (traditionally, tobacco, sultanas and figs were also produced for the market). Nowadays, notwithstanding the continued usage of most land for crop farming, the income share of crops in agriculture income has declined to around the same level as that of vegetable/fruits and husbandry (including dairy and processed meat products).

Risk management for peasant farmers was easier before the neo-liberal period insofar as input costs were comprehensible and product prices stable. This suggests another survival mechanism Vegetable/fruit and animal farming have the advantage of more predictable product figure and future product prices. Inevitably, there are some fluctuations in the market price of fruit and vegetables, and animals and animal products – the fluctuations of nut, meat and milk prices in recent years have deeply effected to many farmers. Nevertheless, productivity in animal husbandry is not dependent on weather conditions, and fruits and vegetables are mostly produced in irrigated areas where the drought risk is thus minimised. Moreover, especially in fruit production, the production cost is at a lower level, meaning reduced lossesin years of bad harvest. These agriculture product composition considerations both operate as one of the basic survival strategies for small farmers while also indicating a strong development in terms of product and income for Turkish agriculture generally.

Income from agriculture rose in the period 1950 to 1980. A part of it was used for agriculture investments, like tractors, irrigation systems, pesticides and land improvement; another part was given over to education for the children and youngsters in cities; and another part went to building up commercial activities and buying real-estate, mostly in cities. Thus, farmer households received greater incomes than in the past, but this was directed via the young and other excess populations to cities so as to prevent excess labour force in agriculture, at least, indirectly. Parents knew that upon their death the land would be distributed among their children, indicating the likelihood of farm fragmentation problems, especially in families with a dozen or more would be inheritors in a (Muslim) culture that has very specific arrangements for fair (equal) division – so packing off the younger males especially to city relatives and extended schooling became an entirely practical option. Of course, a large mass has migrated out of the countryside to cities or abroad with very limited or no land. The image of the ubiquitous smallholder family should not obscure the reality of the landless. Despite the rise in migration among the rural population up to the 1980s, there was no occurrence of a labour scarcity. A huge work force was needed for farming jobs like sugar beet hoeing and harvesting, and cotton and nut harvesting, which was only met with Kurdish seasonal workers.

The mainly effects of the adoption of neo-liberal policies in agriculture were diminishing agricultural support and privatisation of the public institutions from where to obtain agriculture inputs and buy the agricultural products. Due to diminishing price supports and the discontinuation of certain institutions that provided secure buying guarantees for specified agricultural products, a fall in agriculture product prices and rise in market condition and price uncertainty developed. It was after the 2000's, when rises in input prices joined the uncertain market conditions to make survival in agriculture even more difficult for small farmers That the 'Direct Income Support' (DIS) system was adopted and extended. Farmers were face with the dilemma of whether to cultivate or give their land over to rent and receive a guaranteed (risk free) income and DIS. Consequently, rises in rented cultivated land and small plot land sells occurred, especially in the crop farming areas.

Survival for small farmers in the more difficult conditions of the 1980s and 1990s and yet more difficult after 2000 required resourcefulness. Options lay within agriculture as outlined, and also in getting a job or learning an occupation out of agriculture, including women, or children receiving education and going on to a profession and regular work in relatively well paid salaried jobs in the city, or some migrants giving their lands to those who stayed and thus reducing inheritance based land division. These options were all facilitated by a variety of expression of solidarity from city and abroad to the village. For many – millions – it did become impossible survive through it agriculture incomes in the village: they had to seek another job and migrate. Arriving in the provincial cities and regional metropolises, this mass found more serious problems wait for them. Before 1980 adequate conditions for newly entering migrants were to be fund, with job possibilities enabled by the rapid economic growth in cities, manageable city populations, *gecekondu* shanty housing, and a natural strong solidarity between country folk facing the same difficulties and helping each other. After 1980, however, this changed. Poverty filled the cities and overflowed with each newcomer.

Meanwhile, new types of agricultural entrepreneurs began to arise, composed of those who were able to adapt to these new conditions within agriculture or that come from outside. Those from agriculture were traditionally medium or big farmers or new generation farming households who tried to improve their activities, use new methods, make detailed cost-benefit analyses, seek new markets and products and increase their cultivated land by purchase or rent. The others were a novel breed in Turkish agriculture. Some had some jobs in commerce or industry or the service sector, agricultural professional white-collar workers. These could gain a measure of accumulation through their paid employment which they then used as sources of agricultural investment. They established modern farms as relatively large scale operations (by buying land from small farmers and whoever else desired to sell). A third type of new entrepreneur was national or foreign big agribusiness. Investing mainly in animal husbandry, irrigated lands and vegetable and fruit production, these companies have strong finanacial foundations, and ties and partnerships with various business organisations to further their access to and maximisation of markets and capital.

On the supply side, the market share of multinational companies in pesticides, fertiliser and seed has boomed. Company size and number has risen in the dairy, meat (products), and fruit and vegetable growing and marketing sectors. The agriculture based industrial demand for agriculture products is rising in tandem with the increase in contract farming and processed agriculture product exports. Turkey imports some agriculture products and sells other agriculture products both processed and non-processed to realise a trade surplus in agriculture. In the homely market, rapidly developing retail chains (most of them foreign direct investment companies) impact on the agriculture product prices. If these issues were – or are – handled from the hegemonic position of foreign agricultural input monopolies, integration with the world market can be claimed; regardless, Turkish agriculture is certainly exposed and vulnerable to the price, supply and demand fluctuations and speculations in the world agriculture product and food markets.

In this economic environment, against a long term background of falling agriculture prices, and thus incomes, and rising uncertainty, and thus risk, family enterprises try to compensate with productivity gains and the farming of high value added products. Notwithstanding per capita agriculture income continuance as absolute number, the rate of increase is lower than in the past and especially so relative to domestic per capita income rises. This was a factor in the flow from agriculture to non-agriculture based jobs and from rural-to-urban migration. The absolute rural population number plummeted and some villages lost their whole population. The forced migrated of Kurdish people also added to this flow.

Meanwhile, because of the young people leave to get non-farm jobs – blue collar wage labour, white collar employment or establish petty entrepreneurship in the city – the average age of the declining rural population rises. People are retiring (from farming or non-farming jobs) to the country leading to the development of what may be termed 'retirement villages'. The combination of relatively low retirement ages and pension payments in Turkey more often than not means working with the luxury of needing to earn less. Thus it is that most of the retirees moving to the village survive also on small scale agriculture activities. The balance of pensions to earnings varies. Overall, the total of retirement incomes is actually over that of agriculture income in most villages – yet it is not enough to more than minimally support the retired population who do live there. The result is a labour engagement midway between subsistence farming and hobby gardening.

Another non agriculture income in rural localities comes from out of farm jobs from around villages and like populations are aged the child number is falling and with it student and school numbers, which leads to further – long term – depopulation. Other than the elderly and retired, most people in most places do not want a village life. In this respect the young in Turkey are no different than the young anywhere else in the world. One particular upshot of this situation emerges as young women not wanting to marry men in village or at least without plans and prospects of getting out. The women prefer marriage with a man who has regular job and income in cities, even if the income level may actually be lower than that obtainable in the locality. These images of the villages are the – more or less – specifically Turkish expressions of processes of depeasantisation and depopulation of the rural akin to other countries with similar structures in these neo-liberal times.

Another change is observed in Turkey as elsewhere but in specific cultural contexts – meaning, Turkey cannot be described as a unified nation with a single homogenous culture – occurs in the division to labour within the household in the context of the migration and agricultural structure changes. Traditional farmer households do the farming all together as family. In the family farm, non-paid household individuals (mainly women and also children, as shown in the statistics) function as a cheaper labour force, supporting the survival of small scale agricultural production. In the family farming system, production is something done by and as family, with income, equally, something used by and as a family. Resources and outgoings have value within the family framework, even if distribution within the family is not fair (e.g. it usually operates in a very patriarchal context). This situation strengthens family solidarity. Family solidarity is bidirectional, from family to migrants or the non-employed or low waged in farm jobs, and to family from non-farm workers or transferences from cities and abroad. Doubtless this is not only a matter of economic relations: it is also harmonised with family values, social values and culturally relations between individual, family. And this family is traditionally – and still – a large (many children) entity and extended family weave of complex networks linked to the village, local town and certain cities, composed of members who, depending of the viscidities of personal relationships, support and may be expected to support each other in a multitude of ways. This solidarity type is also weakened in the neo-liberal times.

The technological development indicating the inexorable fall in family labour, especially that of women in crop farming, taken together with the family size decrease blazes the base of the family farming system. Beyond this destruction of Çayanov's 'exploitation of himself by himself' – farmers' weakened potential for self-exploitation, the smaller family and weakening family solidarity is seen especially between the new urban poor and among the rural-to-city individual and family migrants. Consequently, another distinctive characteristic of the new urban poverty, the permanently poor and excluded embedded in the geographical and cultural peripheries of the metropolis, is an ever weakening solidarity not only within the urban context but also between the urban and the rural. The fragmentation of labour is expressed through the greater observation of class distinctions in cities than in rural space. In fact, before the 1980s, the weight of the rural mass knew little social distinction because of the limited scale of rural enterprises and incidence of property-farming. The main structure was small scale production and social class distinction grew only very slowly. Changes in class structure in the rural were the generations slow transfer (accumulation) of production means ownership and labour force sale. Rural household life styles and income levels were not hugely different from each other, as a rule, and because of the low income levels households had solidarity defined possibilities to slow down evolutionary changes in the direction of labour.

After 1980, however, weakening solidarity, small rises in agricultural incomes and relatively small non-farm incomes led to rises of a worker class in the rural. The rise in rural worker numbers was also informed by new agricultural farming actors, as defined above, the three types of new agricultural entrepreneurship that developed – successful traditional farmers, urban dweller investors and farmers and agriculture corporations – all farming structure in need of waged labour. Hence the waged labour increases in agricultural jobs. There is, currently, a delicate balance. The new entrepreneurs are not dominant. Circumstances favour the corporation that uses wage labour but small and medium size family farms survive and continue to prosper. And a third mass in this equation is the small producer/worker type cultivating a little land, with a few animals, growing garden vegetables and fruits as a family and/or with family members working as waged labour in agricultural and/or non-agricultural employment. This mass, namely the marginal working class or global unrecorded working class (Bernstein 2008) oscillate in and out of agriculture, between jobs and place: when the job possibilities weakens in the city they return to the village and do farming, to find a good job again go back to the city and non-farming work again. The future of this mass is unclear. This mass has not got politics or labour union organisation, the political structure or ideology found among other poor people. The political attitudes of this mass are expressed according to religious beliefs or cultural values.

This is a picture not of the urban poor or the rural poor, but of a life style and farming type that represents a kind of transition, a differentiation or bridge between the world of yesterday and of tomorrow. The greater part of this category in Turkey is formed of retired farmers or villagers. They are retired from agricultural or non-agricultural work, live in the village or both village and local town/provincial capital/metropolitan city, do farming but not with the aim and intention of growing his farm to any scale of consequence, preferring to live in village for the social and natural environment and sometimes for the living cost. Mostly these are older people; their children live in the city and whether their family members will continue to farm quite unclear. Maybe one more generation will come and survive, but thereafter the future is unknown. This mass, the coming generation, may also eventually come to subsist through agriculture or retirement incomes or both and in solidarity with their family members.

Another specifiable phenomenon is of those people who have regular on-farm jobs and incomes, live in urban spaces and also do farming. Some of these, in fact, farm with relatively high capital investments and display modern entrepreneur characteristics. Another identifiable group consists of those who subsist on the farm with support from family and/or villagers use wage labour and rented tractors on small plots. These types of groups constitute a mass in the agrarian domain and yet can hardly be deemed to fall under the category of 'farmer': their incomes from agriculture are relatively small. Accordingly, the meaning of their farming is as much if not more related to cultural, family values and relationships than an economic base.

We come to Bernstein's problematizing of 'the people of the land' and the peasantry as a class. It is clear that the majority of the rural population is older and retired. It can be predicted that some, in all likelihood an increasing number of people will retire to villages after their active working lives. But these kind of people go to rural or holiday region to spend their retirement, raising animals or vegetables and fruits as much as for recreation as for farming. They can hardly be championed as the people of the land. Likewise in the case of another transition category, those who live in the city and do farming but their children only learn where milk comes from as they get older.

The residuals are capitalist entrepreneurs, waged labour workers in capitalist corporations and seasonal agriculture jobs, small producers who cannot find or imagine another way in life or prefer to survive through agriculture in the rural environment. Especially in crop farming, the central Anatolian land mass has low productivity and weather condition dependency, conditions that act as a break to capital investment in agriculture. The limited capital investment in dry agriculture areas indicates that these areas are open to change in relation to market conditions and internal dynamics. Conversely, comparative increases in capital investment can be expect to go into irrigated areas and the high added value sectors of, vegetable and fruit production and animal husbandry (along with niche markets). These activities are strongly interrelated to international markets. If the land and production scale is sufficiently economically efficient, small producers will survive in this area. But it is uncertain. It seems more likely that the competitive sector – capital

– will continue to develop and further dominate in animal husbandry, dairy and meat (product) markets. This development constitutes a threat to small animal husbandry. Accordingly, decline in agriculture income is further increasing uncertainty in regard to the mass survival of the small producer, which will depend on the complex of market conditions, whether big capital come to these areas, and whether small scale peasant farmers can again adapt and adopt new strategies of survival.

References

Internet sourced statistics

BDDK   www.bddk.org.tr/WebSitesi/turkce/Istatistiki_Veriler/Istatistiki_Veriler.aspx
DPT   http://www.dpt.gov.tr
OECD   www.oecd.org/document/0,3746,en_2649_201185_46462759_1_1_1_1,00.html
TMO   www.tmo.gov.tr/Main.aspx?ID=1
TÜİK   www tuik.gov.tr
UN   www.un.org/millenniumgoals/
WB   http://data.worldbank.org/indicator

General

Abadan Unat, N., R. Keleş, R. Penninx, H. Van Renselaar, L. Van Velzen and L. Yenisey (1975). *Göç ve Gelişme*. Ankara: Ajans-Türk Matbaacılık.

Adaman, F. (with C. Bahar) (2003). *Country Study Turkey*. In: Social Protection in the Candidate Countries: Country Studies Cyprus, Malta, Turkey. Berlin: Akademische Verlagsgesellschaft.

Adaman, F., Ç. Keyder and S. Müderrisoğlu (2006). *Türkiye'de Büyük Kentlerin, Gecekondu Ve Çöküntü Mahallelerinde Yaşanan Yoksulluk Ve Sosyal Dışlanma*. Istanbul, research report.

Akşit, B. (1987). Kırsal Dönüşüm ve Köy Araştırmaları 1900-1980. *11. Tez Kitap Dizisi -7*: 11-30.

Aksoy, S., G. Eraktan, S. Eraktan, F. Kuhnen and W. Winkler (1994). *Türkiye'de Kırsal Nüfusun Sosyal Güvenliği*. Ankara University, cited by Gülbuçuk (2005: 98-99).

Aksoy, S., G. Eraktan, S. Eraktan, F. Kuhnen and W. Winkler (1994). *Türkiye'de Kırsal Nüfusun Sosyal Güvenliği*. Ankara: Ankara University (cited by Gülbuçuk 2005: 98-99).

Akyüz, Y. and K. Boratav (2001). The Making of the Turkish Financial Crisis. Presented at the conference *Financialisation of the Global Economy*, PERI, University of Massachusetts, December 7-9, Amherst, MA, USA.

Amin, S. (2009). Dünya Yoksulluğu. Yoksullaşma ve Sermaye Birikimi. *Mülkiye 2009, Cilt: XXXIII*, sayı 262: 89-99.

Angang, H., L. Hu and Z. Chang (2003). China's economic growth and poverty reduction (1978-2002). Presented at the IMF/NCAER (India) sponsored conference *A Tale of Two Giants: India's and China's Experience with Reform and Growth*, New Delhi, India, Nov. 14-16, 2003. Available at: http://www.imf.org/external/np/apd/seminars/2003/newdelhi/angang.pdf.

References

Avcı, G. and K. Kirişci (2008). Turkey's Immigration and Emigration Dilemmas at the Gate of the Europen Union. In: Castles, S. and R. Delgado Wise (eds.) *Migration and Development: Perspectives from the South.* Geneva: IOM. Available at http.//www. estudiosdeldesarrollo.net/revista/rev7ing/6.pdf.

Aydın, C. (2004). *Dünya Ticaret Örgütü Tarım Müzakereleri. AB ve Türkiye'nin Pozisyonları.* Ankara: AB Genel Sekreterliği.

Aydın, Z. (1986). Kapitalizm Tarım Sorunu ve Azgelişmiş Ülkeler (I). *11 Tez Kitap Dizisi 3. Mayıs 1986:* 126-156.

Aydın, Z. (2001a). Bu sayıda. *Toplum ve Bilim. Bahar 2001, sayı 88:* 3-9.

Aydın, Z. (2001b). Yapısal Uyum Politikaları ve Kırsal Alanda Beka Stratejilerinin Özelleştirilmesi; Söke'nin Tuzburgazı ve Sivrihisar'ın Kınık Köyleri Örneği. *Toplum ve Bilim. Bahar 2001(2), sayı 88:* 11-31.

Aysu, A. (2002). Tarladan Sofraya Tarım. Istanbul: Su Yay.

BDDK (2007). *Bankacılık Düzenleme ve Denetleme Kurumu.*

Bernstein, H. (2008). Who are the 'people of the land? Some Provocative Thoughts on Globalisation and Development, with Reference to Sub-Saharan Africa. Paper presented at conference on *Environments Undone: The Political Ecology of Globalisation and Development,* University of North Carolina, Chapel Hill, USA, February 29 – March 1, 2008.

Bernstein, H. (2010). *Tarımsal Değişimin Sınıfsal Dinamikleri.* Yordam Kitap.

Boratav, K. (1981). *Tarımsal Yapılar ve Kapitalizm.* Ankara: İmge Kitabevi.

Boratav, K. (1985). *İstanbul ve Anadolu'dan Sınıf Profilleri.* Istanbul: Tarih Vakfı-Yurt Yay.

Boratav, K. (2009). Tarımsal Fiyatlar, İstihdam ve Köylülüğün Kaderi. *Mülkiye 2009, Cilt: XXXIII, sayı 292:* 9-23.

Bozoğlu, N. (1987). İşçileşmeye Karşı Köylülüğün Devamı. *11, Tez Kitap Dizisi 7:* 30-34.

Buğra, A. (2008). *Kapitalizm, Yoksulluk ve Türkiye'de Sosyal Politika.* Isatnbul: İletişim Yay.

Buğra, A. and Ç. Keyder (2003). *New Poverty and The Changing Welfare Regime of Turkey.* Ankara: UNDP.

Buğra, A. and Ç. Keyder (2006). Sosyal Yardım Uygulamaları ve Topluma Yararlı Faaliyet Karşılığında Asgari Gelir Uygulaması. *BM Kalkınma Programı için hazırlanan rapor.* Available at: http://www.undp.org.tr/publicationsDocuments/socialassistancereports. pdf.

Buğra, A. and S. Adar (2007). *Türkiye'nin Sosyal Koruma Harcamalarının Karşılaştırmalı Bir Analizi,* Research Report, Sosyal Politika Forumu. Available at: http://www.spf. boun.edu.tr/docs/SocialPolicyWatch_Rapor__TR_.pdf.

Candaş, A., Y. Volkan, G. Sevda and Ç. Burcu Yakut (2010). *Türkiye'de Eşitsizlikler: Kalıcı Eşitsizliklere Genel Bir Bakış.* Istanbul, Boğaziçi Unv, Socyal Politika Forumu.

Carm, E., E. Mageli, L. Nyman Berryman and R. Smith (2003). *Education and Its Impact on Poverty: An Initial Exploration of the Evidence.* Oslo: The International Education Centre at Oslo University College. Available at: http://www.lins.no/db/pdf/report200307.pdf.

Chayanov, A.V. (1966). The Theory of Peasant Economy. In: D. Thorner, B. Kerblay and R.E.F. Smith (eds.), *A.V. Chayanov on the Theory of Peasant Economy*. Homewood, IL: Richard Irvin for the Ameriacan Economic Association (first publishing in 1925).

ÇSGB (nd). *Çalışma ve Sosyal Güvenlik Bakanlığı Sosyal Sigortalar Genel Müdürlüğü, İstatistik Yıllığı 1989-2003.* unpublished report by T.C. Çalışma ve Sosyal Güvenlik Bakanlığı Bağkur Genel Müdürlüğü Kayıtları, Ankara.

Dağ, B.S. (2006). Return to Village and Rehabilitation Project. Presentated at the UNDP/ Turkish Ministry of Internal Affairs sponsored *Internally Displaced Persons (IDP) Conference*, Ankara, Turkey, Feb. 23, 2006. Available at: http://www.undp.org.tr/undp/_ bulletin_archive/2006/03/Engdownload/B.PPT#27.

DİE (1994). *1991 Genel Tarım Sayımı Tarımsal İşletmeler (Hanehalkı) Araştırma Sonuçları.* Devlet İstatistik Enstitüsü, T.C. Başbankanlık, Ankara: DİE.

DİE (2003). *GTS Sonuçları, 1963 ve 2001.* Devlet İstatistik Enstitüsü, T.C. Başbankanlık, Ankara, DİE.

DİE/SIS (2004). *Türkiye İstatistik Yıllığı, 2004,* Devlet İstatistik Enstitüsü, T.C. Başbankanlık (*Turkey's Statistical Yearbook, 2004,* State Institute of Statistics, Prime Ministry, Republic of Turkey), Ankara: DİE.

DPT (1963). *Birinci Beş Yıllık Kalkınma Planı, 1963-1967.* Devlet Planlama Teşkilatı, T.C Başkanlı, Ankara: DPT.

DPT (1968). *İkinci Beş Yıllık Kalkınma Planı, 1968-1972.* Devlet Planlama Teşkilatı, T.C Başkanlı, Ankara: DPT.

DPT (1973). *Üçüncü Beş Yıllık Kalkınma Planı, 1973-1977.* Devlet Planlama Teşkilatı, T.C Başkanlı, Ankara: DPT.

DPT (1979). *Dördüncü Beş Yıllık Kalkınma Planı, 1979-1983.* Devlet Planlama Teşkilatı, T.C Başkanlı, Ankara: DPT.

DPT (1984). *Beşinci Beş Yıllık Kalkınma Planı, 1985-1972.* Devlet Planlama Teşkilatı, T.C Başkanlı, Ankara: DPT.

DPT (1989). *Altıncı Beş Yıllık Kalkınma Planı, 1990-1995.* Devlet Planlama Teşkilatı, T.C Başkanlı, Ankara: DPT.

DPT (1995). *Yedinci Beş Yıllık Kalkınma Planı, 1996-2000.* Devlet Planlama Teşkilatı, T.C Başkanlı, Ankara: DPT.

DPT (2000a). *Uzun Vadelii Strateji ve Sekizinci Beş Yıllık Kalkınma Planı, 2001-2005.* Devlet Planlama Teşkilatı, T.C Başkanlı, Ankara: DPT.

DPT (2000b). *Sekizinci Beş Yıllık Kalkınma Planı, Tarımsal Politikalar ve Yapısal Düzenlemeler Özel İhtisas Komisyonu Raporu.* Devlet Planlama Teşkilatı, T.C Başkanlı, Ankara: DPT.

DPT (2010). *Dokuzuncu Kalkınma Planı, 2010 yılı programı.* Devlet Planlama Teşkilatı, T.C Başkanlı, Ankara: DPT.

DSİ (2009). *2008 Yılı Faaliyet Raporu.* DSİ Genel Müdürlüğü, Ankara: DSİ.

EAF (2010). *Ekonomik Araştırma Forumu, Tusiad Koç Unv.* Politika Notu 10-14. Temmuz 2010.

References

Emrence, C. (2000). Politics of Discontent in the Midst of the Great Depression. *New Perspectives on Turkey 23* (Fall): 31-52.

FAO (2007). *Avrupa ve Orta Asya Bolge Ofisi Pollulku Yardımları Şubesi, Türkiye Cumhuriyeti Tarım ve Köy İşleri Bakanlığı, Birleşmiş Milletler Gıda ve Tarım Örgütü, AB Giriş Süreci Çerçevesinde Türkiye'de Süt ve Süt Ürünleri Sektörüne Genel Bakış.* Rome: FAO.

Friedman, H. and P. McMichael (1989). Agriculture and the State System, The Rise and Decline of National Agricultures, 1870 to the Present. *Sociologia Ruralis* 29(2): 93-117, cited by Yenal, N.Z. and D. Yenal (1993).

Ghosh, J. (2010). *Poverty reduction in China and India: Policy implications of recent trends.* DESA Working Paper No. 92ST/ESA/2010/DWP/92. available at: http://www.un.org/esa/desa/papers/2010/wp92_2010.pdf.

Gökşen, F., G. Özertan, İ. Sağlam and Ü. Zenginobuz (2008). Impacts of the tax system on poverty and social exclusion: A case study on Turkey. *New Perspectives on Turkey* 38 (Spring): 159-179.

Gülçubuk, B. (2005). Kırsal Kalkınma. In: Yavuz, F. (2005) *Türkiye'de Tarım.* Ankara: Tarım ve Köy İşleri Bakanlığı, pp. 68-93.

Günaydın, G. (2009). Türkiye Tarım Politikalarında 'Yapısal Uyum': 2000'li Yıllar. *Mülkiye 2009, Cilt: XXXIII, sayı 262:* 175-223.

Gürsel, S. and U. Karakoç (2009). *Türkiye'de Tarımın Yapısı Değişiyor.* Bahçeşehir Üniveritesi, Ekonomik ve Toplumsal Araştırmalar Merkezi, Araştırma Notu 24, Istanbul: BETAM.

Hann, C. and I. Beller Hann (2001). Mazlum olan kim? Rize'de çay üreticileri örneği. *Toplum ve Bilim, Bahar 2001, sayı* 88: 55-68.

Harrison, G. (2006). Peasantries, Globalisation and Capitalism. *New Political Economy* 11(3): 383-385.

Hobsbawm, E. (1995). *The Age of Extremes: The Short Twentieth Century, 1914-1991.* New York, NY: Penquin.

Hulme, D., K. Moore and A. Shepherd (2001). *Chronic poverty: meanings and analytical frameworks.* Birmingham: University of Birmingham Chronic Poverty Research Centre.

Işık, O. and M. Pınarcıoğlu (2001). *Nöbetleşe Yoksulluk: Gecekondulaşma ve Kent Yoksulları: Sultanbeyli.* İletişim Yayınları.

İslamoğlu, H., E. Güloksüz, Y. Kaya, A. Çavdar, U. Karakoç, D. Nisam and G. Yazıcı, (2008). *Türkiye'de Tarımda Dönüşüm ve Küresel Piyasalarla Bütünleşme Süreçleri.* (Proje No: 106K137, İstanbul, Haziran 2008), Istanbul: unpublished report.

Jongerden, J. (2007). *The Settlement Issue in Turkey and the Kurds: An analysis of Spatial Policies, Modernity and War.* Leiden: Brill.

Kartal, S.K. (1984). *Ekonomik ve Sosyal Yönleri ile Türkiye'de Kentlileşme.* Ankara: Yurt Yayınları.

Kazgan, G. (1988) 2000 Yılında Türk Tarımı: Biyoteknoloji ve GAP Ne Getirebilecek. In: Toprak, Z. and S. Pamuk (eds.) *Türkiye'de Tarımsal Yapılar 1930-2000.* Ankara: Yurt Yay, pp. 257-271.

Kepenek, Y. and N. Yentürk (2000). *Türkiye Ekonomisi.* Istanbul: Remzi Kitabevi.

Keyder, Ç. and Z. Yenal (2004). Kalkınmacılık Sonrası Dönemde Türkiye'de Kırsal Dönüşüm Eğilimleri ve Sosyal Politikalar. *Küresel Düzen: Birikim, Devlet ve Sınıflar (3. Bas),* Istanbul: İletişim Yay, pp. 357-382.

Koç, A. (2005). Türkiye'de Tarımsal Ürün ve Girdi Piyasaları. In: Yavuz, F. (ed.) *Türkiye'de Tarım.* Ankara: Tarım ve Köy İşleri Bakanlığı, pp. 130-159.

Köymen, O. (2008). *Kapitalizm ve Köylülük: Ağalar, Üretenler, Patronlar.* Istanbul: Yordam Kitap.

Macovei, M. (2009). *Growth and economic crises in Tukey: leaving behind a turbulent past?* Economic Papers 386, October 2009, Directorate-General for Economic and Financial Affairs Publications, Brussels: European Commission.

Makal, A. (2001). Türkiye'de 1950-1965 Döneminde Tarım Kesiminde İşgücü ve Ücretli Emeğe İlişkin Gelişmeler. *Ankara Üniversitesi Siyasal Bilgiler Fakültesi Dergisi, Cilt: 56, Sayı: 3, Temmuz-Ağustos-Eylül:* 103-140.

Manço, M.U. (2002). Turks in Europe: From a garbled image to the complexity of migrant social reality. Presented at Entretitien de MEDEA, Brussels, 14th June, 2002), European Institute for Research on Mediterranean and Euro-Arab Cooperation, abstract available at: http://www.medea.be/index.html?page=2&lang=en&doc=1160.

McKinley, T. (2003). *The Macroeconomics of Poverty Reduction, Initial Findings of the UNDP Asia-Pacific Regional Programme.* Discussion Paper, Bureau for Development Policy, New York, August 2003.

McMichael, P. (2006). Peasant Prospects in the Neoliberal Age. *New Political Economy,* 11(3): 407-418.

McMichael, P. (2008). Peasants Make Their Own History, But Not Just as They Please. *Journal of Agrarian Change* 8(2/3): 205-228.

MEB (2007). Bütçe Raporu. Ankara: MEB.

Middle East Technical University (METU) (2002). *Assessment of Social Solidarity Fund Beneficiaries: Final Report.* Sosyoloji Bölümü.

Miran, B. (2005). Tarımsal Yapı ve Üretim. In: Yavuz, F. (ed.), *Türkiye'de Tarım.* Ankara: Tarım ve Köy İşleri Bakanlığı.

Murdoch, J. and A.C. Pratt (1993). Rural studies: Modernism, postmodernism and the 'post-rural'. *Journal of Rural Studies* 9(4): 411-427.

OECD (2008). *Growing Unequal? Income Distribution and Poverty in OECD countries.* Paris: OECD Publishing.

Oyan, O. (2009). IMF ve Dünya Bankası'nın Tarım Reformu Uygulama Projesi'nin Bilançosu. *Mülkiye 2009, cilt: XXXIII, sayı* 262: 237-254.

Özkaya, T. (2009). Türkiye Tohumculuğu ve Tarım İşletmelerinin Tasfiyesi. *Mülkiye 2009, cilt: XXXIII, sayı* 292: 255-274.

Öztürk, M. (2010). 1980 Sonrası Yıllarda Türkiye Tarımında Değişme Eğilimleri: Köysüzleşen Kırlar, Banliyöleşen Köyler, Zayıfların Sığınağı Köyler. *Monthly Review* (Turkish Edition), *Haziran, 2010, sayı* 23: 113-183.

Öztürk, M. (2011). Neo-liberal Policies and poverty: Effects of policy on poverty and poverty reduction in Turkey. Presented at *1. International Conference of Social Economy and Sustainability*, 21-26 September, 2010, at Maringa University, Parana, Brazil.

Pamuk, Ş. (1988). İkinci Dünya Savaşı Yıllarında Devlet, Tarımsal Yapılar ve Bölüşüm. In: Toprak, Z. and S. Pamuk (eds.) *Türkiye'de Tarımsal Yapılar 1930-2000.* Ankara: Yurt Yay, pp. 91-108.

Roep, D. and J.S.C. Wiskerke (2004). Reflecting on Novelty Production and Niche Management in Agriculture. In: Wiskerke, J.S.C. and J.D. Van der Ploeg (eds.), *Seeds of Transition: Essays on novelty production, niches and regimes in agriculture.* Assen: Van Gorcum, pp. 341-356.

Ruivenkamp, G. (1989). *De Invoering van Biotechnologie in de Agro-Industriele Productieketen, De overgang naar een nieuwe arbeidsorganisatie* [The introduction of biotechnology into the agro-industrial chain of production, Changing towards a new labour organisation], cited in Ruivenkamp, G. and J. Jongerden (2011), *From prescription to reconstruction: Opportunities for subpolitical choices in biotechnological and genomics research,* Utrecht: Jan van Arkel.

Ruivenkamp, G. (2008). *Biotechnology in Development: experiences from the South.* Wageningen: Wageningen Academic Publishers.

S.A.M, A.Ş. (2004). *Sosyal Yardımlaşma Ve Dayanışmayı Teşvik Fonu (Sydtf) Kamuoyu Araştırması, Nihai Rapor.* Istanbul, research report.

Saçlı (2009). Türkiye'de tarım istatistikleri: gelişimi, sorunlar ve çözüm önerileri, Devlet Ankara, Planlama Teşkilatı, yayın no. 2792.

SAPRIN (2004). *Structural Adjustment – The SAPRIN Report: The Policy Roots of Economic Crisis, Poverty and Inequality.* London: Zed Books.

Şenses, F. (1999). Yoksullukla Mücadele ve Sosyal Yardımlaşma ve Dayanışmayı Teşvik Fonu. *ODTÜ Gelişme Dergisi* 26 (3-4).

Şenses, F. (2003). Yoksullukla Mücadlenin Neresindeyiz? Gözlem ve Öneriler. In: Köse, A.H., F. Şenses and E. Yeldan (eds.), *İktisat Üzerine Yazılar I, Küresel Düzen: Birikim, Devlet ve Sınıflar.* Istanbul: İletişim, pp. 287-318.

Şenses, F. (2009). Neoliberal Küreselleşme Çağında Yoksulluk Araştırmalarındaki kayıp Bağlantılar: Türkiye Deneyiminden Çıkarılacak Dersler. In: Şenses, F. (ed.) *Neoliberal Küreselleşme ve Kalkınma, Derleyen.* Istanbul: İletişim Yay, pp. 679-705.

Shafaeddin, M. (2010). *Trade Liberalization, Industrialization and Development: Experience of recent decades.* Speech delivered at the Fourth ACDC (Annual Conference on Development and Change), University of Witwatersrand, Johannesburg, South Africa, April 2010.

Sirman, N. (2001). Sosyal Bilimlerde Gelişmecilik ve Köy Çalışmaları. *Toplum ve Bilim, Bahar 2001, sayı* 88: 251-254.

Sönmez, A. (2001). Doğu Karadeniz Bölgesi Fındık Üretim Kuşağında Toprak Ağalığı, Köylülük ve Kırsal Dönüşüm. *Toplum ve Bilim, Bahar 2001, sayı* 88: 69-104.

Sönmez, Ü. (2004). *Independent Regulatory Agencies: The World Experience and the Turkish Case*. MSc thesis, Ankara: METU.

Stedile, J.P. (2009). Çokuluslu Şirketlerin Tarıma Karşı Saldırısı. *Mülkiye 2009, Cilt: XXXIII, sayı 262:* 99-106.

Stiglitz, J.E. (2009). Küreselleşen Dünyada kalkınma Politikaları. In: Şenses, F. (ed.), *Neoliberal Küreselleşme ve Kalkınma, Derleyen*. Istanbul: İletişim Yay, pp. 281-307.

Tanrıvermiş, H. (2005). Tarımda Sosyal Politikalar. In: Yavuz, F. (ed.), *Türkiye'de Tarım*. Ankara: Tarım ve Köy İşleri Bakanlığı, pp. 94-119.

Tarım, Ş. (2004). *Tarımsal Yapıda Değişme ve Gelişmeler*. II. Tarım Şurası, II. Komisyon Raporu, Ankara.

TEG (n.d.). *Toplumsal ve Ekonomik Gelişmenin 50 Yılı*. (no publishing information).

Tekeli, İ. (2008). *Göç ve Ötesi*. İstanbul: Tarih Vakfı-Yurt Yayınları.

Tekeli, İ. and S. İlkin (1988). Devletçilik Dönemi Tarım Politikaları (Modernleşme Çabaları). In: Toprak, Z. and Ş. Pamuk (eds.) *Türkiye'de Tarımsal Yapılar 1930-2000*. Ankara: Yurt Yay, pp. 37-90.

Tezcan, S. and İ. Koç (2006). *Turkey Migration and Internally Displaced Population Survey (TMIDPS)*. Ankara: Hacettepe University Institute of Population Studies.

TMO (2010). Buğday, Arpa, Çavdar, Yulaf Alım Fiyatları.

Togan, S., A. Bayener and J. Nash (2005). Analysis of the Impact of EU Enlargement on the Agricultural Markets and Incomes of Turkey. In: Toga, S. and B.M. Hoekman (eds.) *Turkey: Economic Reform and Accession to the European Union*. Washington, DC: World Bank.

Toprak, Z. (1988). Türkiye Tarımı ve Yapısal Gelişmeler 1900-1950. In: Toprak, Z. and Ş. Pamuk (eds.) *Türkiye'de Tarımsal Yapılar 1930-2000*. Ankara: Yurt Yay, pp. 19-36.

TÜİK (1987-2011). *Veritabanları, Gelir Yöntemi İle GSYH* (Databank, GNP-GDP with Production Method).

TÜİK (1989-2011). *Hanehalkı İşgücü İstatistikleri* (Household Labour Force Survey Results).

TÜİK (2000). *Genel Nüfus Sayımları* (TSI, General Population Census), 1927-2000.

TÜİK (2001). *Genel Tarım Sayımı 2001* (General Agricultural Census 2001).

TÜİK (2007a). *Tarımsal Yapı: Üretim, Fiyat, Değer* (Agricultural Structure: Production, Price, Value).

TÜİK (2007b). *Çocuk İşgücü Anketi Sonuçları 2006* (Child Labour Force Survey 2006).

TÜİK (2008-10). *Bitkisel Üretim İstatistikleri, Veri* (Crop Production Statistics, Data).

TÜİK (2008-11). *Adrese Dayalı Nüfus Kayıt Sistemi Sonuçları* (TSI Results of Address Based Population System).

TÜİK (2008a). *Türkiye İstatistik Yıllığı 2008* (Turkey Statistics Yearbook 2008).

TÜİK (2008b). *Tarımsal İşletme Yapı Araştırması 2006* (Agricultural Holdings Wage Structure 2006).

TÜİK (2009a). *Gelir ve Yaşam Koşulları Araştırmasına, 2005* (Income and Living Conditions Survey, 2005).

TÜİK (2009b). *Gelir ve Yaşam Koşulları Araştırması, 2008* (Results of the 2008 Poverty Study).

TÜİK (2009c). *Gelir ve Yaşam Koşulları Araştırması, 2009* (Results of the 2009 Poverty Study).

TUİK (2010a). *İstatistik Göstergeler 1923-2009* (Statistical Indicators 1923-2009), Ankara: Türk İstatistik Kurumu.

TÜİK (2010b). *Tarım İstatistikleri Özeti 2000-2009* (The Summary of Agricultural Statistics 2000-2009), Ankara: Türk İstatistik Kurumu.

TÜİK (2011a). *Bitkisel Üretim İstatistikleri, 2010* (Crop Production Statistics, 2010).

TÜİK (2011b). *Tarımsal İşletmelerde Ücret Yapısı, 2010* (Agricultural Holdings Wage Structure, 2010).

TÜİK (2011c). *Haber Bülteni 66, 31 Mart 2011* (News Bulletin 66), 31 March 2011.

TÜİK (n.d.). *Sayım /Araştırmanın Kimlik Bilgileri*, TÜİK Araştırma Bilgi Sistemi (Available at: http://tuikrapor.tuik.gov.tr/reports/rwservlet?mthtmlcss&report=Metarp2.rdf&p_aras=1210).

Türkekul, B. (2007). *Potential alliances for Turkey in coming WTO agricultural negotiations.* CIHEAM Analytic note No. 20, June 1977, Paris: CIHEAM.

Türk-İş (2007). *Çalışanların ekonomik ve Sosyal Durumu*, 20. Genel Kurul İçin Hazırlanmış rapor.

Ulukan, U. (2009). *Türkiye Tarımında Yapısal Dönüşüm ve Sözleşmeli Çiftçilik: Bursa Örneği.* Istanbul: Sav.

UN (2000). *Resolutions Adopted by the General Assembly 55/2, United Nations Millennium Declaration, 8 September 2000.* New York: UN.

UN (2005). *Millenium Development Goals Report 2005.* New York, NY: UN.

UN (2008). *Millenium Development Goals Report 2008,* New York, NY: UN.

UN (2009). *Millenium Development Goals Report 2009,* New York, NY: UN.

UN (2010). *Millenium Development Goals Report 2010,* New York, NY: UN.

UNDP (2000). *Poverty Report 2000, Overcoming Poverty.* New York, NY: UNDP.

UNDP (2003). *Human Development Report 2003.* New York, NY: OUP.

UNDP (2005). *Investing in Development: A Practical Plan to Achieve the Millennium Develpoment Goals,* New York, NY: UNDP.

UNDP (2010). *Beyond the Midpoint: Achieving the milennium development goals.* United Nations Development Program, New York, NY: UN. Available at: http://content.undp.org/go/cms-service/stream/asset/?asset_id=2223855.

Van der Ploeg, J.D. (2008a). *The New Peasantries: Struggles for Autonomy and sustainability in era of empire and globalisation.* London: Earthscan.

Van der Ploeg, J.D. (2008b). Empire and The Peasant Principle. Paper presented at the plenary session of the *XXI Congress of the European Society for Rural Sociology,* Keszthely, Hungary.

Von Flügge, W. (1948/1949). Anadolu'da Zirai İşletme Meseleleri. *İstanbul Üniversitesi Iktisat Fakültesi Mecmuası,* Cılt: LO, No.I-4, Ekim 1948-Temmuz 1949: 122-165, cited by Makal, A. (2001): 115.

World Bank (2002). *Turkey: Greater Prosperity with Social Justice.* Washington, DC: World Bank. Available at: http://www-wds.worldbank.org/servlet/WDSContentServer/ WDSP/IB/2003/12/05/000160016_20031205171347/Rendered/PDF/273790English0 1ver0P07825901public1.pdf.

World Bank (2009). Development Research Group. Available at: At: http://data.worldbank. org/indicator/SI.POV.DDAY,   http://data.worldbank.org/indicator/SI.POV.GAP2/ countries and http://data.worldbank.org/topic/poverty.

Yaltırık, A. (2002). *Turkish Agricultural Machinery Market Research Report.* PhD thesis, Ankara. Available at: www.icex.es/staticFiles/maquinaria%20agricola_11675_.pdf.

Yaqub, S. (2000). *Intertemporal Welfare Dynamics. Background paper for HDR 2001.* Brighton: Sussex University. Available at: http://hdr.undp.org/en/reports/global/ hdr2001/papers/yaqub-1.pdf.

Yenal, N.Z. and D. Yenal (1993). 2000 Yılına Doğru Dünyada Gıda ve Tarım. *Toplum ve Bilim, 56-61, Bahar 1993*: 93-114.

Yükseler, Z. and E. Türkan (2008). *Türkiye'de Hane halkı: İşgücü, Gelir, Harcama Ve Yoksulluk Açısından Analizi.* İstanbul: TÜSİAD Yay.

Appendices

Appendix 1. Elevation and topograpic map of Turkey[93]

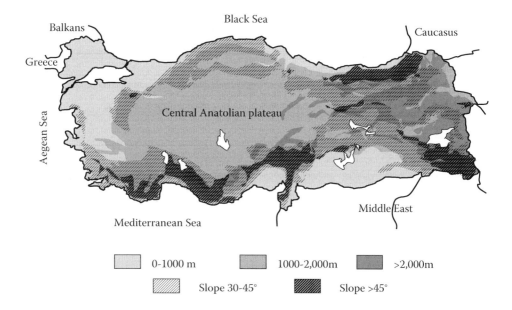

---

[93] While effort is made for this map to be reasonably accurate, it is only best approximations. See FAO, Wageningen UR (World Soil Information Database), Wikimedia Commons, http://www.fao.org/countryprofiles/maps.asp?iso3=TUR&lang=en and http://upload.wikimedia.org/wikipedia/commons/d/db/Turkey_topo.jpg for better detail (and the sources these are drawn from).

Appendix 2. Map of ecological zones in Turkey[94]

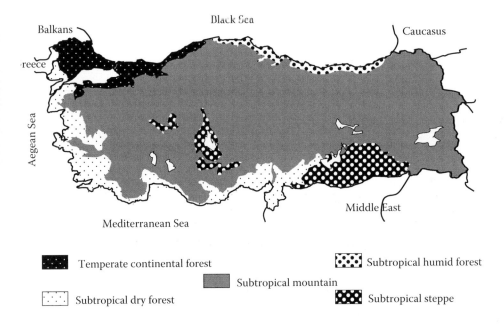

Temperate continental forest

Subtropical dry forest

Subtropical mountain

Subtropical humid forest

Subtropical steppe

[94] While effort is made for this map to be reasonably accurate, it is only best approximations. See FAO, Wageningen UR (World Soil Information Database), Wikimedia Commons and http://www.fao.org/forestry/country/19971/en/tur/ for better detail (and the sources these are drawn from).

Appendix 3. Drought and soil degredation map of Turkey[95]

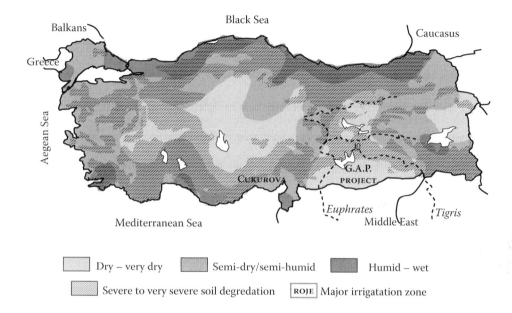

Dry – very dry   Semi-dry/semi-humid   Humid – wet

Severe to very severe soil degredation   ROJE   Major irrigatation zone

[95] While effort is made for this map to be reasonably accurate, it is only best approximations. See FAO, Wageningen UR (World Soil Information Database), Wikimedia Commons, http://www.icemtour.com/weather_in_turkey and http://library.wur.nl/isric/index2 for better detail (and the sources these are drawn from).

Appendix 4. Map of agricultural product production in Turkey[96]

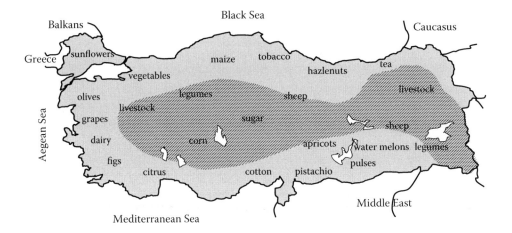

[96] While effort is made for this map to be reasonably accurate, it is only best approximations. See FAO, Wageningen UR (World Soil Information Database), Wikimedia Commons and http://www.fao.org/countryprofiles/maps.asp?iso3=TUR&lang=en for better detail (and the sources these are drawn from).

Appendix 5. Map of agricultural zones in Turkey[97]

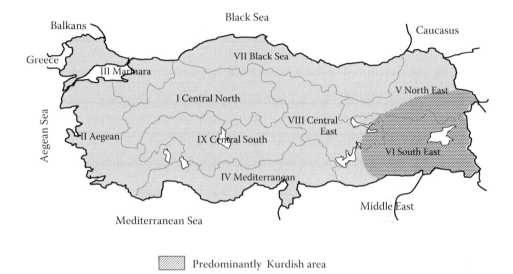

Predominantly Kurdish area

[97] While effort is made for this map to be reasonably accurate, it is only best approximations. See sources FAO, Wageningen UR (World Soil Information Database), Wikimedia Commons, http://www.fao.org/countryprofiles/maps.asp?iso3=TUR&lang=en and http://www.fao.org/ag/AGP/AGPC/doc/Counprof/Turkey/Turkey.htm for better detail (and the sources these are drawn from).

Index

Printed in the United States
by Baker & Taylor Publisher Services